Global Alliances in the Motor Vehicle Industry

Leslie S. Hiraoka

Q

QUORUM BOOKS
Westport, Connecticut • London

Library of Congress Cataloging-in-Publication Data

Hiraoka, Leslie S., 1941–
    Global alliances in the motor vehicle industry / by Leslie S. Hiraoka.
        p.   cm.
    Includes bibliographical references and index.
    ISBN 1–56720–346–9 (alk. paper)
    1. Motor vehicle industry—Mergers.   2. Strategic alliances (Business).   3. Globalization.
    I. Title.
    HD9710.A2H57   2001
    338.8′87292—dc21   00–037269

British Library Cataloguing in Publication Data is available.

Library of Congress Catalog Card Number: 00–037269
ISBN: 1–56720–346–9

First published in 2001

Quorum Books, 88 Post Road West, Westport, CT 06881
An imprint of Greenwood Publishing Group, Inc.
www.quorumbooks.com

Printed in the United States of America

The paper used in this book complies with the
Permanent Paper Standard issued by the National
Information Standards Organization (Z39.48–1984).

10 9 8 7 6 5 4 3 2 1

Copyright Acknowledgment

The author and publisher gratefully acknowledge permission to reprint extracts from the 1997
General Motors Annual Report. Copyright 1998 GM Corp. Used with permission of GM Media
Archives.

Every reasonable effort has ben made to trace the owners of copyright materials in this book, but
in some instances this has proven impossible. The author and publisher will be glad to receive information leading to more complete acknowledgments in subsequent printings of the book, and
in the meantime extend their apologies for any omissions.

This volume is dedicated to the memory of my parents
George Y. and Ellen F. Hiraoka

Contents

Illustrations

Chapter 1

Industry Globalization

As national boundaries proved too confining for the growth and competitiveness of principal manufacturers (General Motors, Ford, Toyota, Volkswagen, Chrysler, and Daimler-Benz), globalization of the motor vehicle industry markedly accelerated in the last half of the 1990s through the construction of major complexes abroad and the forging of international megamergers. The expansion in foreign business had its origins in the technological transfer of Ford's mass-production paradigm from the United States to Western Europe and Japan following World Wars I and II and its subsequent use in significantly advancing the industrialization of high-growth recipient nations like Japan and Germany. Production was initially concentrated on heavy industrial trucks for reconstruction and development as well as taxis and buses for mass transportation, and as incomes rose, the U.S. pattern of mass production and marketing of passenger automobiles ensued. In Western Europe, the proximity of heavily populated areas to German production sites led to profitable export markets, especially to smaller countries that lacked sufficient economies of scale to support the development of their own industries. Japan, in contrast, focused on the development of its domestic market and then sought expansion overseas. This began the second major movement in industrial globalization as small-car exports from Japan to the United States reached massive proportions resulting from the Arab oil embargo of 1973–1974 and the Iranian revolution of 1979. The growing transpacific trade prompted the development of complex transportation, marketing, and physical distribution systems to serve the huge U.S. market and initiated the global competition among what had largely been domestically oriented automakers. The Japanese exporters also introduced their lean production methods as an adaptation of the Ford manufacturing model, reversing the flow of technology and management methods that had been going from Detroit to the rest of the world. This reversal accelerated when the U.S.

government threatened to impose protectionist measures on cars from Japan, resulting in a major flow of direct foreign investments into North America and the construction of numerous production facilities in the New World. The huge complexes, an ocean away, were financed from profits earned from domestic operations and the transpacific trade and ushered in the current and most important move toward globalization, whereby business abroad vied with domestic concerns for the attention of multinational corporations.

The degree of difficulty encountered in competing in a huge, unfamiliar area like the United States—or Brazil, India, and China, for that matter—in a technologically sophisticated, capital-intensive industry like motor vehicles forced major firms to consider radical approaches to their ways of conducting business. Companies as different and far apart as Chrysler and Daimler-Benz decided to merge, and smaller firms like Mazda and Volvo cars have been taken over by larger ones (Ford). International equity alliances have also advanced, such as the joint venture between Toyota and General Motors to produce compact cars at the latter's Fremont, California, plant, with technology and management oversight provided by Toyota. The large equity stake taken by Renault SA in Nissan Motor probably best demonstrates the need for partners to compete globally. Nissan is strong in Asia, Mexico, and England, with considerable production capacity in the United States, while Renault has major markets in Western Europe and South America but little presence in the United States. The current situation represents a tentative step toward full merger because each partner has glaring weaknesses that could undermine the alliance, in which case Renault could dissolve it by selling its stake. In the DaimlerChrysler merger, the original partners had sufficient financial reserves to underwrite solutions to problem areas caused by the union, with the prestige of the Mercedes-Benz nameplate and popularity of Chrysler's sport utility vehicles in the affluent U.S. market adding to the impetus to merge.

NATIONAL INDUSTRIES

As globalization proceeds, the shortcomings of the major corporate entities arise from their development as national industries to principally supply the needs of the domestic economy. Renault, for example, is still owned in part by the French government, and Nissan has always had strong backing from Japan's Ministry of International Trade & Industry (MITI). During the latter's financial crisis in early 1999, the industrial ministry "sent the clearest signal to date today that it would not allow the struggling Nissan Motor Company, Japan's second-largest auto maker to collapse" (Strom 1999, C2). The clear intentions notwithstanding, MITI had little recourse but to take a back seat to Renault's $5.4 billion bailout of Nissan since it lacked the financial resources and industrial experience to be of much use to the carmaker. The industry's globalization has thus weakened the oversight power that national governments once exercised. Nevertheless, the automakers are still important factors in their domestic economies, as illustrated by the keen interest that official agencies tend to have in their well-being. This importance is further magnified by the small number of highly advanced nations that have been successful in producing viable motor vehicle industries. Among the eight nations listed in Table 1.1, Canada does not have an indigenous industry, with almost all of its output being produced at satellite plants of foreign manufacturers like GM, Ford, and Honda. In the United Kingdom, its once independent firms have been taken over by foreigners, with Ford now controlling Jaguar and Aston Martin and BMW buying Rover and Rolls-Royce, the latter with Volkswagen.

The exceptional role of motor vehicles in the revival of postwar economies through industrialization and trade prompts the question, Why would the U.K. permit the loss of such corporate "crown jewels" as Rolls-Royce and Jaguar to foreign ownership? The magnitude of the Nissan bailout provides most of the answer. In the current era, government subsidies for tottering firms with taxpayers' money are prohibitively expensive and, consequently, politically precarious for elected officials. Moreover, the liberalized regimes covering international trade and investments frown on protectionist barriers keeping out foreign goods and capital ownership, especially when these are erected by the more affluent countries listed in Table 1.1. The barriers also invite retaliatory measures by trading partners that could escalate into trade wars and seriously injure the economic well-being of the warring countries. For example, when the United States unilaterally imposed higher tariffs under the Smoot-Hawley Act of

Table 1.1
Selected Motor Vehicle-Producing Countries with Their Gross Domestic Product (GDP)

Country	Estimated 1996 Gross Domestic Product (in $trillions)	1997 Motor Vehicle Production (in $millions)	% of World Production
United States	7.66	12.118	22.7
Japan	2.85	10.975	20.5
Germany	1.70	5.022	9.4
South Korea	0.65	2.818	5.3
France	1.22	2.581	4.8
Canada	0.72	2.571	4.8
United Kingdom	1.19	1.936	3.6
Italy	1.12	1.816	3.4

1930, the measure unfortunately deepened the Great Depression, which had just begun. With this in mind, the United States became a leading proponent for liberalized trade and investment rules following World War II, and these became codified for the free world in the General Agreement of Tariffs and Trade, now known as the World Trade Organization. With its large consumer market, the United States has frequently threatened countries that keep out U.S. goods and investments with retaliatory measures against their exports to the United States. Such pressure was successful in opening the Japanese automobile industry to U.S. equity investments at the beginning of the 1970s, with Chrysler buying a 15% interest in Mitsubishi Motors, General Motors acquiring 35% and 5.3% in Isuzu and Suzuki, respectively, and Ford buying 24% of Toyo Kogyo, later renamed Mazda. These American moves, however, still kept auto manufacturing within the handful of advanced nations (Western Europe, North America, and Japan) and were consequently similar in substance to Japanese transplants being built on U.S. soil.

A tangent to the globalization efforts of the industry occurred when multinational enterprises in the West and Japan undertook direct foreign investments in less-developed nations where legal, business, and social systems are amorphous and frequently corrupt and mistrustful of foreign profit motives. Nearly all Third World nations have vivid memories of "Yankee exploitation" and imperial colonialism and have adopted highly restrictive measures to curb the freewheeling excesses that occurred in the past. This is to ensure that when foreign investors depart—as they usually do—the host country is left with a viable enterprise and business infrastructure to continue profitable operations. Because of government restrictions, which they regard as onerous, automakers were initially content to compete in their own affluent markets and shunned the high risks of venturing into communist or socialist states with their daunting, bureaucratic approval agencies. This corporate attitude could exist provided demand remained high and operations were profitable in domestic markets, a situation that was jeopardized in the United States when foreign carmakers exported heavily to North America and when Japanese transplants added significant capacity that threatened domestic suppliers.

To compete against the low-cost producers of small cars, General Motors, Ford, and Chrysler attempted to automate existing facilities and downsize product lines and, after these failed to regain market share from the Japanese, began a significant migration of factories to Mexico, thus beginning the globalization phase to low-cost developing nations. For Detroit, Mexico was an ideal production location because of its relatively stable, democratically elected central government, long history of trade with the United States, and official willingness to industrialize with U.S. capital, technology, and managerial expertise. Its main attraction, however, remained its nearby, low-cost production environment, where output could be exported to the United States. As industrialization proceeded and national income rose, local Mexican demand would became a factor in Detroit's planning.

EMERGING MARKETS

As Third World, less-developed nations adopted the high-growth policies used by the advanced economies such as importation and use of technology to rapidly industrialize, economic activity grew strongly and paralleled the development of significant consumer markets. As in Mexico, these changes attracted the attention of motor vehicle manufacturers in the United States, Western Europe, and Japan, where consumer markets were maturing, and, consequently, sales outlets abroad were increasingly sought.

While North America and Western Europe will continue to be very important markets given their volume, most of the growth in vehicle sales will occur outside of these markets. Growth in vehicle sales is very closely tied to growth in real GDP [gross domestic product]. In Asia Pacific, Latin America, and Central and Eastern Europe, real GDP is projected to grow at twice the 2.5% average rate forecasted for the next ten years in North America and Western Europe. As a result the share of real world GDP will shift from North America and Western Europe to Asia Pacific, with some slight increase in Latin America and Central and Eastern Europe. Vehicle sales growth should reflect this shift. (Strauss 1997)

The estimated linear relationship between real GDP growth and vehicle sales growth for four emerging economic regions and two mature ones is depicted in Figure 1.1.

In addition to rising income, the low degree of market saturation and little available production capacity to supply the potential demand have placed developing countries high on the agenda of motor vehicle firms. As indicated on Table 1.1, world output is concentrated in the advanced economies because of their once-heavy domestic demand. Even in countries (Japan and Germany) where output is dedicated to the export trade, a significant proportion is sent to North America, where supply is already ample from existing and new plants coming on stream. In the regions where potential demand is high, such as China, India, Southeast Asia, and Latin America, government officials have erected trade barriers to keep exports out and induce foreign firms to build operating plants to supply domestic markets. Capital, advanced technology, and managerial expertise are then brought in, giving further impetus to industrial development, employment of local workers, and rising income levels. While such transfers have been beneficial to the host countries, sales and earnings from these costly investments have not materialized for the foreign auto firms, with the current recessions in Asia and South America further plaguing market outlook. This has been especially true for Japanese companies, like Nissan and Mitsubishi Motors, that witnessed both domestic and other Asian demand evaporate following financial turmoil in the region in 1997–1998. The value of their foreign investments declined as steep devaluations occurred in the Thai

Figure 1.1
Projected Vehicle Sales and Real Gross Domestic Product

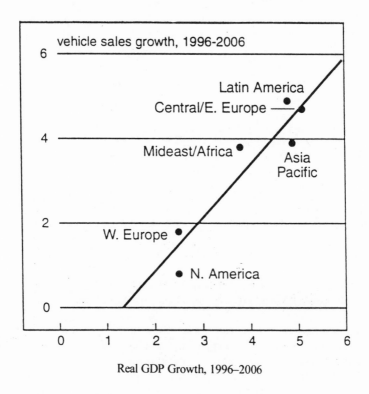

Real GDP Growth, 1996–2006

Source: Federal Reserve Bank of Chicago, *Chicago Fed Letter*, Number 121 (September 1997): Figure 3.

baht, Malaysian ringget, Indonesian rupiah, and South Korean won. In Indonesia operations had to be suspended because of civil unrest and acts of violence, and in Korea, local firms like Hyundai, Kia, and Daewoo—in which Japanese and American firms hold equity stakes—have been brought to the brink of bankruptcy. Such are the current grim realities of areas of the world for which there are very bright forecasts, and the striking contrasts compound the risks for carmakers that are operating on a global basis.

Tiger Economies

Following its successful postwar reconstruction and development of heavy industry and export markets, Japan, with its policy of supporting high-value-added manufacturing, became the role model for other Asian "tigers" wishing to close the economic gap between them and the advanced, Western nations. South Korea, Taiwan, Singapore, and Hong Kong were the first tier of industrializing nations using the Japanese blueprint, with the success of Korea in entering the U.S. export trade in motor vehicles, consumer electronics, and semiconductors galvanizing similar action in Thailand, Malaysia, Indonesia, and even China. All professed to have open-market economies with unfettered trade, but, in reality, industries and imports were carefully regulated. Malaysia's New Economic Policy of 1971 even attempted to allocate high-paying jobs resulting from its industrialization to indigenous Malays in order to rectify the low standard of living of its native population relative to non-Malays, mainly Chinese and Indians. Malays were also given specific ownership stakes in manufacturing firms amounting to 30% of the capital stock. The wholesale redistribution of assets and income in the country was underwritten by the rising value of Malaysia's considerable gas and oil reserves during the energy shortages of the 1970s, which also attracted foreign investors such as Japanese automakers that were interested in supplying motor vehicles to this emerging market. Ordinarily, the heavy-handed regulations of a small country like Malaysia would deter foreign manufacturers, but the high yen exchange rate and saturation of Japan's domestic market prompted numerous carmakers to set up factories throughout Southeast Asia. Malaysia's high economic growth rates of 7–8% per year, boosted by rising world prices for its natural resources, were also attracting outside investors, and by 1984 over 83% of the country's passenger cars was being supplied by Japanese companies, led by Nissan with 27.5%, Toyota with 22.2%, and Honda with 13% (Torii 1991, 393).

Government Intervention. The extent of foreign dominance of this flagship industry proved unacceptable to Malaysia's prime minister Mahathir Mohamad, who in 1979 initiated a national car project that would be owned and operated by native Malays. When his engineers and managers were found incapable of carrying out the huge undertaking, Kuala Lumpur turned to Mitsubishi Motors, then a minor enterprise, to develop the Proton national car. The auto firm seized the opportunity, even though a 70% majority ownership in the joint venture would be held by a state corporation, HICOM, and Mitsubishi Motors and Mitsubishi Corporation, the huge trading house, would each own 15%. With strong support from the state in the form of a 40% exemption on duties for completely knockdown auto kits from Japan and a 50% reduction on excise taxes, Proton, which began production in 1985, quickly grabbed the lion's share of the market, which reached 73% in three years. This success, however, did not turn the company into a major global competitor because its share in more important areas like Japan, the United States, and Europe remained small. Toward the end of the 1990s, as its sales and profits continued to slump even in Malaysia, Mitsubishi, like its larger compatriot Nissan, sought bailout capital in order to remain viable.

MARKET DYNAMICS

At this early stage in the industry's globalization, the large home markets of the major manufacturers frequently dictate their performances. The preceding case of Mitsubishi in Malaysia is illustrative of how a major foreign presence cannot compensate for sales lost in Japan. Robust sales in the United States, on the other hand, have prompted record sales and profits for Detroit's automakers. In addition, while General Motors and Ford have invested heavily in immigrant plants in Mexico, most of this output had been earmarked for export to the United States, with the firms profiting from low-cost Mexican production and exceptionally strong demand in the United States that was undergirded by falling unemployment, inflation, interest rates, and gasoline prices and further stimulated by rising stock and bond markets. The reverse was true in Japan, the locomotive of East Asia, and as it sputtered and proceeded into negative growth, all surrounding, smaller countries like Malaysia and South Korea followed, illustrating the powerful effect that such major economies like Japan, the United States, and Germany had on their respective regions. Not all Japanese automakers, however, were sucked in by their recession's vortex. Strong U.S. sales for Toyota, Honda, and Subaru cushioned these firms from the deterioration in Asia, and the reason for this success can be attributed to their product offerings in larger sport utility vehicles and well-designed sedans. These are also the attributes that are responsible for Detroit's record profits, which the car firms are using to diversify their products and geographical markets. The development of hybrid vehicles, particularly light trucks that are larger and have the driving comfort of a passenger sedan, has been highly successful in spurring customer sales. The developmental costs of their "world car"—a compact vehicle that can be manufactured and sold in poorer, emerging markets—are also being underwritten by the munificent stream of revenues derived from the United States, as are plant investment costs in China, Latin America, and other emerging markets. The exceptionally bright U.S. sales picture can be seen in the following numbers: "Light vehicle sales for 1994–1997 averaged 14.9 million units, with unprecedented stability. Sales for 1994, 1995, 1996, and 1997 were 15.0 million, 14.7 million, 15.0 million, and 15 million, respectively. Sales for 1998 were higher at 15.5 million and forecasts for 1999 and 2000 are expected to be 15.6 million and 15.5 million respectively" (Strauss and Motyka 1999). The sustained demand for their output has given the Detroit firms the financial resources that strongly advance their globalization programs, and some of these strategies include:

1. Equity ownership in faltering Asian firms, such as Ford's takeover of Mazda.

2. Partnerships with foreign firms as in the DaimlerChrysler merger, with subsequent integration to form a powerful global company.

3. Equity and production arrangements with local suppliers that form a global sourcing network for raw materials, parts, and assembled modules.

4. Streamlined production processes that can be duplicated in other parts of the world, such as GM's Eisenach, Germany, plant and its successor, the "Blue Macaw" facility in Brazil.

5. Research and development of a small "world car" for emerging markets.

6. Investment, testing, and production of hybrid vehicles for the robust North American market as well as in low-polluting autos that can meet stringent emission standards already on the books in California.

7. Refinements of intrafirm distribution and trade systems where excess vehicle supplies in one depressed area can be shipped to areas of high demand.

8. Production and distribution channels that cross national boundaries in order to take advantage of regional free-trade pacts such as the North America Free Trade Agreement (NAFTA), Mercosur (the large South American bloc), the European Union, and the Association of Southeast Asian Nations (ASEAN).

GLOBAL PLANNING

The preceding moves by the American automakers were necessitated by the shifting regional demand dynamics shown in Table 1.2, where from 1986 to 1996, growth in North America fell behind that of other regions. Adding to their woes, exports from Japan and Korea took large shares of the U.S. market. In the succeeding "crisis" years, 1996–1998, growth returned to North America and Western Europe, while substantial recession occurred in Asia and South America. Furthermore, those regions experiencing negative growth were expected to rebound smartly beginning in 1999 with developing markets in Asia and South America forecast to have huge sales increases of 116.7% and 81.5%, respectively, returning to earlier trend lines of the 1980s. The robust percentages make forecasts for North America's increase of 13.3% and Western Europe of 9.8% appear anemic, but the comparison is disingenuous. Western markets may be maturing, but their motor vehicle industries have undergone considerable production rationalization through mergers, acquisitions, and departing firms, leaving a few strong producers that can operate successfully even in a moderate or slow-growth environment. Japan, Korea, and almost all developing countries, in contrast, have a host of domestic or foreign manufacturers unprofitably serving small percentages of their national markets. For most of these companies, the wrenching downturn in sales and profits is their first such experience, and many are unwilling to implement needed retrenchment and cost-cutting programs. Some automakers were paralyzed by the sudden onset of adverse economic conditions, leading to further deterioration of corporate balance sheets and ultimate bailouts by the government or foreign firms. Success in the huge U.S. market, on the other hand, has kept Toyota and Honda in high gear to the extent that both companies are building facilities in Indiana and Alabama, respectively, to meet the increased demand for their popular sport utility vehicles. This is the type of diversification that global companies are striving for in which downturn in one major region is offset by thriving

Table 1.2
Vehicle Sales Growth Rates by Region (%)

Region	Boom Years 1986-1996	Crisis Years 1996-1998	Recovery Years 1998-2008 (projected)
North America	-5.6	6.5	13.3
South America	81.3	-6.9	81.5
Western Europe	9.9	13.9	9.8
Japan and Korea	45.0	-24.1	42.4
Other Asia	102.7	-20.0	116.7
Other	16.7	12.2	56.5

Source: Federal Reserve Bank of Chicago *Chicago Fed Letter*, Special Issue, Number 145a (September 1999): Table 2.

circumstances elsewhere. Simply investing everywhere, however, is not sufficient to guarantee success, especially in sophisticated markets, like the United States, where consumer preferences are rapidly changing. Local affiliates must consequently be given appropriate decision-making authority to implement plans geared to their market's conditions. Thus, Honda and Toyota have succeeded in the United States because they not only have been adept at constructing facilities that produce vehicles in great demand but have excelled at designing compact and sedan passenger cars that have great appeal to the American driving public.

FOREIGN INVESTMENTS AND ALLIANCES

In the midst of record sales and earnings, the Big Three American firms (General Motors, Ford, and Chrysler) have briskly moved to diversify their assets before the inevitable recession strikes their principal market. Executives at Chrysler, remembering the trying period when the company was bailed out by the U.S. government, have moved to ensure the automaker's future by outright merger with Daimler-Benz of Germany, which is prominently known worldwide for its luxury sedan lines. In spite of this considerable recognition, it was the German company that initiated the merger, undoubtedly to solidify its base in the huge American market. It had already shown a serious interest in the region with its first U.S. manufacturing investment in Alabama, together with the listing of its stock on the New York Stock Exchange. In the first year following the merger, DaimlerChrysler used its presence on Wall Street to raise $4.5 billion through the sale of its corporate notes with the assistance of two American investment banks, Credit Suisse First Boston and Salomon Smith Barney. The large issue, denominated in U.S. dollars, is an example of the former Daimler-Benz AG now being able to diversify its source of capital by tapping America's large financial market, with the opportunity to do this clearly enhanced by its alliance with Chrysler. The dollar issue further indicates that the raised funds will probably be earmarked for investments in North and South America or Asia; otherwise, the notes would have been denominated in euros or deutsche marks. It also indicates that the merged company, DaimlerChrysler, will be working in those areas—Asia and South America—where the company is especially weak and where forecasts for vehicle sales are particularly bright. The company already trails non-Asian companies, like General Motors, Ford, and Volkswagen, that have invested heavily in both South America and Asia. The forte of DaimlerChrysler, moreover, carries over from strengths of the individual partners, with Chrysler known for its large, sedan and Jeep sport utility vehicles and Mercedes-Benz (of Daimler-Benz) for its luxury nameplates. Expertise in these product categories, however, will be of little help in poor countries like China and India, where Volkswagen and Suzuki—both known for small, inexpensive, durable cars—are sales leaders.

World Financial Centers

In addition to emerging vehicle markets in developing countries, major financial markets like New York's Wall Street, will have a significant voice in the success of the DaimlerChrysler merger, with unrelenting scrutiny undertaken by the media, large brokerage houses, and pension and mutual funds. Monthly sales figures and quarterly earnings reports are closely watched, with disappointments in either prompting fund managers to sell their extensive stockholdings, causing the price of the company's stock—a principal barometer of financial health—to fall. If events continue to spiral downward, credit ratings are lowered, and access to financing is slowed or terminated. Chrysler Corporation had a history of such financial crises, and, consequently, the merged DaimlerChrysler will be carefully monitored when the U.S. economy enters into recession or when recovery in Asian markets leaves the company behind.

The growth of international trade and investments as well as the turn to capitalist-based, free-market economies by the former USSR and the People's Republic of China have increased the influence of major equity, debt, and monetary exchanges in underwriting the growing number of international transactions and alliances. Development of these financial institutions, such as equity markets in developing nations, was also a necessary precursor in the process to globalize by domestically based motor vehicle firms. Emerging economies, lacking financial resources, tapped foreign sources of capital, like the World Bank, and regional development institutions for extensive infrastructural building projects, like roads, ports, communication, transportation, and other public utility systems, in addition to paying for advanced foreign technology needed for industrialization. Rising standards of living subsequently attracted private funds, both portfolio investments for domestic equity markets and longer-term capital from foreign industries, like motor vehicles, for plant and equipment. A large share of the portfolio investment money came from U.S. mutual and pension funds as sustained bull markets in equities accelerated the flow of new money into these investment and retirement accounts while greatly increasing their underlying asset values. Asset managers, in turn, continually searched for high-return stocks, whether in growth industries like Internet-related business or foreign equity exchanges in countries experiencing economic expansion. When these portfolio funds come into newly industrializing economies like Thailand, Malaysia, Mexico, or Brazil, the inflow usually accelerates economic development, but the reverse is true when such investments, frequently referred to as "hot money," abruptly exit the country, as they have done in nearly all developing nations of Asia (including Russia) and Latin America. The rapid exodus from Southeast Asia in 1997 resulted in financial paralysis as both domestic currencies—inherently weak to begin with—and stock markets promptly nose-dived. Operating capital in the form of hard-currency loans denominated in yen or U.S. dollars became unavailable as banks in Japan and the United States suspended the extension of new debt to the tottering economies, forcing local banks and companies to default on existing loan arrangements. With a wrecked consumer economy, sales of expensive items like automobiles evaporated, with car sales slumping around 50% from 1997 to 1998 in Thailand, Malaysia, and Indonesia and 21% in the Philippines ("Car Trouble" 1998, 48). The economic maelstrom also devastated South Korea and its fledgling auto industry and proceeded westward to shatter a feeble Russian economy in 1998, then plunging Brazil into recession as its currency, the real, was devalued in 1999.

Altered Business Plans

In the resulting carnage, major motor vehicle firms acted quickly to scale back plant construction in affected areas or consider exporting from regions where inventory was rapidly accumulating because of languid sales. For example, investment plans for a large General Motors assembly plant in Thailand, announced in May 1996, are being reassessed by corporate headquarters in light of the new economic realities. Some decisions already made in January 1998 include:

1.   Delayed opening of the plant, which had been scheduled for 1999.

2.   Scaling back of project costs from $750 million to $450 million.

3.   Reduction of plant capacity from an annual rate of 100,000 vehicles to less than one-half, or 40,000 units.

4.   Possible assembly of a less-expensive vehicle than the $15,000 Opel Astra, which GM had planned to build (Blumenstein 1998).

More heavily affected has been Toyota, which had to stop production at its two Thai plants because of the slump in car sales. Its Hilux brand, furthermore, is the sales leader for the country, and the company has begun to make plans to export the Hilux pickup truck to New Zealand and Australia, which had been supplied by Japanese factories prior to the Thai currency crisis. The steep devaluation of the Thai baht has prompted Toyota to source more of its parts from local manufacturers instead of importing them from Japan, where the strong yen–weak baht rate has made components priced in yen too expensive for use in Thai manufacturing. The diverging currency values, moreover, make Thai-made parts cheaper in export markets, and Toyota is using this to also export diesel engines, which it makes in a joint venture with Siam Cement, to Malaysia, Portugal, and New Zealand. The export plans have the fervent backing of the Thai government, which specifically asked the Japanese automaker to restart production at its factories as well as export output to help reduce the nation's high unemployment rate and to bring foreign money into the cash-poor economy. These requests were acceded to by Toyota as a way of strengthening relations with Bangkok and demonstrating its intention of staying in Thailand during good and bad times (Shuchman 1997).

Ford's huge, $1.3 billion plant construction program in southern Brazil is another project undergoing reassessment in a major emerging market experiencing adverse economic times. The large American automaker had originally planned to locate the facility in Rio Grande do Sul, in an industrializing Brazilian state that is close to nearby trading partners of the country, namely, Argentina, Uruguay, and Paraguay. The Mercosur free-trade agreement covering the four nations had already drawn General Motors to the area, and state officials were intent on doing the same with Ford, using such incentives as tax breaks and subsidized loans amounting to $260 million. In the aftermath of the real devaluation and with capital fleeing the country, the governor of Rio Grande do Sul, citing ruinous economic conditions, reneged on the incentives, prompting Ford to consider other options. Slowing car sales in the Mercosur region meant that the company did not need output from the proposed facility, and because plant construction was in a preliminary stage, the project could be moved elsewhere. This option was enhanced by a range of financial incentives offered by other Brazilian states attempting to attract the compact car plant with its 5,000 new jobs. Two months after quitting its first site, Ford chose the northeastern state of Bahia, which South Korea's Asia Motors had also selected as the site of a new car plant prior to its implosion in Korea's fiscal crisis of 1997. The resulting circumstances of the two firms, Ford and Asia Motors, were indeed striking. The Korean manufacturer, a part of Kia Motors, was placed in court receivership and eventually sold to Hyundai Motors. The new parent of Asia Motors was so short of cash that little thought was given to resurrecting the Brazilian plant (Yamaguchi 1999). No such delay awaited Ford's plans in South America. Within days of choosing the Bahia site, the firm announced moves to assemble its Laser cars in Bogotá, Colombia, even though that nation was under the same financial duress as Brazil (Ford Motor Co. 1999).

SURGING HOME MARKETS

More support for Ford and General Motors (GM) is coming from huge profits derived from booming North American markets, as shown in Table 1.3. Even though Ford recorded losses of $120 million in Latin America for the second quarter of 1999, these and its small Asian loss were easily covered by the nearly $1.9 billion of net income from North America. Latin American losses for GM were much less than Ford's, with the latter, as indicated earlier, incurring major problems in the location of a large Brazilian plant. GM's losses in Brazil were also cushioned by the equity stakes in its new plant held by local suppliers, with the early negative returns apportioned among various owners. Business risk during bad economic times is reduced when there are multiple owners invested in a major project. The converse is also true during strong economic periods when profits are diluted by the number of equity holders. Loss of some control by the multinational corporation over operations can also hinder GM's management of the plant, but if differences between partners become too intense, the American firm can easily buy out any recalcitrant partner, replacing it with other local interests more amenable to GM's management. GM can also do what Ford did: build a wholly owned subsidiary in another part of the country.

The Asian losses for General Motors are considerably more than for Ford, reflecting the greater investment program that GM has undertaken, especially in China. Here, too, the Asian losses are easily underwritten by the income from North America and Europe. Moreover, the early losses are anticipated as the Detroit automakers diversify their assets by building in foreign areas where potential business is anticipated to be good. In so doing, valuable experience is

Table 1.3
Second-Quarter 1999 Net Income for Ford and General Motors by Region

Region	Net Income (in $millions)	
	Ford	General Motors
North America	1,900	1,530
Europe	88	187
Latin America	-120	-40
Asia	-9	-83

Source: *Wall Street Journal*, July 21, 1999, pp. A3, A6.

gained, and the firms keep up with foreign competitors, like Volkswagen and Toyota, that already hold large segments of the Latin American and Asian motor vehicle markets. The Asian market, in particular, is now abreast of Western Europe in sales, with both regions having annual totals of 13.4 million vehicles, somewhat below booming North American sales of 17 million units. South America trails with 3.3 million units sold, but production capacity vis-à-vis sales lags there, with only 2.5 million vehicles produced per year. Asian output, in contrast, exceeded sales by a sizable 3.7 million units, mainly due to prevailing recessionary forces ("The World" 1998). The shortfall in North and South America means that excess output from Western Europe and Asia is capable of supplying export markets in the New World until investment projects come onstream. In attempting to manage these global dynamics, the motor vehicle manufacturers have not only implemented large direct foreign investments but negotiated major cross-border deals as well. The globalization tends to follow two tracks, with multinational firms from the industrialized countries building new operating capacity in emerging markets, such as the Ford and GM plants in Brazil and Thailand. Among themselves, the principal firms are negotiating significant cross-border deals like the DaimlerChrysler merger, with the Renault-Nissan alliance and Ford's takeover of Volvo cars following closely on the heels of the big merger.

INDUSTRY CONSOLIDATION

The hectic and very expensive business of securing markets abroad and building foreign capacity has divided the world's automotive industry into three levels, led by a first tier of large, very profitable firms, like General Motors, Ford, Toyota, Volkswagen, and Honda, that is undertaking most of the foreign direct investments and acquisition of smaller firms. In the Indonesian crisis, for example, Volkswagen (VW) purchased Lamborghini, the originally Italian luxury sports carmaker, from a son of President Suharto even as VW was attempting to outbid BMW for control of Britain's Rolls-Royce. A second tier of firms includes Chrysler, Mercedes-Benz (automotive arm of Daimler-Benz), Renault, Nissan, and Fiat which have sought or negotiated alliances with each other to increase their coverage of global markets and compete with first-tier companies. A third tier consists of nameplates such as Volvo, Mazda, Kia, Mitsubishi Motors, and even Fiat, which have lost or stand to lose, their independence as they become subsidiaries of other companies. These deals, furthermore, are so costly that only a few participants have the financial resources to compete in the world bidding. The Renault-Nissan alliance, for example, called for a $5.44 billion cash infusion to debt-ridden Nissan, while Ford's purchase of the car operations of Volvo AB amounted to $6.45 billion.

In the global rationalization, corporate size becomes an important parameter as smaller companies join forces to compete against the giants or are taken over in whole or in part by bigger firms. These moves have altered the 1994 list of top-twenty motor vehicles manufacturers published by the

Organization of Economic Cooperation and Development (see Table 1.4). The top four firms—General Motors, Ford, Toyota, and Volkswagen—are the usual pacesetters as they implement billion-dollar plant construction programs or acquire smaller companies. This top group will expand to include DaimlerChrysler and eliminate the two individual partners, #6 for Chrysler and #16 for Mercedes-Benz (Table 1.4). A Renault (#9) combination with Nissan (#5) will also be included in the group provided the pairing is successful and yields greater returns. Otherwise, the alliance may fission and each side may go its separate way. With Mazda and Kia no longer independent, these two listings in Table 1.4 may be eliminated. Volvo's passenger car business, now integrated with Ford, is also disappearing as an individual entity, but even with the addition of Volvo's truck output to the car business, the automaker was too small to make the top-twenty listing. Ford, therefore, paid a hefty sum not for Volvo's operating capacity but for the carmaker's luxury nameplate.

The Contest for Volvo

Volvo's strong presence in Europe and reputation for well-built, safe vehicles were also attributes sought by the Dearborn, Michigan, headquarters of Ford. A further impetus to bid for the company derived from the moves that had already given General Motors a 50% equity stake in Saab, Sweden's other auto firm, and compelled Renault of France to take a 25% stake in Volvo Car, a 45% share in Volvo Truck, and a 10% holding in Volvo AB, the parent firm, which, in turn, held a 20% stake in Renault (see Figure 1.2 for intercorporate shareholdings). The extensive interconnections between Renault and Volvo led to a near-merger between the two companies, and following the publicized collapse of the talks, the smaller Volvo found itself "in play," with the Swedish firm being courted by Volkswagen of Germany and Fiat of Italy before its decision to join Ford. With General Motors rumored to be interested in Volvo, Ford was forced to make a preemptive bid; otherwise, it could forever lose the opportunity of adding this new "jewel" to its corporate "crown," which already included its Lincoln luxury car line, Mazda of Japan, and Jaguar and Aston Martin of the United Kingdom. The highly profitable Dearborn firm could also dip into its $24 billion of retained earnings to execute a cash purchase of Volvo Car and subsequently forego difficult negotiations regarding a stock deal or debt financing. The solid financial foundation also endeared the smaller Volvo to the Ford proposal, especially since it had undoubtedly resigned itself to foreign ownership ever since the ill-fated discussions with Renault. The smooth outcomes of Ford's prior acquisitions were also an important factor: "Ford has been unusually successful at international mergers, having bought Jaguar a decade ago and made it profitable while fixing the chronic quality problems that long tarnished Jaguar's reputation. . . . Ford's success at Jaguar and its international staff were the main reasons why Volvo chose Ford's bid over a slightly higher offer from Fiat S.p.A. of Italy, people close to negotiations say" (Bradsher 1999, C4).

Table 1.4
Production Leaders in 1994

Rank	Company	Worldwide Production
1	General Motors	8,035,000
2	Ford	6,518,000
3	Toyota	5,164,000
4	Volkswagen	3,153,888
5	Nissan	2,784,000
6	Chrysler	2,774,718
7	Fiat	2,410,000
8	PSA Peugeot Citroen	1,989,810
9	Renault	1,914,682
10	Mitsubishi	1,797,000
11	Honda	1,744,000
12	Mazda	1,227,000
13	Hyundai	1,174,000
14	BMW Rover	1,051,185
15	Suzuki	970,300
16	Mercedes-Benz	886,533
17	Kia	675,461
18	Isuzu	544,303
19	Auto vaz (Russia)	535,000
20	Fuji Heavy (Subaru)	488,093

Source: OECD, *Globalisation of Industry:Overview and Sector Reports* (Paris, 1996, p. 171, Table 4.5). Copyright OECD, 1996.

Figure 1.2
Cross-Equity Holdings in the Automobile Industry, June 1992

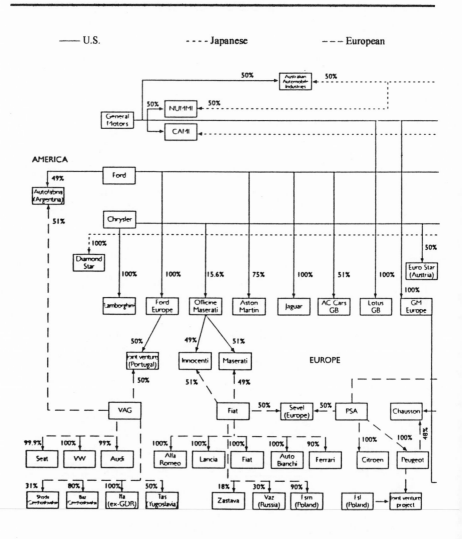

Source: OECD, *Globalisation of Industry: Overview and Sector Reports* (Paris, 1996, p. 189, Figure 4.9). Copyright OECD, 1996.

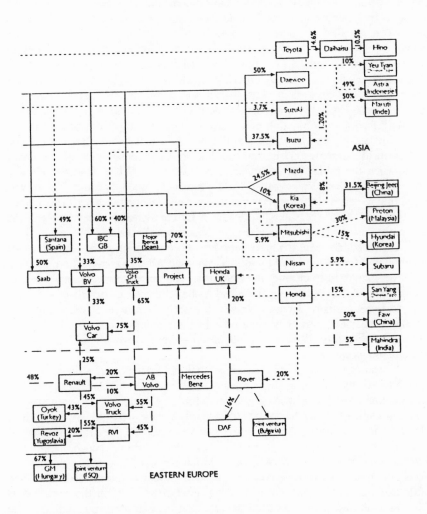

Prior to the Fiat bid, Volvo held discussions with the chairman of Volkswagen, and both Italian and German mass producers of small cars, like Ford, were eager to add the prestigious Volvo nameplate to their product line. Ford, however, was interested only in the car division of Volvo, for which it would pay $6.45 billion, whereas Fiat and VW were bidding for Volvo's profitable truck division as well. "Although there are few synergies between cars and trucks in terms of parts, auto makers like to be involved in both areas because demand for the two can move in different cycles. A bad year in cars can be offset by a good year in trucks, and vice versa. Moreover, car dealers like to be able to sell fleet customers a whole range of vehicles, not just part of the range" (Latour and Mitchener 1998, A3, A8). Consequently, Fiat's bid of approximately $7 billion may have been slightly more than Ford's, but the Italian company was actually offering much less because it was intent on securing Volvo's business in heavy trucks, buses, and construction equipment as well as cars. Fiat's bid was also weak because of reduced profits at home resulting from the termination of government-sponsored rebates offered to car buyers. Its sizable foreign markets in Poland and Brazil are also languishing due to the world's currency crisis, and Fiat had to delay construction of a Russian plant when the ruble was devalued in August 1998. While financially much stronger than Fiat, Volkswagen's bid ultimately failed because Volvo was unwilling to part with its non-car operations. This intention was reaffirmed when it purchased a 12.8% stake in Scania AB, the Swedish truck maker, and announced plans to possibly merge truck operations (Bradsher 1999, A1, C4).

Considerable credit for developing Ford's winning bid goes to its international staff established by former chairman Alex Trotman, who initiated a massive global restructuring in 1994 that combined the company's North American and European operations and assigned the development of a "world car" to Lebanese-born Jacques Nasser. Formerly in charge of the company's European business, Nasser became president and chief executive officer of the entire corporation on January 1, 1999, and made the Volvo deal one of his first major announcements.

In contrast to the Ford success at making foreign acquisitions, Renault stumbled badly when it had management control of American Motors Corporation (AMC) and when it got into a bruising battle with Volvo managers and stockholders in its heavy-handed efforts to take over the Swedish firm. Some of the blame for these miscues can be traced to the nationalization of Renault by the French government in 1945, which added significant bureaucratic control to the car firm's decision-making process, especially in foreign markets, where both corporate executives and government officials had little experience. Cultural and managerial clashes occurred in the early 1980s after Renault took a 46% controlling stake in American Motors, resulting in the departure of AMC's chairman and chief executive officer. Bereft of an experienced leader, the U.S. firm, which had been floundering badly, could not be turned around, and by 1987 mounting losses forced Renault to sell AMC to Chrysler. The latter company, then under the shrewd direction of Lee Iacocca, was quick to realize the potential of AMC's Jeep sport utility vehicles, making his new acquisition highly profitable in a few short years.

Volvo, unlike American Motors, had profitable niches in both North America and Europe and was therefore not particularly eager to have Renault, with its spotty record in the two areas, come in and dictate how its business should be conducted. Renault also offered a buyout consummated with an exchange of shares, making Volvo shareholders somewhat dubious about receiving stock in a company controlled by the French government. In the end, the Volvo owners voted against the merger with Renault, although the union had gained the support of Volvo's chief executive, who was then discharged. A year after the failed merger, the French government began the sale to private interests of part of its majority stake in Renault, thus tacitly acknowledging that state ownership had become a burden to the globalization plans of the carmaker. Moreover, the protectionist barriers erected by Paris to keep foreign cars and investors from entering the country were being eroded. This dismantling was required if France wished to continue membership in the European Union and the World Trade Organization and receive the benefits that membership conferred, such as lowered duties on French goods exported to other countries. The government's yielding action to foreigners prompted Toyota, Japan's largest automaker, to invest in a $700 million car plant in the country, and Renault, in turn, took a major stake in Nissan, Japan's second largest motor vehicle firm.

The Renault–Nissan Alliance

With the government opening its borders to foreign competitors and with limited presence outside Europe, Renault realized that it could be left behind as the mélange of international deals eliminated potential partners. Even with respect to the $5.44 billion purchase of Nissan shares that it consummated, the French auto company was Nissan's second choice behind DaimlerChrysler, which was negotiating to have Nissan fill its own gaping absence in Asia. The listing of leading vehicle manufacturers in Table 1.4 presents the industry after the Renault-Volvo merger talks collapsed and prior to the huge deals at the end of the 1990s, namely, the DaimlerChrysler merger announced in May 1998, Ford's takeover of Volvo, and the Renault equity alliance with Nissan. Combinations involving Fiat (with GM), PSA Peugeot Citroen, and Mitsubishi (with DaimlerChrysler) are expected in the near future because of weaknesses in their global strategies. General Motors, taking advantage of the economic crisis in Asia, has increased its equity ownership in Suzuki, Isuzu, and Fuji Heavy Industries as it attempts to keep pace with Ford's takeover of Mazda. Volkswagen, the German leader, also has a large presence in Asia, with its share of the China market exceeding 50%.

May 1998 can arguably be cited as a principal inflection point in the globalization of the industry, with the DaimlerChrysler merger announced at the beginning of the month. Within a week of the announcement, Chrysler's head, Robert Eaton, "insisted the new company would be a force in Asia. It would consider all available means to expand its Asian presence, Mr. Eaton said, including investments, partnerships and acquisition" (Sapsford 1998). At the time, Mitsubishi Motors was thought to be the target company of the merger partners, but attention quickly shifted to the bigger Nissan Motor Company, the fifth largest vehicle producer in the world, particularly when, on May 20, it announced another annual loss, this time for the 1998 fiscal year. Both Japanese firms had been losing money in the wake of the country's prolonged recession and were coming to the conclusion that each would not be able to pull itself out of the financial quagmire without outside assistance. Therefore, even before the consummation of its own megamerger, DaimlerChrysler began planning an alliance with the faltering Nissan. So was Renault of France. A tortoise-and-hare race subsequently evolved, with media attention focused on the outspoken Juergen Schrempp, who—giddy in the aftermath of his union with Chrysler— was expected to pull a Japanese "rabbit" from his acquisition hat. The bureaucratically encrusted Renault, plodding along in endless meetings with French government officials, was left in the speedy hare's dust but still emerged victorious at the finish line.

A Good Fit. For both companies, a deal with Nissan seemed ideal because each lacked a commanding presence in the Asia market. In addition to its number two hold on the Japanese market, Nissan had viable operations in the United States, Great Britain, Mexico, and Southeast Asia that included some of the most efficient vehicle assembly plants in the world. Nissan Diesel, the truck-producing affiliate of Nissan Motor, also held the fourth largest share of the Japanese truck market, with annual sales of $2.8 billion. Such a position was highly attractive to Daimler's Juergen Schrempp, who had initially targeted Nissan's truck business even with its heavy losses. The ensuing Chrysler merger fueled more ambitious plans, however, and by January 1999 Schrempp had "opened the door to something more. 'We do not exclude an equity participation' in Nissan Motor itself, Mr. Schrempp said, in response to questions at an industry conference" (Simison and Schuchman 1999). In rapid-fire sequence, Daimler-Benz, within months of completing its $35 billion Chrysler merger, was planning another massive deal with Nissan Motor, whose annual sales exceeded $49 billion, orders of magnitude bigger than those of Nissan Diesel Motor. Unfortunately, DaimlerChrysler was already beginning to feel merger pains when shareholders and top executives began leaving the company, and its stock price moved downward as planned synergies and cost savings remained elusive. The reality checks forced Schrempp to abandon negotiations with Nissan in March 1999. Nissan, meanwhile, had been conducting separate talks with Renault for an infusion of cash for its deteriorating condition.

Heavy Debt Load. Nissan's downward spiral had been caused by a sustained recession in Japan's economy that had resulted in losses not only for the automaker but for its industrial affiliates as well—many of whom were suppliers highly dependent on Nissan business. These include 201 firms in which Nissan has sizable ownership like the 39.8% stake in Nissan Diesel Motor, and the liabilities of these close affiliates are in the consolidated financial statements of the parent company. This indebtedness as well as potential liabilities in the form of guarantees signed by Nissan for loans taken out by affiliates to cover pension fund shortages came to $21.2 billion as of March 31, 1998. Not included on Nissan's balance sheet were the potential liabilities of a larger group of 389 affiliates for which the parent firm is probably responsible, and estimates of this second-tier debt load run to about $15 billion. Heretofore, the rise of the Japanese economy never threatened the viability of the Nissan *keiretsu* or industrial group because the few economic downturns that occurred, such as during the Arab oil embargo of 1973–1974, were vitiated by expanding overseas markets. In the current crisis, the domestic and Southeast Asian markets were simultaneously devastated by recession, and Nissan was further losing sales in the United States because it had few big sellers in the booming sport utility vehicle market, and the designs of its sedans were not appealing to buyers. Moreover, Japan's banking sector, also suffering from the recession and a surfeit of bad loans, was in no position to backstop the huge Nissan and its constellation of affiliated firms. The Japanese government was similarly affected and could not give much attention to the automaker.

A Global Combination. Nissan was consequently forced to seek assistance from abroad and despite its shaky financial situation, it was successful in attracting $5.4 billion from Renault because of its worldwide, name-brand recognition. Even in Western Europe, Nissan managed to garner sales of 490,000 vehicles in 1998 compared to Renault's sales of 1,760,000 units. In North America, where Renault has no business, Nissan sold 660,000 vehicles. In Central and South America, Nissan sold 190,000 vehicles compared to Renault's sales of 130,000. The bulk of Nissan's business, of course, came from sales in Asia and Australia totaling 1,090,000 vehicles. The capacity to build cars for a new Renault–Nissan global system is also impressive and placed the combined automakers ahead of Volkswagen and DaimlerChrysler and behind only General Motors, Ford, and Toyota (Shirouzu 1999). This can be determined in Table 1.4 by adding production totals of Nissan and Renault and those for Chrysler and Mercedes-Benz. The combination thus has the potential for producing a global competitor provided the wide expanse separating the companies and their management cultures can be bridged. In this, the circumstances leading to the alliance may prove to be beneficial because during the intense negotiations:

1.   Most of the financial liabilities of Nissan were exposed.

2.   Nissan, although the bigger partner, was forced to make changes in its troubled operations, particularly after it suffered a humiliating refusal by DaimlerChrysler to form an alliance.

3.   Opening Nissan to foreign investment starts the globalization of the firm as it brings foreign managerial oversight as well as joint production projects with Renault and foreign sourcing of parts that will disentangle it from its *keiretsu* relationships that nearly forced the company into bankruptcy.

4.   The troubled financial situation in Asia has accustomed once-closed economies to seek foreign assistance and investment that could accelerate the growth prospects in the region.

5.   The Japanese government—finally realizing the depths of the nation's economic malaise—has initiated massive fiscal and monetary programs to stimulate its lethargic economy and is having some measure of success.

Renault's prior failures in global deal-making (with American Motors and recently Volvo) have also conditioned its top executives to the challenges of joining with the much bigger Nissan and its alien management culture. The specific terms call for Renault to pay $5.4 billion for a 36.8% stake in Nissan, including warrants that, when exercised, could increase the Renault share to 44%. The current percentage does not give Renault management control of the Japanese company, a point reaffirmed by Louis Schweitzer, chairman and chief executive officer of the French company, because he "'did not think that would be good for Nissan'" (Strom 1999, 6). Schweitzer also believed that the Japanese company would carry the principal burden of turning itself around, but he insisted that Nissan accept three experienced executives from Renault, who would also sit on Nissan's board. The individuals are:

1.   Carlos Ghosn, who would be chief operating officer and second in command to Toshikazu Hanawa, the chief executive officer (CEO). Ghosn would oversee total quality management, corporate communications, and the legal department and would be supported by a staff of forty Renault executives in his immediate task of returning Nissan to profitability.

2.   Patrick Pelata, executive vice president in charge of product planning and design, production cost control, and corporate planning and strategy.

3.   Thierry Moulonguet who would be senior vice president and deputy chief financial officer and whose principal efforts would be directed at getting control of Nissan's enormous debt problems and implementing a debt reduction program. (Nissan Annual Report 1999)

Renault's Leaders. In exchange for the Japan-bound team, Renault elevated Nissan's CEO to its board of directors and a former member of Nissan's board became adviser to Renault's chairman and joined its management committee. A top-level global alliance committee was established, chaired by the CEOs of both companies and including five other executives from each side, that would oversee global synergies prepared by cross-company teams in the areas of vehicle engineering, power trains, purchasing, product planning, and marketing. This rapid response by Renault to its new alliance, including the dispatching of three key players to Tokyo and identification of problem areas, can be ascribed to its own billion-dollar loss in 1996 and the stringent efforts to turn itself around. In this, the company was guided by Schweitzer and Ghosn, who initiated an effective cost-cutting program that helped Renault earn $1 billion as early as 1998. Both leaders are planning a similar recovery at Nissan.

Louis Schweitzer, Renault's urbane chairman, is further distinguished by being the great-nephew of Dr. Albert Schweitzer, winner of the 1952 Nobel Peace Prize for his humanitarian work in Africa. Both Louis Schweitzer and Ghosn—who was appointed by the former to spearhead the Renault turnaround—are graduates of France's elite universities, and although Schweitzer's prior work experience was with the government, as head of Renault he has made and implemented difficult decisions. This was especially evident in the 1996 closing of the Vilvoorde plant in Belgium, an action that elicited stern protests not only from the president and prime minister of France but from the king and prime minister of Belgium as well.

In the end, all leaders had to yield to the inexorable global forces affecting automotive markets in Western Europe, especially those countries, like Belgium and France, that were members of the European Union (EU). Membership in the EU customs union meant that governments would refrain from erecting protectionist barriers against imports and investments from member nations, leaving formerly protected markets like those in France and Italy vulnerable to competition from U.S. and Japanese carmakers. Older plants, like the Vilvoorde facility (built in the 1930s), were also being measured against more recently constructed ones like the General Motors Opel plant in Eisenach, Germany, and the Sunderland, U.K., plant put up by Nissan. These had yearly output per employee of 71.9 and 56.7 vehicles, respectively, compared to 46.9 units for Renault's most productive facility at Flins, France. In addition to having more productive operating capacity, the Americans and Japanese were introducing their competitive marketing strategies, particularly more newly designed models that were taking sales away from older cars. With more entrants competing for greater shares of the mature European market, excess capacity became an inevitable result. Renault's overall operating rate, estimated at below 78%, placed added pressure on the company's management to reduce capacity and employment at one or more plants. Along these lines, Ford acted before Renault and closed its U.K. operations in Halewood following a $291 million loss in 1996 for its European division. Renault followed suit on February 27, 1997, with an announcement to close the Vilvoorde plant on July 31, in part because of an expected large loss ($925 million) for 1996 (Beamish, Morrison, Rosenzweig, and Inkpen 2000).

The denunciation from labor and political leaders was immediate and included a six-week strike at the Vilvoorde site and a campaign by the French Socialist Party against such capricious business practices that shatter the social compact that had brought harmonious labor relations to the region in the past. In March Schweitzer met with Belgium government officials and reiterated his intention to close the plant on July 31 and helped ease the turmoil by stating that $400 million would be allocated to cover severance pay and related closing costs. On March 19 the chairman met with leaders of the striking union and rejected a call for a 10% reduction in paid work hours in lieu of closing the plant, later indicating that Vilvoorde had always been a candidate for closure given its proximity to other operating facilities as well as the faltering markets it served. These steadfast, up-front, face-to-face points made by Schweitzer convinced French union members not to strike Renault and also prompted the Vilvoorde workers to return to work. In the aftermath of the plant closing, the chairman and Ghosn (the new executive vice president) vigorously cut $3.5 billion from the company's bloated costs, returning the company to profitability. By 1998, 48% of the savings from the corporate restructuring had been attained, and earnings for the year were expected to exceed $1 billion. In the stunning turnaround, Renault's leaders, besides closing the Belgian plant, accomplished their feat in the following ways:

1.   Streamlining purchasing costs by reducing the number of suppliers and giving them added responsibilities in quality and production control.

2.   Building more models using a common vehicle platform.

3.   "Designing appealing new vehicles [like] its most recent hit the Scenic, Europe's first minivan, . . . that is more compact than American monster vans, while being roomier than European hatchbacks" (Andrews 1999, C1, C2).

Global Synergies. The improved economic picture of Western Europe, particularly France, where Renault derives 48% of its revenues, played a crucial role in the firm's recovery. During the second quarter of 1996, France had negative growth of 1.6%, as reported by *The Economist*, followed by a strong 3.5% gain in its gross domestic product by the succeeding third quarter. For Nissan, Japan's economic revival is similarly important as the Renault executives attempt to reinvigorate their new partner. In the Far East, the Japanese economy is anticipated to bottom out in its long recession and begin growing slowly in 1999. The slight reversal will present a more benign backdrop to Nissan's domestic business but will be insufficient to effect recovery. The company's turnaround will therefore depend on global synergies that the two partners must extract from their fledgling alliance. In the endeavor, the booming American market offers some opportunities, especially since Renault does not operate there and can now use Nissan's established channels of distribution to reintroduce its vehicles, which it plans to do under the Nissan marque. Renault will also share design ideas with the Japanese company in order to make Nissan's models more appealing in the highly competitive U.S. market, where its sales fell 14.7% in 1998 while other makers were having a banner year. In the equally important area of excess plant capacity and bloated payroll, both companies' executives will take their cue from Schweitzer's difficult, but necessary, closing of the Vilvoorde plant. The shifting global dynamics have obviously made some facilities obsolete, particularly in Japan, a maturing market in recession where Nissan has most of its oldest factories and most of its employees. The company's president, Yoshikazu Hanawa, already understands what decisions need to be made and has conceded the possibility of closing plants in its efforts to cut costs quickly and consolidate operations with Renault. In so doing, it will be forsaking the lifetime employment system that was a hallmark of Japanese industry during its economic heyday as it comes to terms with the rapidly changing international milieu.

Occurring within the short time span of ten months beginning in May 1998, the Renault–Nissan alliance, together with the DaimlerChrysler merger and the Ford takeover of Volvo, constitutes a defining moment in the global motor vehicle industry. National boundaries, domestically oriented business, and insular management that heretofore characterized the world's most important manufacturing sector have yielded to the imperatives of operating globally. These include the diversification away from large home markets, like the United States, Western Europe, and Japan, in order to reduce business risk caused by a single, stagnating economy. Emerging markets with considerable profit opportunities have simultaneously attracted industry giants as they diversify production, supplier, and consumer bases. In international acquisitions, some corporate identities will be subsumed as smaller firms become wholly owned subsidiaries, and, in mergers, new organizations will arise.

Before the Arab oil embargo, oceans separated Ford and Mazda as well as Daimler-Benz and Chrysler, and, for the most part, the firms were primarily interested in the regional areas they served. After the Japanese carmakers began exporting and operating plants successfully in North America, a global perspective was suddenly thrust upon the industry, yielding the recent acceleration of global alliances. These and other decisive moments are analyzed in the ensuing chapters, beginning with the export blitz of small Japanese cars to the United States in the 1970s.

REFERENCES

Andrews, Edmund L. "Nissan Looms Large for Renault's 'Cost Killer.'" *New York Times*, March 27, 1999, pp. C1, C2.

Beamish, Paul W., Allen J. Morrison, Philip M. Rosenzweig, and Andrew C. Inkpen. *International Management*. New York: Irwin McGraw-Hill, 2000, Chapter 42.

Blumenstein, Rebecca. "GM Delays Plans to Open Big Thai Plant." *Wall Street Journal*, January 6, 1998, p. A2.

Bradsher, Keith. "Ford Buys Volvo Car Unit in Bid to Lift Profile of Luxury Models." *New York Times*, January 29, 1999, pp. A1, C4.

"Car Trouble." *Business Week*, March 9, 1998, pp. 48–50.

Ford Motor Company press release. "Ford to Assemble Vehicles in Colombia," via http://biz.yahoo.com/prnews/ July 27, 1999.

Latour, Almar, and Brandan Mitchener. "VW, Volvo Talks Could Lead to Merger." *Wall Street Journal*, July 1, 1998, pp. A3, A8.

Nissan Annual Report 1999. "A New Alliance for the Millennium."

Sapsford, Jathon. "Chrysler-Daimler Merger Fuels Speculation of a Japanese Deal." *Wall Street Journal*, May 11, 1998, p. A17.

Shirouzu, Norihiko. "Renault, Nissan Seal Their $5.44 Billion Deal." *Wall Street Journal*, March 29, 1999, p. A19.

Shuchman, Lisa. "Toyota, Shifting Gears in Asia, Plans to Boost Thailand Exports." *Wall Street Journal*, December 9, 1997, p. A19.

Simison, Robert L. and Lisa Shuchman. "DaimlerChrysler Seems to See a Good Deal in Mess That Is Nissan." *Wall Street Journal*, January 12, 1999, p. A1.

Strauss, William A. "Auto Industry Cruises On." *Chicago Fed Letter* Number 121, Federal Reserve Bank of Chicago, September 1997.

Strauss, William A., and Keith Motyka. "Sixth Annual Auto Outlook Symposium." *Chicago Fed Letter* Number 145a, Federal Reserve Bank of Chicago, September 1999.

Strom, Stephanie. "Japan Signaling Its Intention to Keep Nissan Motor Going." *New York Times*, March 3, 1999, p. C2.

———. "In Renault-Nissan Deal, Big Risks and Big Opportunities." *New York Times*, March 28, 1999, p. 6.

Torii, Takashi. "Changing the Manufacturing Sector, Reorganizing Automobile Assemblers, and Developing the Auto Component Industry under the New Economic Policy." *The Developing Economies*, 29(4)(December 1991): pp. 387–413.

"The World Is Their Showroom." *New York Times*, May 8, 1998, p. D1.

Yamaguchi, Noriko. "Brazil May Pave Way in Days for $1.3 Billion Ford Plant." Reuters news release via http://biz.yahoo.com/ July 19,1999.

Chapter 2

Postwar Growth and Exports of the Japanese Industry

Prior to World War II, Japan's motor vehicle industry concentrated on the production of large commercial units like trucks and buses as opposed to passenger cars, which a poor populace could hardly afford and for which there was an equally poor system of roads to drive on. Foreign technology was imported by Toyota and Nissan, and rudimentary techniques in production and cost control were developed. Much of the industry's effort was co-opted by the military for the war, and market development did not resume until the return of civilian rule. The limited impact of wartime activity on the industry can be seen in the case of the Honda Motor Company, which was incorporated only in September 1948, after the war, and then only as a motorcycle producer. Yet the company grew to be in the vanguard of exporters when the huge U.S. small-car market suddenly opened in the 1970s.

U.S. OCCUPATION

Geopolitical events in occupied Japan, in contrast to the war period, greatly impacted the nascent motor vehicle industry, especially the development of its export trade, which was geared to overseas markets in the United States after the Chinese mainland fell to communists in 1949. The "who lost China?" debate raging in congressional and State Department anterooms in Washington had direct bearing on the U.S. occupation of Japan, forcing its supreme allied commander, Douglas MacArthur, through a series of major policy changes from an initial idealistic democratization and demilitarization, to economic reconstruction and self-sufficiency, to the return of sovereignty and U.S.–Japanese cooperation in trade and industry that transformed the latter into an effective ally in the containment of world communism. U.S. policy even overrode the views of Shigeru Yoshida, Japan's pragmatic prime minister, who in 1951 spoke

of the long term necessity of trading with China, and while he realized that in view of the present communist domination of that country it would not be possible to expect great results in the near future, nevertheless he believed that in the long run the Chinese would adopt the attitude that "war is war and trade is trade" and that it would be possible for a reasonable degree of trade to take place between Japan and China. (*Foreign Relations of the United States 1951*, vol. 6, part 1, 827–828)

These thoughts, expressed by the prime minister to various State Department diplomats, were an effective means of playing the "China card" used by Tokyo in an attempt to coax more aid from Washington as the Japanese slid closer to the brink of mass starvation and social revolution. In addition, the Japanese prime minister was protesting the "virtual strangulation" of the country's economy engendered by "draconian anti-inflation measures" of 1949–1950 implemented by Washington in an effort to "stabilize" the war-torn economy (Johnson 1982, 198–200). The measures that the United States sought to end included:

1. Monetizing of bonds issued by the Reconstruction Finance Bank and purchased by the Bank of Japan using printed money, resulting in severe inflation.

2. Government budgetary deficits, which also accelerated inflation.

3. Pegging the Japanese yen to the U.S. dollar at the arbitrarily high rate of 360 yen to the U.S. dollar, immediately pricing imports of much-needed food and other necessities out of the reach of the Japanese consumer.

EARLY TRADE INITIATIVES

The aim of the new exchange rate was the balancing of the nation's trade accounts, which in 1949 saw exports of $500 million running well behind imports of $900 million, with the U.S. government financing the deficit because creditors were unwilling to accept the nearly worthless Japanese notes and currency. In addition to making imports prohibitively expensive, the 360-yen rate made Japanese exports cheaper in foreign markets—the latter outcome becoming a major stimulus for export drives that would wreak havoc on U.S. industries in ensuing decades.

Liquidity for export financing of capital equipment was also provided by the Washington-approved Export-Import Bank of Japan as a means of encouraging trade networks between Japan and noncommunist countries in

South and Southeast Asia. The Yoshida government, failing in its attempt to convince a rapidly anticommunist United States of the need to trade with China, began planning for basic imports from poor, noncommunist countries on the continent as a way of counteracting the 360-yen rate, which placed imports from the United States out of the reach of Japan. Since the yen and most other Asian currencies were nearly worthless on foreign exchange markets, trade would essentially occur on a barter basis where Japanese machinery and technology would be exchanged for raw materials. Trade, particularly exports, would also be advanced at the highest levels of government by the formation of the Ministry of International Trade & Industry (MITI) and the Japan Development Bank (JDB), whereby the former would adopt an industrial policy favoring the development of heavy and chemical industries, with these sectors capitalized with government funds funneled through the latter. From 1953 to 1955, MITI designated electric power, shipbuilding, coal, and steel as strategic industries, and 23.1%, 33.6%, 29.8%, and 10.6%, respectively, of each industry's capital needs were supplied by the JDB (Johnson 1982, 211). In such manner, the country's industrial phoenix began its rise from the ashes of postwar Japan.

In contrast to the progress at home, the Asian trade initiative, though pursued aggressively by the new trade ministry, had lackluster results:

Due to the economic backwardness of most of non-communist Asia, however, coupled with unresolved reparations negotiations, lingering nationalistic suspicion of Japan's ulterior objectives, and Japan's own paucity of capital, most of the ambitious overseas development schemes advanced between 1951 and 1954 failed to materialize. By the time of the last Yoshida cabinet, the sense of failure and frustration in this area was immense.... Although such central agencies as MITI, the Japan Export-Import Bank, and the Japan Development Bank had drafted detailed plans for joint overseas development of such resources as iron ore, coal, magnesium, bauxite, copper, nickel, petroleum, rubber, salt, timber, sugar, tea, and various other agricultural products—and dispatched missions to such countries as India, Pakistan, Malaya, Indonesia, the Philippines, Thailand, and Taiwan—most of these schemes remained on the drawing boards, if they had not already been abandoned (Dower 1979, 476–477).

The Asian trade initiative—the abandoned schemes notwithstanding—nevertheless demonstrated that the government apparatus was functioning in a meaningful, cooperative manner and spearheading the opening of trade with a number of countries. These contacts eventually grew into highly productive arrangements once the Japanese industrial machinery began consuming inordinate amounts of fuel and raw materials. The lack of results in undeveloped Asian areas also put added emphasis on developing trade with advanced countries, especially the United States, since these were the markets that could absorb a significant amount of Japan's exports.

GOVERNMENT–INDUSTRY COOPERATION

The relatively industrialized state of Japan's economy, despite the war's devastation, can be ascribed to the historical cooperation that developed between the government and powerful industrial cartels (known as *zaibatsu* and led by Mitsubishi, Mitsui, and Sumitomo) that peaked during World War II and continued in circumscribed form as the American occupation attempted to keep the economy from completely disintegrating. The *zaibatsu*, now under a looser arrangement known as *keiretsu*, still held considerable power in basic mining, metal, chemical, machinery, and shipbuilding—but not motor vehicles industries—with their positions enhanced as powerful government agencies like MITI were established. MITI itself was an amalgam of the Ministry of Commerce & Industry and the Board of Trade and had long ties with the cartels, which it supposedly regulated and would look to for assistance in lifting the economy from its devastated state. As such, the *keiretsu* received priority production authorization and financing from the government as both sides with their established influence continued their mutually beneficial cooperation. Germany, in contrast, was a divided nation after the war with its cartels, like the chemical giant I.G. Farben, broken into competing firms, effectively terminating the national socialism formed by Adolf Hitler and big industry. U.S. government backing for Japan's state–industry arrangement would also materialize with the outbreak of the Korean War on June 25, 1950, and elevated motor vehicles to a strategic industry.

Prior to the Korean hostilities, the auto and motorcycle business had been lumped with electrical appliances as a consumer goods industry by official Japan and consequently was of low priority in terms of development. The Bank of Japan and even the Ministry of Transport felt that funds used for the development of a passenger car could be more productively spent on more basic industries like power generation and steel, and the auto industry—nonexistent at the time—would be left to more advanced American and European firms. The powerful *keiretsu* groups that were forming around large commercial banks naturally supported this argument since their prowess did not include motor vehicles, and the limited financing available from their banks would be insufficient for the purchase of technology for the capital-intensive automaking industry. On the other hand, the fledgling Ministry of International Trade & Industry, well aware of the importance of the automobile in the United States, was not willing to have its sphere of influence curtailed by the abandonment of this potentially powerhouse industry and succeeded in getting the Bank of Japan to financially support Nissan, Toyota, and Isuzu—but not Honda— during this difficult period. Only a nonstrategic motorcycle manufacturer in 1951, Honda had difficulty in getting MITI's approval for increasing production at its Tokyo factory to 300 units per month, even though demand for the Honda Type E motorcycle would soon reach three times this monthly rate. In typically myopic fashion, MITI bureaucrats suspected that Honda was using the greater production to increase its allocation of government-rationed fuel supplies. Later, the industrial ministry attempted to stop the highly innovative company from building passenger cars because it had arbitrarily decided that Honda should stay in two-wheeled vehicles (Sakiya 1982, 71).

During this formative period, Japan's automobile industry was dividing along discrete lines, with government backing having limited influence on the success of each firm, particularly Honda, which made its mark overseas in the hotly competitive U.S. car market. The three principal *keiretsu* groups yielded only one entrant, Mitsubishi Motor, in this dynamic field despite resources from their banks and experienced trading companies. Toyota and Nissan, makers of trucks and other military vehicles during the war, received considerable MITI backing for moves into passenger cars, again with totally different outcomes by the end of the century. Toyota's sales and profits remained high in both U.S. and domestic markets, while Nissan's tumbled, forcing the company to sell a $5.44 billion equity stake to Renault SA of France in order to stay financially afloat. These results pointedly demonstrated the government's very limited abilities in the selection and guidance of new, strategic industries, and even with its successful reconstruction of Japan's postwar economy in older, basic industries, MITI's influence waned as powerful firms in motor vehicles and consumer electronics (Sony and Matsushita) formulated global plans without soliciting much input from the trade ministry. As a result, in this most strategic of Japanese industries, Washington—maneuvering in the Cold War and fighting communists in the Korean War—set the framework for their corporate and international development.

COLD WAR GEOPOLITICS

With Americans dying in Korea, most idealistic notions about democracy and free enterprise bereft of state-sanctioned monopolies were purged from the still-U.S.-occupied kimono closet. The rallying cry became "better dead, than red!" loudly articulated in the McCarthy hearings as the U.S. senator from Wisconsin continued his routing out of communist sympathizers in official Washington. Out of this turmoil, John Foster Dulles from the New York law firm of Sullivan and Cromwell emerged as a major architect of U.S. foreign policy, and, consequently, of Japan's industrial and trade policy for the 1950s, coincident with the country's "economic miracle" in reconstruction and development under MITI's administrative guidance.

Even prior to becoming secretary of state in the Eisenhower administration (1952–1960), Dulles was designated as a special representative of the president (Harry S. Truman) "with the personal rank of Ambassador, with the responsibility for conducting, on behalf of the United States, the further negotiations which are necessary to bring a Japanese Peace Settlement to a satisfactory conclusion" (*Foreign Relations of the United States 1951*, vol. 6, part 1, p. 788). The peace settlement, signed in September 1951, ended the U.S. occupation and returned sovereign rule to the Japanese, both part of an overall plan to integrate the nation into an anticommunist bloc being organized by the United States. Washington was also hoping to remilitarize its former adversary in order for Japan to carry a fair share of the war burden on the Korean peninsula. Yoshida, on the other hand, was primarily concerned about his still-shaky economy and appealed to Dulles for aid along the lines of the Marshall Plan in Europe. Dulles would have none of this but conceded to the U.S. Congress:

With the loss of the normal trading areas of China and Manchuria and the threatened loss of Southeast Asia with its rice bowl and other raw materials needed by Japan, Japan's economic future was indeed precarious. It might become necessary, if the Southeast Asian area fell to Communism, for Japan to fill most of its food and raw material needs from the United States at considerable expense, to say nothing of the problems of transportation over some 5,000 miles of ocean. In such case, Mr. Dulles explained that our economists figured that there might be an additional $250 million a year burden on the United States, and Mr. Dulles wanted the members of Congress to know what might be before them in the future.

Mr. Dulles then explained that the real purpose of his trip [to Japan] was to find out how dependable a commitment could be obtained from the Japanese Government to align itself with the nations of the free world against Communist imperialism, and what the cost to the United States would be. (*Foreign Relations of the United States 1951*, vol. 6, part 1, p. 791)

In 1952 Dwight D. Eisenhower was elected president of the United States and negotiated an end to the Korean War, which had begun under his predecessor, Harry Truman. Dulles, now secretary of state, still confronted the "extremely dangerous current economic position" of Japan and in a cabinet meeting of August 6, 1954, chaired by Eisenhower suggested "the need for negotiating international trade agreements [like the General Agreement on Tariffs and Trade, GATT] favoring Japan, with a review of the importance of Japan to the free world," even with hostilities ended in Korea. In terms of export markets, the secretary suggested Southeast Asia and frankly thought that Japan "should not expect to find a big U.S. market because the Japanese don't make the things we want. Japan must find markets elsewhere for the goods they export." The secretary then cited:

the need for the entire Administration rather than just the State Department to effect a workable program. The President commented that no single action would solve the Japanese economic problem but that a variety of approaches must be made. He suggested that it was an absolute fallacy to say that there should be *no* East–West trade. Instead, some Japanese trade with her Communist neighbors might be encouraged. . . .

Following remarks by the Department of Commerce on the above problems, the President then emphasized the need for making the attacks on this problem on a broad front, and he asked all Cabinet members to review this material for the purpose of contributing new ideas and the urgency of working this subject into their public addresses. He indicated the controversy which would arise in connection with foreign economic policy legislation in the coming year and stressed that to ban all competitive products would result, in the long run, in the disaster of war . . . and that if forced too far,

Japan would become ripe for Communism. (*Foreign Relations of the United States 1952-54*, vol. 14, part 2, pp. 1693–1725)

In terms of both the communist and economic problems, however, the "heaven-sent" Korean War placed both topics at the top of the agenda at the highest levels of Tokyo and Washington, and far-reaching decisions were made for their resolution, especially in Japan. Premier Yoshida concluded that communist China posed no military threat to his nation and brushed aside the U.S. request to send 300,000 troops to the peninsula. Material orders to support the war effort, on the other hand, jump-started the moribund Japanese economy, where from 1952 to 1953 such expenditures brought to the cash-poor nation 37% of its total foreign exchange earnings. Buying of goods from allied Asian nations also lifted their economies, enabling greater trade possibilities between Japan and Southeast Asia. In order to meet retooling needs of its factories, Tokyo created six government banks, including the Japan Development Bank, whose capitalization of 10 billion yen was provided by the still-in-force, American-led occupation authorities. The bank, in turn, supplied much of the capital requirements of MITI's basic, strategic industries. Still, the sudden need for manufacturing capacity overwhelmed the lending abilities of the government banks, prompting the industrial ministry to employ its "overloan" policy at the central bank (the Bank of Japan) and *keiretsu* city banks of the private sector to meet the greater liquidity demands of manufacturers. The *keiretsu* firms essentially overborrowed from their principal commercial bank, and the *keiretsu* bank did the same at the central bank's loan window (Johnson 1982, Chapter 6). The extra liquidity proved necessary in igniting industrial recovery from the postwar depression, but the system continued and eventually atrophied as weak firms were kept afloat by funds from the main bank and stronger members of the *keiretsu*. In the 1990s several *keiretsu* banks were left with sizable numbers of bad loans caused by the crash of the real estate market, and the weakened state of these financial institutions kept the entire economy in a depressed state for the entire decade.

INDUSTRIAL REVIVAL

The effect of $2.37 billion of military purchases on the Japanese economy caused industrial production to nearly double from 1950 to 1955, and the increased employment prompted recovery in consumer spending and the domestic economy in general. The growing consumer needs forced MITI to alter its policy favoring only heavy and chemical industries, especially with the Korean armistice achieved in 1953, and approve as strategic such industries as synthetic textiles in 1953, plastics and petrochemicals in 1955, automobiles in 1956, and electronics in 1957. The ministry's belated strategic designation of automobiles is one indication of how the government was losing control of this important industry to the private sector. Another was financing for retooling and development: $23 million came in from U.S. military orders to support the need for trucks and jeeps compared to only $4.2 million of new equipment funds provided by the Japan Development Bank. With the ending of the Korean War the revived consumer market for motor vehicles inevitably supplanted the military orders, with the new demand prompting a host of firms like Fuji Heavy Industries (Subaru), Toyo Kogyo (Mazda), Shin-Mitsubishi, and Daihatsu to enter the field. When MITI sponsored a competition among car firms for a new people's minicar, few, if any, of the manufacturers submitted prototypes, probably because industry in general was busy catering to the domestic boom times initiated by the Korean War. MITI was thus left behind in its efforts to rationalize the industry, with entrants in truck and carmaking growing to seven in 1965: Nissan, Toyota, Isuzu, Hino, Mitsubishi, Prince, and Toyo Kogyo, with four others—Honda, Daihatsu, Suzuki, Fuji—making smaller vehicles. The scramble to enter the growth industry was aided by the abundant supply of technical and entrepreneurial talent in postwar Japan, along with MITI's protectionist policies to keep this infant industry closed to imports and foreign ownership. The burgeoning domestic demand for automobiles did the rest, with domestic sales keeping up with production until 1973, when exports became a major outlet as the Arab oil embargo paralyzed the large-car market in the United States. For this sudden turn of events, MITI's failure to more effectively rationalize the industry and eliminate competition through mergers and alliances proved highly opportunistic for the country's many car firms that had built enough production capacity to seize the suddenly opened foreign market for small cars (Cusumano 1985, Introduction).

DOMESTIC DEMAND

Table 2.1 indicates how Japan's auto industry proceeded through its two distinct growth phases, in which the 1960s saw concerted investment in productive capacity and methods to meet the exponential increase in domestic demand caused by rising national income. The 1970s and 1980s detailed the impact of strong export drives, which as a percentage of domestic production reached a peak of 30% in 1986 and fell sharply as overseas production and protectionist policies curbed exports from the home islands. The marked transitions of Japan's motor vehicle industry (including trucks, buses, and cars) can be further inferred from data of the early 1960s, when the industry made substantially more trucks and buses, until 1968, when demand finally shifted to passenger cars. In 1965, for example, production of trucks numbered 1,160,090 units, followed by cars at 696,176 and buses at 19,348 (*World Motor Vehicle Data 1995*, 49). In these turbulent early years, firms (some just entering the industry) grappled with major decisions involving the need for:

1.   Increased investment in production capacity.

2.   The product transition from industrial trucks, to affordable passenger cars.

3.   Marketing and management planning and implementation to succeed in what was quickly becoming a highly competitive market.

Toyota's Accelerated Production

In 1950 Nissan and Toyota were principal producers with Nissan slightly ahead of Toyota in total production: 12,458 units for the former against 11,706 for the latter. Nissan had 54.8% of its production in standard trucks and a mere 6.9% in small cars, while the percentages for Toyota were more skewed at 62.4% and 4.0%, respectively (Cusumano 1985, 12–13). The war in Korea spurred domestic economic activity, and, in response, Toyota sent two managing directors—one of them, Eiji Toyoda, would become company president in 1967—to Ford's River Rouge plant to study and form an accelerated production plan based on Ford's pioneering mass-production methods. With home demand about to take off, nearly all industrialists were rushing to adapt foreign technology and business strategies to short-circuit development times. The advanced state of American industry made it only natural that Toyota would

Table 2.1
Japan's Passenger Car Production and Exports to the United States

Year	Total Production	Exports to U.S.	Exports as % of Production
1960	165,094	942	0.57
1965	696,176	22,127	3.18
1967	1,375,755	66,417	4.83
1968	2,055,821	152,100	7.40
1970	3,178,708	323,671	10.18
1973	4,470,550	583,861	13.06
1975	4,567,854	711,902	15.58
1976	5,027,792	1,050,685	20.90
1980	7,038,108	1,819,092	25.85
1986	7,809,809	2,348,456	30.07
1990	9,947,972	1,876,055	18.86

Source: Japan Automobile Manufacturers Association, Inc. as published in *World Motor Vehicle Data*, 1995 ed. (Washington, DC: American Automobile Manufacturers Association), pp. 49, 51.

seek the high-speed production instituted and experimented with by its founder, Henry Ford, over twenty years ago. The executives from Toyota arrived with an interest in doubling existing production levels without significant costs in new facilities and with little addition to employment rolls. One obvious solution to these decision parameters lay in the River Rouge plant's development and use of state-of-the-art, automated equipment, and Toyota quickly implemented the purchase of such equipment to begin the retooling of its antiquated facilities. The new capital stock also enabled plant employees to operate more than one machine at the same time, thus allowing for sizable gains in labor flexibility and productivity. Finally, the layout of the plant was fundamentally altered by placing machines and operators along the production line according to the sequence of operations needed to make the vehicle. Heretofore, layout was along the lines of a job shop, where similar equipment pieces were found in the same area, and work in process was moved from one machine type to another. These modifications were implemented to enable Toyota facilities to lower per unit operating costs and achieve economies of scale along the lines of Ford and General Motors. From 1950 through much of the 1960s it was consequently "a period of close imitation and implementation of the Ford system for the production of passenger autos for Toyota" (Shiomi and Wada 1995, 37). During this early stage, the importing of U.S. technology and production methods further represented a unique opportunity for Toyota and other firms that had not sunk much money in prior facilities that could hinder the building of new, grassroots plants with modern designs, processes, and layout. Toyota in its effort to become Japan's major automobile manufacturer also adopted the full-line product offerings used by GM to overtake Ford's early lead in becoming the world's premier vehicle company. The expanded marketing strategy, however, had to wait until the company had sufficient capacity to permit the large-scale production of different car lines, which numbered only three in 1966—the Crown, Corona, and Publica (Shiomi and Wada 1995, Chapters 1, 2).

Production Networks. The wholesale use of advanced, foreign technology by itself was insufficient to transform Toyota into a leading producer, and the company proceeded to develop highly innovative networks and processes to streamline operations during this formative period. With little infrastructural support (financial capital, land, plant, experienced personnel) in its drive to become a mass producer, Toyota and other automakers developed a *keiretsu* of parts suppliers where the company (instead of the traditional commercial bank) would be in the center surrounded by independent suppliers whose primary, if not only, customer would be the automotive company. Ties between Toyota and its *keiretsu* member firms would be strengthened by substantial intercorporate stockholdings as well as the sharing of trade secrets regarding future car designs and engineering modifications. The development costs of new models could subsequently be shared with the supplier, and, in addition, much of the subassembly of major components would be done at supplier factories because work area was at a premium at the main Toyota assembly site. This proved to be a much more efficient setup compared to Detroit's highly integrated manufacturing arrangement where all parts and work in process were developed and done in-house. The clustering of parts suppliers around the central assembler further enabled the employment of Toyota's *kanban,* or just-in-time inventory system for parts delivery, which not only reduced operating costs and space but improved quality control as well. Line workers were careful not to ship or use defective parts because such items would be detected at the next workstation and returned, with accompanying delays in production charged to the defective part supplier.

For most of the 1960s, however, the sophisticated *kanban* system with suppliers could not be implemented because the company lacked sufficient assembly capacity and had to distribute consignment work to eight independent assemblers, among them Kanto Auto Works, Central Motor, Hino Motors, Daihatsu Motor, and Toyota Automatic Loom Works, the industrial predecessor of Toyota Motor. Hino and Daihatsu were smaller firms with their own nameplates and essentially had operating capacity to take on another company's assembly work. Toyota found the system so efficient that it continued these production arrangements, resulting in as many as 50% of its cars being assembled by outside firms. With MITI's approval, quickly given since the ministry was actively attempting to rationalize the industry, Toyota became the largest shareholder in both Hino and Daihatsu in 1967–1968, thus bringing the smaller firms into its *keiretsu* orbit.

The manufacturing network offered Toyota both the output expansion and the production flexibility that the company needed during this time of increased demand. These attributes arose in the simultaneous development of:

1. The volume assembly of standard sedan models by some of the subcontractors dedicating their lines to continuous output of a popular model.

2. Small-lot production of related versions of the basic sedan line such as pickup trucks, vans, and station wagons, depending on demand. The small-lot producers, of course, had to have the capability of producing multiple products on the same production line.

This dual capability gave Toyota the ability to offer the consumer a full line of product choices in order to capture a major share of the market, and a sizable share was needed to distribute the expanded output from the production system that' the company was rapidly building. As the consignment companies accumulated product and process experience, Toyota began using them for product development of offshoot vehicles of its basic sedan lines, the Crown and Corona. As early as 1955, Kanto Auto Works undertook development of a taxi, pickup truck, and van for the Crown and a compact taxi for the Corona (Shiomi and Wada 1995, Chapter 2). In reality, Toyota, at the time, lacked the engineering depth for doing all the work by itself and, therefore, had few qualms about spreading needed research and development among allied firms.

Shorter Setup Times. By the mid-1960s, Toyota was reaching volume production levels in three of its most popular models: 50,000 units per month for both Corona and Publica and 80,000 for the Crown, with the greater scale enabling the automation of the assembly line and a move to double shifts. To increase customer satisfaction and loyalty, especially at the critical purchase time, the firm instituted a ten-day waiting period separating receipt of the customer's order and delivery of the car. To cut waiting time and achieve the ten-day goal, especially on the multiple-product lines, production had to be streamlined to implement rapid changeover and setup times, particularly for the heavy dies used in the metal stamping of body parts. Fluctuating and low demand also meant that production in small-lot sizes without the cost-reduction benefits of scale economies necessitated minimal downtime, particularly when dies were changed in order to make production cost-effective:

The only drawback to mixing models in assembly and having previous processes manufacture in small lots was that machines and workers had to be able to switch from one job to another quickly. Compared to manufacturers in the United States and Europe, all Japanese automakers developed the capability, in varying degrees, during the 1950s and 1960s, after serving a closed market that required an increasing number of car and truck models. Each discovered that the key to accommodating diversity was to manufacture in small lots, and that only fast machinery setup and production lead times made this type of production economical. (Cusumano 1985, p. 284)

Assisting Toyota in its efforts to streamline small-lot production were two notable engineers, Taiichi Ono and Shigeo Shingo, who, like the first Henry Ford, relished the hands-on opportunity for increasing plant output. While Ford accelerated production by pushing material through his increasingly automated lines, Ono relied on a just-in-time, *kanban* card control system for pulling work-in-process along the production line. This is done when the *kanban* card signals when a component is needed on the assembly line, in effect, pulling material to where it is needed. Ono's long career at Toyota, most of which occurred at high management positions, ensured the implementation of his productivity-enhancing measures, especially since new production capacity to which he had considerable input was continuously coming onstream to match the growth in demand. Top management was naturally supportive of his work and that of Shingo, who, as a company consultant, lacked Ono's authority. Nevertheless, Toyota readily accepted Shingo's suggestions on reducing setup times, and these revolved around the following:

1.   Preparation and standardization of dies to reduce machine downtime during die installation and adjustments.

2.   Use of carts, supporting fixtures, and experienced teams for the faster movement and mounting of the dies.

3.   Development of hydraulic or pneumatic tools to assist in accurate and more efficient changeovers.

Shingo's suggestions, when employed, reduced setup times from hours to minutes, thus making feasible the production of small lots of varied products. At the consumer end, Toyota instituted extensive marketing surveys in an effort to forecast demand for specific models, which also aided in production scheduling. In its later foray into the huge U.S. market, the firm did not attempt such surveys and relied instead on product attributes like price, quality, vehicle design, and mass advertising (television, newspapers, magazines) to lure customers into its showrooms.

Competition with Nissan

Prior to the transpacific export drives, Toyota's principal competitor came from the older Nissan Motor for the expanding domestic market, in which the lead in production as shown on Table 2.2 seesawed until 1963, after which Toyota secured the top position. Though much has been written about its vaunted production system, the preceding account of its development indicates that it was a rapidly assembled construct taking advantage of foreign technology and outside suppliers and subcontractors to keep up with demand. In this competition, furthermore, the product offerings of front-runners Toyota and Nissan were indistinguishable, small, boxy, affordable vehicles of white passenger cars and black taxicabs. The lack of consumer choice continued during the initial period of exports to the United States, when threadbare Japanese subcompacts all looked the same simply because they had all been designed for the stolid home market. The contrast with big, flashier vehicles from Detroit would be startling with the small cars having little chance of selling had it not been for the gas shortages and economic recession in the American market.

In the home market, Toyota's triumph over Nissan would be marked by its better sales organization and customer service—abilities that it hustled to implement, even prior to World War II, when it encouraged dealers from General Motors Japan to switch to Toyota. At the time, the Japanese company's trucks were not as well known as its American counterparts from GM and Ford, and Toyota resorted to price cutting to sell its vehicles. Such marketing moves were not effected by Nissan because the latter's truck output was bought primarily by the Japanese military. After the war, Toyota moved quickly to double its number of new dealers by pursuing Nissan dealers. Many were attracted by the advice and training in sales promotion and management offered by Toyota as well as by pricing methods and the implementation of an installment buying program, which had been well received by a poor, buying public. Another successful development was the purchase of a bankrupt driver's education school that instructed future drivers on Toyota cars, resulting in a nearly captive market, especially since the automaker was willing to sell cars to its students under easy credit payment plans. Most of these competitive marketing programs were instituted by Shotaro Kamiya, who was president of Toyota Motor Sales from 1950 to 1975 and, even prior to this long tenure,

Table 2.2
Company Share of Japanese Production and Exports

Year	% of Japanese Production		Exports (units)	
	Toyota	Nissan	Toyota	Nissan
1950	29.0	54.3		
1953	40.6	34.7		
1956	37.4	40.4		
1960	25.5	33.3	6,397	10,944
1963	31.6	29.1	24,379	44,911
1966	36.0	26.4	105,145	98,219
1970	33.6	28.3	481,892	395,300
1975	37.5	33.6	868,352	884,864
1980	32.7	27.6	1,785,445	1,465,827

Source: Adapted from Michael A. Cusumano, *The Japanese Automobile Industry* (Cambridge: Council on East Asian Studies, Harvard University Press, 1985), pp. 98–99 Table 25; Appendix E, pp. 394–395.

implemented the price reduction on Toyota trucks before the war to gain market share from GM and Ford. Kamiya also formulated a pricing policy for the new Toyopet in 1953 that would undercut other Japanese carmakers and then coordinated with design and production engineers to achieve sufficient cost cutting in order to maintain the competitively low price. Such tactics, synchronizing demand forecasting, product cost cutting, and scale production runs, necessitated in-depth surveys of consumer demand, which were undertaken by a planning and research department established by Kamiya. The department had "a central role in determining the designs and prices for the Publica and the Corolla, and encouraged a vigorous export policy during the middle and late 1960s after predicting, correctly, that growth in domestic sales would slow down considerably during the 1970s" (Cusumano 1985, 130).

HONDA'S RESEARCH AND DEVELOPMENT

"In 1946, when Japan was still in a state of total destruction from the war, Soichiro Honda set up a tiny ramshackle plant, called it the Honda Technical Research Institute, and started manufacturing small engines and motorbikes" (Sakiya 1982, 7). As with most mechanical geniuses, the lowly circumstances of Honda's beginning did not bother its founder and namesake, but even the socially aloof inventor would have been shocked if he could glimpse the future multinational giant that he was creating. While Honda Motor Company would become noted for its technical innovation in both motorcycles and automobiles, its maverick, go-it-alone attitude would serve the young, impertinent company well since it would start behind Toyota and Nissan and still doggedly pursue the automobile business over the objections of the Japanese bureaucracy. In this pursuit as well as its earlier success in motorcycles, Honda Motor had the shrewd organizational and financial abilities of its first managing director, Takeo Fujisawa, who assumed the position in 1948 and, together with the founder, beat out some 200 two-wheel-vehicle makers that were also attempting to begin viable enterprises in exceptionally bleak surroundings (Sakiya 1982, Chapter 3).

Honda's initial products were two small engines as opposed to finished vehicles, with the smaller 50 cc engine attached to a bicycle and the larger 98 cc engine sold to a motorcycle manufacturer. Development of its first motorcycle occurred in 1949, and it used the 98 cc engine, which had 3 horsepower output. Further sustained work on the engine upgraded its displacement to 146 cc, having 5.5 horsepower. The more powerful engine was mounted on the Dream Type E motorcycle in 1951, and it became the first commercially successful vehicle made by the fledgling firm, with sales greatly assisted by the economy's improvement during the Korean War.

As recovery advanced, the energetic Honda toured the United States to examine its highly developed consumer market and industrial facilities where machinery was purchased to augment his own jerry-built plant, where inspection of finished vehicles was done on the road in front. The foreign technology was immediately utilized in the three new motorcycle plants that Honda Motor was constructing in pursuit of the rising demand for the "high performance vehicles" that the inventor was continuously developing. Capital investments made by the small firm totaled $1.5 billion from 1952 to 1954 and exceeded the expenditures of the larger automakers, Toyota and Nissan, which were already looming as rivals. Honda's global presence was also rapidly advancing with invention of the Super Cub motorbike and construction of the ten billion-yen Suzuka plant in 1960, the largest motorcycle plant in the world, which would supply both international and domestic demand. "Considered by many to be Soichiro Honda's masterpiece, the Super Cub has often been compared to the Model T Ford and the Volkswagen Beetle" because it was not designed for the few "speed maniacs" but to provide easy, affordable transportation for all users (Sakiya 1982, 118). In so doing, the company successfully melded the founder's insatiable penchant for speed and high-powered engines with the more mundane aspects of mass-marketing its products to first-time buyers. To compress development time, Honda Motor entered its motorcycles and racing cars in Isle of Man and Formula II international racing trials, which doubled as testing grounds for the better-performing engines that Honda was developing for its commercial vehicles. Even the Suzuka plant, originally built for motorcycle assembly, was retooled to produce the Civic subcompact, which raced onto U.S. highways in Japan's blitz of the small-car market. Prior to its entrance into automobiles, the firm planned on establishing a sales subsidiary in the New

World for its burgeoning motorcycle business, a move that failed to get needed approvals from MITI or its bureaucratic sister, the Ministry of Finance. By the end of the 1950s, however, Honda Motor had already become such a powerhouse that it could make an end run around the government ministries by asking a member of the Japanese Diet to intervene on its behalf. The rogue firm shunned the exporting services of Japan's large trading houses—never becoming associated with their closely knit circles—and even used an old-line American firm (Grey Advertising) to launch a highly successful marketing campaign for its new Super Cub, which opened the huge U.S. market to motorcycle use.

U.S. CAR WARS

There were a number of reasons that Honda and other firms in the industry began to seriously consider the U.S. export market at the beginning of the 1960s:

1.   Sufficient manufacturing capacity was being added to keep up with domestic demand and handle some foreign demand as well as enable economies of scale to make internationally competitively priced vehicles.

2.   As the country entered multilateral trade agreements like the GATT, it was forced to lower protectionist barriers, resulting in the entrance of foreign imports. To gain experience in meeting the competition, motor vehicle firms tested their models and business strategies in the highly competitive and unfamiliar U.S. market.

3.   In 1960 Prime Minister Hayato Ikeda announced a goal for doubling the nation's GNP in ten years, to be accomplished by a significant increase in exports spearheaded by MITI, the large trading companies, and selected industries like automobiles.

4.   In 1949 the Volkswagen Beetle was successfully exported to the United States, taking the lion's share of the small-car market.

5.   In retaliation, the American carmakers were planning to launch small cars in 1960, and the Japanese felt compelled to establish their own franchises before competition from Detroit set in.

Energized by the preceding circumstances, Toyota—even though it had exported only 300 cars in 1957—and Nissan sent their Toyopet and Datsun 210 models to Los Angeles for test-marketing on its urban freeways. While suitable for the austere, relatively primitive driving conditions in Japan, the two cars were no match against the sleek, high-powered vehicles found everywhere in Los Angeles, and the vehicles, whose small engines collapsed while attempting to keep up with traffic on busy freeways, were sent back to Japan, and export plans were put on hold until the development of more powerful cars. To add to their problems, the American automakers successfully introduced new minicars, the

Pinto, Vega, and Gremlin, with disastrous consequences for foreign firms, like Renault, that, like the Japanese, were trying to duplicate VW's success. In easily beating back the foreigners, Detroit facilely assumed that the import problem was manageable and returned its energies to the profitable, big-car models and the nearly monopolistic hold that General Motors, Ford, and Chrysler had on the market. Some erosion in the early 1950s, however, had occurred as the Beetle's small share in the United States continued to grow and as Toyota and Nissan did establish their Land Rover Cruiser and half-ton pickup truck as commercially viable exports. More importantly, the Japanese firms could dip into their profits derived from the booming domestic market to carry out concerted development programs to upgrade export models for the American market. Their reliable imports, furthermore, pushed product quality issues to the fore as American buyers and the consumer activist Ralph Nader vocally complained about defects in Detroit's cars, but these were simply ignored at corporate headquarters.

The Corona

By 1965 Toyota had fielded a new entrant, the Corona, to crack the U.S. export market and restricted its introduction to Los Angeles, where it appeared that the glamorous Hollywood set was tiring of the slow-moving and noisy Beetle, whose unchanged design was becoming boringly familiar. While American car buyers were still interested in an affordable, two-door hardtop, marketing research indicated that the cramped space for adults in the back seat of the Beetle made it virtually worthless as a selling feature. The Corona was designed to address these concerns: it was under $2,000 in price, had a quiet engine that had almost twice the horsepower of the Beetle, offered options like air conditioning and automatic transmission, and had greater space in the back for more comfortable adult seating (Rukeyser 1969, 78, 135). In its first year (1965) in the United States, sales of the Corona were only 6,400 units, placing it a distant twenty-first on the list of foreign imports. Sales, however, climbed exponentially, reaching 130,000 four years later, putting Toyota second only to the front-running VW. By then Toyota's marketing area covered the East Coast and Midwest, and it offered a roomier, four-door Corona in a fuller product lineup. To showcase its inexpensive, quality-built cars, Toyota outspent the American Motors Corporation $18.5 million to $12 million for mass television advertising, even though AMC had more than twice the U.S. sales as the Japanese company. Toyota's profits from its domestic market were thus being used to advance abroad as the company's share of the U.S. import market climbed to 13% ("The Fast Pace" 1970, 44).

Datsun Models

Despite its earlier fiasco in the U.S. market, Nissan (maker of Datsun cars) doggedly pursued the huge California market by upgrading its servicing and parts availability, but not its engine performance to handle the long trips at sufficient speed common in the American West. Nissan headquarters saw no need for the engine upgrade since lesser-powered ones had proven adequate for the Japanese market, and it took the new 90 horsepower of the Corona model to convince Nissan to act. Nissan's Datsun 510 with its 96 horsepower engine consequently premiered in the United States three years after the Corona, with the high-performing newcomer immediately taking off in sales as an inexpensive alternative to the BMW 1600. Nissan followed the 510 with the Datsun 240Z, a landmark Japanese sports coupe that also got the attention of car enthusiasts, with the heightened demand placing Nissan as the third largest independent importer, behind Volkswagen and Toyota. The Japanese cars not only blunted the growing market share of the VW Beetle, which began a precipitous fall in 1973, but firmly recast their image from cheap, flimsy boxes on wheels to sporty, high-performance, attractive cars just in time for the oil crisis that overwhelmed the entire U.S. auto market.

Honda Civic

As graphically shown in Figure 2.1, Honda Motor was a primary beneficiary of the gasoline shortages accompanying the Arab oil embargo of 1973–1974, displacing VW as the third largest importer in 1978. The company had concentrated its energies on motorcycles and racing cars prior to entering the Japanese car market, and because it was so behind Toyota and Nissan, it focused on the high-performance American market, where it could use its racing and work experience on engines. Fortunately for Honda, the U.S. government had become highly concerned about air pollution emitted in the exhaust of motor vehicles and was mandating new guidelines to clear the dirty air in Los Angeles and other urban areas. Manufacturers in Japan were also impacted because Tokyo was following the U.S. lead in cleaning up its own fouled atmosphere. To reduce auto emissions, the carmakers developed and installed platinum catalytic converters that would lead to cleaner combustion of refined petroleum. The catalyst, however, would be poisoned by the lead added by the oil refining companies to reduce engine knocking, and following prolonged wrangling between the two powerful industries and involved government offices like the Environmental Protection Agency, the oil industry was forced to offer a nonleaded fuel. While the debate ensued, Honda Research and Development Company came out with a pioneering CVCC (compound vortex control-led combustion) engine that would meet the stringent new air emissions standards without using a catalytic converter. The new engine was mounted on the Civic subcompact model that was being exported to the United States in 1973, where it commanded a premium price as a fuel-efficient, inexpensive, attractive car that could run on either leaded or unleaded fuel. This dual capability of the Civic became a clear selling advantage during the U.S. fuel shortages because the oil refiners were in the process of switching to unleaded gas, for which they did not have much inventory. The old, leaded fuel, however, was in abundant supply because it could not be used by the new cars with the platinum catalyst.

Figure 2.1
U.S. Imported Car Sales

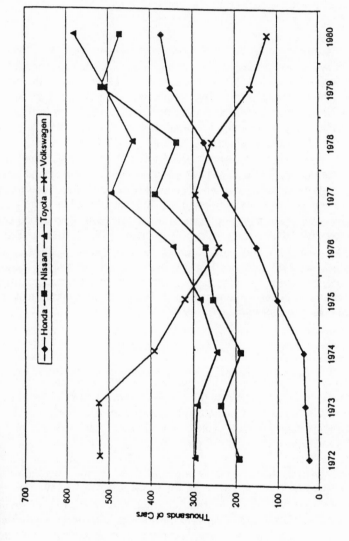

Source: Automotive News (various issues). Automotive News DATA CENTER.

With the immediate success of the Civic, Honda rapidly shifted its attention away from the Japanese market to North America. Output at Sayama and Suzuka [plants] accelerated at a rapid pace during the 1970s, from under 400,000 vehicles [automobiles and trucks] per year in 1970 to almost 1,000,000 in 1980. Every extra vehicle produced went overseas, with exports rising from 5.9 per cent of total output to 69 per cent between 1970 and 1980. By the end of the decade 60 per cent of exports went to the United States alone, which was also consuming 40 and 50 per cent of the company's total output each year, a level maintained during the 1980s. (Mair 1994, 64)

Consequently, even before the construction of its Ohio auto plant, Honda was already heavily focused on the American market, and future models like the bigger Accord and racier CRX sport coupe would be designed with this attention in mind. The pattern of moving upscale and having a full line of car models with periodic design changes was also used by Toyota and Nissan in displacing the Beetle from its top spot among imported cars. In addition, all three Asian firms used their low-cost production methods to maintain market gains by competitively pricing their cars in the United States. Profits from the export trade, furthermore, fueled expansion plans as the Japanese companies moved from their West Coast base to all areas of the United States, "pouring millions into warehouses, dealer-training programs and new office buildings. . . . Nissan [has] signed up more than 300 dealers in the past year, thereby expanding its dealer force by 50% to more than 900" (Camp 1971, 1). The marked success prompted calls from Ford and Chrysler for government controls, which the Reagan administration imposed at the beginning of the 1980s. This, in turn, compelled the Japanese industry, with assistance from the rising yen, to build assembly plants in North America—a program of construction that the firms attacked with gusto for most of the 1980s.

Luxury Exports

Exports from Japan were reinvigorated in 1990, when close analysis of the affluent American market led to the successful introduction of new luxury cars, with Honda's Acura NSX sport coupe racing ahead, carrying a $60,000 price tag. The more conservative Toyota followed with a stately sedan, the Lexus, to rival the Mercedes-Benz, and this product strategy, with a high level of customer service, eventually won out over the Acura and Infiniti, the latter from Nissan. All three entrants became viable, upscale lines in the luxury market niche formerly held by German importers Mercedes-Benz and BMW. The Japanese exporters thus came full circle from an initial mass-marketing of small, cheap cars to oust the Volkswagen Beetle, to the midsize car models represented by the Honda Accord and Toyota Camry, and finally, to luxury lines to challenge the German makers. Because of the quota on Japanese imports, the small and midsize vehicles were primarily supplied by the U.S. transplants, as described in Chapter 3, and these had both positive and negative aspects for Detroit's Big Three automakers.

Chrysler Falters

In the American market, much more than German importers would be gravely affected by the climbing sales of Honda, Toyota, and Nissan, as shown in Figure 2.1. Chrysler and American Motors were especially hard hit, with the latter taken over by Renault in 1978. Chrysler barely survived the onslaught, and although it returned to profitability, the vivid memories of being bailed out by the federal government, its banks, suppliers, and labor union eventually persuaded it to seek a merger with Daimler-Benz. The oligopolistic hold of General Motors and Ford on the Amercan car market was also broken, and both companies initiated massive foreign direct investments, to the dismay of the United Auto Workers labor union, which was left behind. Also dumped were some of the outlandish business practices used by Detroit's Big Three, which made its smallest member, Chrysler, especially vulnerable in the "car wars" between the Japanese and domestic companies.

Chrysler's "sales bank" produced the biggest headache for Lee Iacocca, who was shocked to learn of its existence and magnitude upon joining the firm on November 2, 1978, even though he had spent many years in the industry as an engineer and top executive at nearby Ford. A prior president, Lynn Townsend, had relied on the bank scheme to boost sales at Chrysler by counting all vehicles produced as sold products when they were actually in the sales bank inventory waiting to be purchased by dealers. By mandating production quotas, Townsend, an accountant, could meet his profit goals by counting as sales all vehicles—no matter how badly assembled— that had been pushed through the plant. Product quality was abandoned, and this haunted the company when the reliable imports from Japan arrived. As the company's inventory became bloated with unsold cars, its independent car dealers refrained from ordering, knowing full well that Chrysler would be conducting a fire sale of its huge stock, when they would then buy vehicles at huge discounts. Operating in this manner, using fictitious sales numbers, Chrysler was always short of cash even when profit goals were met, and it would be forced to borrow. In 1970 its debt of $791 million was greater than GM's. As the cash squeeze continued, Townsend was forced to lay off "the people who were critical to the company's future, the engineers and the research-and-development experts" (Halberstam 1986, 554) as a prelude to his own resignation in July 1975.

The devastated company inherited by Iacocca was forced to continue cutting personnel and selling inventory at deep discount because in 1979 the shah of Iran was shoved off the "peacock throne" and the United States was embroiled in its second major oil crisis of the 1970s. The usual, stopgap antics for keeping the company afloat furthermore were not sufficient this time, and Iacocca was forced to lobby the U.S. Congress for a $1.5 billion bailout package. The extraordinary measure came in the form of a loan guarantee program in which private borrowing by the carmaker would be guaranteed repayment by the federal government if Chrysler could not repay. It represented "the largest and most complex effort ever by the Government to assist a private corporation" and permitted "Chrysler to send thousands of checks to the company's unpaid suppliers and temporarily avert default" (Lohr 1980, A1). For its long-term well-being, the new financing allowed the firm to continue development of the K-series of compact, fuel-efficient cars with front-wheel drive that would greatly assist the company's return to profitability without the charade of its sales bank. To support the launching of the K-cars, Iacocca reinstated the five-year-or-fifty-thousand-mile warranty, last used by Lynn Townsend, even though the company pledge might cost the company $100 million in repair bills, which it did not have. The alternative to bona fide sales backed by the company warranty meant slipping back to the gimmickry of the sales bank with deeply discounted vehicle sales, and Iacocca, knowing how disastrous this would be, opted for the warranty. In so doing, the charismatic executive remade the auto company into a "new" Chrysler that made quality, warranty-backed, fuel-efficient vehicles, which Iacocca himself proclaimed in a highly successful advertising campaign that helped turn around his company and made him a celebrity (Halberstam 1986, Chapter 34).

Turn to Quality

One of the major outcomes of the Japanese imports in the U.S. market was the dawning of global competition and the need to build reliable, attractively designed, and reasonably priced vehicles in order to survive in the altered environment.

Two years after coming to believe what millions of American consumers already knew—that Japanese cars are better than American cars in many measures of quality—the domestic auto makers are trying to shift from turning out more cars faster to making more cars better. Their goal is to produce cars that are built better, that run better and that last longer than the two makers many U.S. auto executives concede are the best on the road: Toyota and Honda.

In their quality quest, the auto makers are reorganizing their managements, spending billions of dollars on new plant and equipment, and trying to improve their relationship with workers and suppliers. (Sease 1982, 1)

Ford has been particularly successful in implementing statistical quality control charts on the manufacturing floor, resulting in a 48% drop in defects over the two years they have been used. Simple control charts with upper and lower control limits are placed at workstations, where output is randomly sampled and tested as production ensues. If test results fall outside the limits, thereby indicating defective product, production can be stopped and corrections made. Defective work is thus identified where it originates and the amount of defective work is kept to a minimum because the continuous sampling constantly monitors the output.

General Motors has also used control charts effectively at its Pontiac division but has encountered problems in implementing them company-wide because of its sheer size and the reluctant cooperation of its unionized workforce. The company's huge financial reserves, built over years of dominating the U.S. market, have also shielded GM from adverse effects that the imports have had on smaller firms like Chrysler and even Ford. This has slowed management's desire for change, particularly since better times were expected. Quality control methods were consequently only sporadically used, such as at the Pontiac engine plant, where defective engines dropped from 2.1 per 1,000 produced to 0.6 per 1,000. Inventory costs also fell by $800,000 since the need for spare parts was reduced (Sease 1982, 10). Despite the measurable improvement, management failed to streamline its processes and enhance the competitiveness of its product until wrenching financial circumstances shoved it, like Chrysler, to the brink of bankruptcy. Meanwhile, Ford, through its active learning and improvement programs, which resulted in robust sales saw its pretax earnings surge to $5.1 billion in 1986, nearly twice those of GM's, even though it was 60% of the latter's size. Ford's surging sales continued in the 1990s and, by the end of the decade, reached parity with the latter after GM spun off Delphi Automotive Systems in a move to streamline its operations.

REFERENCES

Camp. Charles B. "Small Japanese Cars Score Big Successes in American Market." *Wall Street Journal*, May 26, 1971, pp. 1, 31.

Cusumano, Michael A. *The Japanese Automobile Industry*. Cambridge: Council on East Asian Studies, Harvard University, 1985.

Dower, J.W. *Empire and Aftermath*. Cambridge: Council on East Asian Studies, Harvard University, 1979.

"The Fast Pace of Japanese Cars." *Business Week*, August 8, 1979, pp. 42–44.

Foreign Relations of the United States 1951. Vol. 6: *Asia and the Pacific*, part 1. Washington, DC: U.S. Department of State, 1977.

Foreign Relations of the United States 1952–1954. Vol. 14: *Japan*, part 2. Washington, DC: U. S. Department of State, 1985.

Halberstam, David. *The Reckoning*. New York: William Morrow, 1986.

Johnson, Chalmers. *MITI and the Japanese Miracle*. Stanford, CA: Stanford University Press, 1982.

Lohr, Steve. "Chrysler Issues First of Its Notes Backed by U.S." *New York Times*, June 25, 1980, p. A1.

Mair, Andrew. *Honda's Global Local Corporation*. New York: St. Martin's Press, 1994.

Rukeyser, William Simon. "The World's Fastest Growing Auto Company." *Fortune*, December 1969, pp. 76–81, 128–135.

Sakiya, Tetsuo. *Honda Motor*. Tokyo: Kodansha International, 1982.

Sease, Douglas R. "Battered by Imports, Car Makers Get Serious about Raising Quality." *Wall Street Journal*, August 26, 1982, pp. 1, 10.

Shiomi, Haruhito, and Kazuo Wada. *Fordism Transformed*. New York: Oxford University Press, 1995.

World Motor Vehicle Data. 1995 ed. Washington, DC: American Automobile Manufacturers Association.

Chapter 3

Transplants from Japan

The watershed event that precipitated Detroit's crisis and ultimately its revival occurred in November 1982. That is when Honda Motor Company started building cars in Marysville, Ohio. Just thirteen months later, Toyota followed by opening its first U.S. assembly plant as a joint venture with General Motors in Fremont, California. It was the Japanese, ironically, who showed that American workers could build quality automobiles, and thus stripped away Detroit's excuses. The Japanese started a new American auto industry. And in the end, Detroit decided to join in. (Ingrassia and White 1994, 13)

In retrospect, the events summarized above appear natural and inevitable, but in reality, the transition from exports to the building of immigrant Japanese auto plants in the United States was marked by tumultuous upheavals that began with the Arab oil embargo and continued to the end of the 1970s, when the shah of Iran vacated the "peacock throne."

INDUSTRY MAELSTROM

The Japanese car companies were not only intensely competing against each other at home—in a market that was rapidly maturing and already had too much output—but also striving to keep their recently won gains in the huge U.S. market. The shah's departure and the return of gasoline shortages, price inflation, and recession to the United States probably became the defining moment in persuading the Japanese to move their plants across the Pacific Ocean. Turmoil in international oil markets and in the Middle East, which supplied a substantial part of U.S. energy requirements, guaranteed that there would be a market for compact cars, their specialty. One unknown remained to be tested: Could these automakers set up their lean production facilities in a high-cost environment like the United States? The question was preempted in May 1981, when the new U.S. president, Ronald Reagan, convinced the Japanese government to limit auto exports to his country to 1.68 million vehicles per year, effectively implementing an import substitution policy generally used by less-developed nations. In such a measure, the government establishes a barrier to imported goods, usually with a tariff or quota limit, forcing foreign companies to build production facilities in the protected market. The policy brings jobs to the country, and this was the raison d'être for Reagan's voluntary export restraints (VER), which were strongly supported by the United Auto Workers union. Support also came from executives of General Motors, Ford, and Chrysler who wanted to curb the number of imports to their domestic territory. Japanese carmakers were thus forced to invest in the United States or forfeit future growth in their prime overseas market.

U.S. AUTO INDUSTRY

The protectionist measure directed against their imports, however, was not totally unexpected. Motor vehicles, after all, constituted the premier American industry that had driven the economy for much of the twentieth century. Moreover, it was concentrated in several large, industrial states surrounding the Great Lakes: Indiana, Illinois, Ohio, Wisconsin, and particularly Michigan. Detroit (and the southeastern part of Michigan) had been the industry's capital city after major firms Ford and General Motors located headquarters and production complexes in the region in the early 1900s because of its proximity to raw material supplies such as iron and steel and a large pool of unskilled workers, "many of whom had recently immigrated from eastern Europe. While the northeast US also contained large numbers of recent immigrants, southeastern Michigan gained a national reputation around 1900 for effectively discouraging unionization" (Rubenstein 1992, 23–24). The fledgling auto industry under the autocratic rule of its founder Henry Ford, followed labor practices adopted in the steel industry by chief executive, Andrew Carnegie, who tolerated no dissent or unionizing activity at *his* facilities in Pennsylvania and West Virginia. Workers were expected to be mindless automatons practicing a strict Protestant (though many were Catholics) work ethic of an honest day's pay for an honest day's work. The semireligious artifices, ingrained in this Bible Belt since earlier pioneering days, however, could not stem the organizing efforts of unions whose promises of a better life and fulfillment of the American dream had prompted the mass migration to the New World in the first place. In the process, the industrial Midwest forged a modus vivendi with the United Auto Workers and its counterpart in steel that permitted organized labor to share in some of the gains through negotiated wage increases, provided strike activity stopping production was curtailed. The compact between big business and big labor was furthermore sanctioned by the community and its elected officials in Washington and state capitals ushering in a golden growth age for Detroit and the American Midwest, which began to dim and imploded during the oil crises of the 1970s.

Even as imports took a sizable share of cars sold in the United States, and a significant number of immigrant plants began operations in North America, the domestic motor vehicle and equipment manufacturing firms still constituted the "largest of all manufacturing industries" and remained the "cornerstone of our nation's industrial base. No other industry has a bigger impact on America's economy. Car and truck sales have averaged 4.4% of our nation's Gross Domestic Product over the past three decades." These assertions were made in a press release issued by the U.S. Trade Representative (USTR) Office on May 10, 1995, as part of an ongoing attempt to open foreign markets to U.S. motor vehicles and auto parts. The outright boosterism by an executive office of the U.S. president was, of course, an outgrowth of Detroit's implosion during the "car wars" of the 1970s and 1980s, in which both labor and management sought advocacy measures from Washington in order to survive the parlous times. Indeed, Congress and the White House would have been irresponsible if they had remained aloof from the problems plaguing the country's biggest manufacturers, which had turned their base of operations in the Midwest into a Rust Belt of closed factories and unemployed workers. The prompt government action by the conservative President Reagan upon entering the White House in moving to assist Detroit was predicated on the industry's depressed conditions in 1981 and the specter of its possible collapse. The carmakers' role in the U.S. economy, moreover, was probably bigger in the early 1980s before Detroit began closing numerous domestic facilities and constructing plants abroad. Hence, the USTR's report reflects the downsized U.S. industry, especially as foreign, mainly Japanese, settled in the American heartland. Despite the diminution, the U.S. auto industry still has a profound impact on its economy, as detailed in the trade office's publication:

Chrysler, Ford and General Motors, with total U.S. employment of 696,000 and a total payroll of $31 billion, are the nation's largest manufacturing employer. With about 90% of the content of our vehicles obtained from the U.S. and Canada, America's car companies also have a very large multiplier effect on employment throughout the auto-supply industry. In fact, Chrysler, Ford and General Motors support 19 out of every 20 jobs related to the production of cars and trucks in the United States. Together with suppliers and dealers, they employ more than 2.3 million Americans in more than 4,000 facilities and 18,000 dealerships across the country.

America's car companies are also essential to the nation's manufacturing infrastructure and many of its most basic and strategic industrial sectors. Chrysler, Ford and General Motors purchase large proportions of the nation's total output of material and synthetic rubber, machine tools, glass, semiconductors, aluminum, iron and steel (see Table 3.1). Over the past five years, they have invested more than $73 million in plants, equipment and workforce training. Since 1990, they have spent more than $44 billion on research and development, and are among the largest employers of research engineers and scientists.

. . . . The hundreds of millions of dollars they pay in local, state and federal taxes and make in philanthropic contributions help meet our nation's educational, social and cultural needs. (U.S. Trade Representative press release, May 10, 1995)

Table 3.1
Inputs to the U.S. Auto Industry

Industrial Input	Auto Industry Consumption as % of U.S. Total Consumption
Natural rubber	75%
Synthetic rubber	50
Platinum	41
Machine tools	40
Iron	35
Screw machines and auto stampings	31
Glass	25
Zinc	25
Fabricated textile products	21
Aluminum	19
Advertising services	15
Steel	14
Paint and allied products	13
Copper	10
Semiconductors	6

Source: Adapted from U.S. Trade Representative press release, "Impact of America's Car Companies on the U.S. Economy," Fax document number 40102 (Washington, DC: Office of Public Affairs, May 10, 1995).

Complementing the domestic picture, Table 3.2 presents the inflow of foreign vehicles and parts giving rise to the U.S.–Japan merchandise trade deficit. The arrival of the immigrant transplants in the 1980s did reduce the percent of finished vehicles in the trade deficit from 45% in 1986 to 36% in 1994, but, in the process, the proportion of imported parts has doubled as Japanese-based suppliers began exporting to carmakers that were now operating in the United States. While this development came as a surprise to the U.S. Trade Representative Office, which had negotiated the voluntary export restraints in an effort to reduce the bilateral trade deficit, it was simply a natural business reaction for the new Japanese facilities to rely on quality supplies from home. Since they had little knowledge of U.S. domestic parts suppliers, they had few alternatives but to turn to shipments from the firms that had supplied them

Table 3.2
The Automotive Share of the U.S.–Japan Merchandise Trade Deficit

Year	Deficit (in $billions)	% of Deficit due to Vehicles	% due to Parts
1986	58.0	45	10
1987	60.0	43	12
1988	52.0	45	17
1989	49.1	46	20
1990	41.1	52	23
1991	43.4	52	21
1992	49.4	43	20
1993	59.3	37	19
1994	65.9	36	20

Source: Adapted from U.S. Trade Representative press release, "Impact of America's Car Companies on the U.S. Economy," Fax document number 40102 (Washington, DC: Office of Public Affairs, May 10, 1995), chart 2.

in Japan. Moreover, these were the only firms they could trust that could make parts of exacting specifications with zero tolerance for defects. Hardly aware of such industry practices, government bureaucrats miscalculated the effect of the VER quota on the bilateral trade account. Big labor was also disappointed at the coming of the transplants, which often located in rural areas and states in the U.S. South to thwart the organizing efforts of the United Automobile Workers (UAW) union. The Japanese, in turn, were followed by the German companies BMW and Mercedes-Benz in the 1990s, which selected the deep southern states of South Carolina and Alabama also to distance themselves from the UAW. More significant for the union, however, was the realization by U.S. executives that global competition had arrived in the United States, prompting their huge foreign investments in low-cost operating areas like Mexico, China, Thailand, and Brazil where the UAW could not follow.

In view of such antagonism shown the Japanese investors by the U.S. government, labor, and business, it may seem perplexing as to why the foreigners would risk the costly transpacific migration in the first place. The obvious answers point to the huge profits that they had already earned in the export trade and the strong demand that existed in the United States for their vehicles. This was the same demand that had been taken for granted by Detroit's Big Three automakers, for which they would sustain numbing losses as international forces like the oil embargo crippled their foundations.

THE FIRST ARRIVAL

In taking on the risky prospects of venturing into the American Midwest against large, established enterprises like General Motors and Ford, the Japanese newcomers were financially cushioned in the following ways:

1.   Significant earnings obtained by the postwar recovery of their own large domestic market, which has frequently been portrayed as an "economic miracle."

2.   Revenues from the merchandise trade (Table 3.2), whose magnitude can be estimated as follows: in 1986, 55% of the $58 billion deficit in vehicles and their parts can be translated into $31.9 billion worth of sales in the United States for the Japanese firms.

3.   The strengthening of the yen on foreign exchange markets, which greatly reduced investment and operating costs in the United States.

4.   Subsidies and tax breaks by local and state governments that were eagerly courting the foreigners to locate in their jurisdictions.

Opposing this abrupt move across the Pacific Ocean was the conservative nature of Japan's industrialists, who had evolved a business paradigm that was peculiar to the home islands and centered on employee loyalty fashioned on a lifetime employment system, seniority pay scales, compliant labor unions, and worker perquisites such as company housing. Moreover, the still-extant nightmare of Japan's humiliating defeat in World War II undoubtedly gave pause to any headlong dash to North America by leading companies, like Toyota and Nissan, that had nearly been obliterated in the conflict and its bitter aftermath. A maverick firm, incorporated after the war and not a major player in the home market, was needed to break the corporate inertia. That pioneering firm, moving before Honda, was Sony, the earliest arrival that shed its Japanese characteristics and remade itself into a quintessential American firm possessing considerable marketing prowess and highly innovative product development skills. The car wars, following the migration of consumer electronic manufacturers, were the culminating "big bang" in a series of trade skirmishes between the two nations that extended back several decades over a number of commodities that, like the restraints on automobiles, ended in a new barrier by Washington to keep Japanese goods out of its market. The car quota failed to dent much of the deficit in vehicles and parts, but it continued the march of special interest groups to Washington to lobby for "temporary" breaks and measures on an ever-lengthening list of commodities, of which the major ones are listed in Table 3.3.

In the earlier agreement governing color television receivers in 1977, a

Table 3.3
Events Affecting the Japanese–U.S. Trade

Year	Commodity	Event
1969	Steel	Voluntary restraint agreement limiting shipments to the U.S.
1971	Textiles	Agreement restricting textile exports to the U.S.
1973	Petroleum	Arab oil embargo
1973	Soybeans	Temporary U.S. embargo
1976	Computers	Japan lifts restriction on foreign investment and imports on mainframe units
1977	Color T.V. receivers	Orderly marketing agreement limits exports to U.S. to 1.75 million units per year
1978	Steel	Trigger price mechanism instituted in the U.S. as an antidumping measure
1979	Petroleum	Iranian revolution
1979	Various	Multilateral trade negotiations reduce tariff and non-tariff barriers among trading nations
1979	Telecom- munications	Mutual reciprocity agreement between the U.S. and Japan providing some access to each other's markets
1981	Automobile	Voluntary quota limiting Japanese exports to the U.S. to 1.68 million units per year
1986	Memory chips	Semiconductor trade agreement sets minimum prices in the U.S. and establishes voluntary import quotas on Japanese chips
1992	Auto parts	Bilateral pact requesting Japanese industry to buy $19 billion of American-made parts by 1995
1995	Automobiles and auto parts	U.S.-Japan trade accord seeking greater access to Japan's market

Source: Adapted from Leslie S. Hiraoka, "U.S.–Japanese Competition in High-Technology Fields," *Technological Forecasting and Social Change*, 26(1) (August 1984): 2, Table 1.

different ramification arose when Sony, anticipating the quota on its U.S. exports, began construction, in 1971, of a landmark manufacturing facility in San Diego. Sony, like Honda, was never part of the Japanese establishment and had always looked to the United States for customers who were willing to buy its latest electronic geegaws. The postwar success made the firm an important global player, and, consequently, when it made its move to San Diego, it was quickly followed by its bigger, more established rival, Matsushita, which purchased an Illinois plant from Motorola in 1973. The drama of direct foreign investments to serve the world's richest market continued when manufacturing costs began to increase because of the petroleum shortages. Sony would move south of the border and begin production at its *maquiladora* plant in Tijuana, Mexico (see Chapter 6). By the 1990s the great majority of television sets sold in the United States were assembled in Mexico, specifically Tijuana, and the multinational corporations established a transpacific logistical system that specified:

1.   The manufacturing of television picture tubes in Southeast Asia, where labor costs are cheaper than in Mexico.

2.   Shipment to Mexico, where the tube and other parts are imported duty-free for final assembly into television sets.

3.   Export of the finished sets for sale in the United States with minimal duties imposed by the U.S. government because of NAFTA.

The Car Companies Arrive

Given the much greater impact of automobiles on the U.S. economy, Japanese manufacturers understood that since the U.S. government had imposed sanctions on lesser items like textiles, steel, and consumer electronics, their product would inevitably be a target. The action would be particularly severe if any of Detroit's companies, even Chrysler, failed. A further consideration for the foreign investors was the economic rebuilding of the depressed U.S. industrial heartland caused by their exports and the movement of domestic facilities to Mexico. These factors would guide Japanese capital in the location of their immigrant plants to the same region favored by Detroit, albeit without the Michigan bias. In addition, joint ventures with their Detroit counterparts would accelerate the transfer of technology to the Americans, thus increasing goodwill and a cooperative spirit in their new environment. With these externalities in mind, the sites of the Japanese plants, as shown in Figure 3.1 are understandable in terms of their dispersion over seven states near or in the American heartland. All are in proximity to major highways that ease the delivery of parts from supplier companies as well as the distribution of assembled vehicles from plants to customers. This followed the logistics established by Detroit in locating in the nation's population center and therefore close to all major American markets except for the West Coast, which, for the

Figure 3.1
U.S. Location of Transplants, 1989

Plant	Location	Cost
Honda	Ohio	$490M
Nissan	Tennessee	$660M
Toyota-GM	California	$450M
Toyota	Kentucky	$800M
Mitsubishi-Chrysler	Illinois	$500M-$800M
Mazda	Michigan	$450M
Fuji-Isuzu	Indiana	$500M

Source: Leslie S. Hiraoka. "Paradigmatic Shifts in Automobile Manufacturing," *Engineering Management Journal* 1(2) (June 1989): 10, exhibit 2. Copyright date 1989 by the American Society for Engineering Management.

newcomers, could be supplied by imports from Japan or Mexico. Furthermore, building in different state jurisdictions, the foreigners would not compete with each other for the attention of state governments and incentives like tax breaks, infrastructural improvements, including access roads, sewer, water, and power lines, and labor training programs funded by local agencies. The new assembly plants could also take advantage of the rich network of U.S. auto parts suppliers south of the Great Lakes. These were, in general, small enterprises confined to a single area and rarely did business out of state. The parts suppliers therefore had to compete against each other for orders from the single, nearby Japanese plant, and the latter could nimbly take advantage of this buyer's market by extracting quality, price, and timely delivery concessions from them. In dispersing their transplants, the car companies would also get the strong support of the state's congressional delegations, which wielded considerable power because they represented such populated states as Ohio, Michigan, and Illinois. With such support, the foreigners could deflect or dilute the numbing trade sanctions emanating from Washington since they were now employing American workers and paying taxes to U.S. jurisdictions. The evolving circumstances were especially noticeable because, concurrently, American firms were closing plants in the same area, leading to layoffs and economic decline. Moreover, the billions of dollars invested in small, rural areas like Smyrna, Tennessee, Georgetown, Kentucky, and Marysville, Ohio, and the hiring of workers at industry wage rates that were much higher than pay at nearby establishments turned the immigrant plant into the community's largest employer. This, in turn, attracted the attention of local, state, national, and even international media, with government bureaucrats and politicians elbowing their way into the spotlight to claim their share of the credit. While some investments would stumble, as did the Mitsubishi plant in Illinois, when it was hit with a sexual discrimination suit, the migration as a whole would be immensely successful in establishing the heretofore-parochial Japanese auto firms in the world's biggest and most cosmopolitan market. The success internationalized the world's principal manufacturing industry, prompting General Motors and Ford to implement a global building program as well as take large equity stakes in foreign companies. Chrysler merged with Daimler-Benz following the opening of the latter's first U.S. plant in Alabama. BMW constructed its facility in South Carolina, Honda expanded in Alabama, and Toyota opened a truck-making site in Indiana. In October 1999 Sony's chief executive officer, Nobuyuki Idei, was elected to the board of directors of the General Motors Corporation.

Honda's Ohio Entry

Honda's fateful decision to produce in the United States was boosted by its early success in exporting both motorcycles and automobiles, with the Civic, Accord, and Prelude nameplates arriving in North America in 1973, 1976, and 1978, respectively. The sales gains of the Civic immediately presented the fledgling automaker with the problem of insufficient capacity to meet burgeoning demand for its domestic and overseas markets. A significant decision was then made by the firm to dedicate most, if not all, of its Japanese production to the U.S. trade, in effect, "betting the farm" in the race for a major share of the American market. Investment support was also committed to enhance its prospects, including:

1. A design studio set up in Los Angeles in 1975.

2. Exclusive Honda dealerships established in the United States after the Accord and Prelude were launched.

3. The building of a $35 million motorcycle plant in Marysville, Ohio, which was announced in 1977 and began production in 1979.

Soon after the start-up of motorcycle production, Honda announced the construction of its $250 million car plant at the same Marysville location. Hence, the earlier, smaller investment was a stalking-horse for the auto plant and the Ohio choice was made while the company was making the decision to serve the U.S. market even at the expense of the one at home. In Ohio the state's highly perceptive governor, James Rhodes, clearly understood what Honda was contemplating and set out for Honda headquarters in Japan to vigorously campaign for the selection of his state. The trip occurred in 1976, when Rhodes offered the Marysville site, which was "next to a big automotive test track that the government of Ohio had constructed during the 1970s precisely in the hope of attracting new automotive investment to the state" (Mair 1994, 77). Financial incentives in the form of tax rebates and infrastructural development totaling $60 million were also offered by the wealthy industrialized state. Another strategic asset available in Ohio was the extensive network of auto parts firms in the geographically compact state, with most of them concentrated in the northern part to service the Detroit car companies. As more Japanese firms moved to states south of Michigan, however, these parts suppliers were forced to cease production in the north and relocate around the new transplants. Honda's site was in southwestern Ohio, with Toyota and Nissan locating even farther south in the border states of Kentucky and Tennessee. General Motors similarly placed its Saturn plant in Tennessee.

The transplants came intent on instituting a just-in-time parts delivery system and mandated that major suppliers be capable of meeting a demanding schedule. For Honda, whose own analysis concluded that early losses would be incurred by its distant Ohio plant, investment costs were pared by having its major suppliers assemble parts modules at their own production sites. Operating costs and space requirements were thus reduced at the Marysville assembly plant. Lacking the financial resources of a General Motors or Toyota, Honda attempted to hedge its bet by keeping plant capacity small. More production lines would be added if warranted by customer demand. The small, rural town environment was also endearing to Honda because such a backdrop was not conducive to labor union organizing efforts. The company therefore continued to base most of its North American expansion plans in Ohio for the next two decades. To service climbing sales, Honda of America Manufacturing (HAM), incorporated in Marysville only in 1978, announced a second production line to boost annual output to 360,000 vehicles. The expansion exhausted space at the site, and in 1984 HAM chose the town of Anna, Ohio, for an engine plant for its Civic subcompact and compact models. The same year, HAM's Canadian counterpart announced plans for a \$200 million (Canadian dollars) plant in Alliston, Ontario, to supplement the fast-selling Accord cars made at Marysville. Both plants supplied the eastern half of North America, while the West Coast received its cars from Japan. To add production capacity for its Civics, also made at Marysville, the company began constructing a second assembly complex in nearby East Liberty, started up in 1992. The output of all Honda facilities was sufficient to accommodate U.S. demand, especially since a recession had gripped the home islands since 1990, releasing capacity at its large plants in Japan for the U.S. export trade. American buyers had also grown attracted to larger vehicles like Ford and Chevrolet pickup trucks, the Ford Explorer sport utility vehicle, and the Dodge Caravan minivan. Ford's redesigned Taurus family sedan became the best-selling car in 1992, dethroning the Accord, which had held the position for the previous three years. Even following this loss, the Accord (and Civic) continued to be well received, with the Accord occupying the runner-up position in U.S. car sales for the remainder of the 1990s. The sales performance of the two nameplates as well as the lean production facilities in Ohio and Ontario contributed handsomely to Honda's bottom line and greatly diluted the deleterious effects of the home market's recession. The downturn in Japan also justified the firm's lean investment projects in North American rural areas and small towns, where costs could be controlled and where space was available not only for expansion but for transplants of parts suppliers, either U.S. or Japanese, to nearby areas. This enabled Honda to set up its just-in-time (JIT) delivery network.

Establishing a Parallel Supply System. Honda's leap into the U.S. heartland was made with the resolve that it would institute the cost, quality, and production control programs that contributed so much to the success of the young firm's motor vehicle ventures. The operating paradigm extended to its parts suppliers and workforce, and Honda expected considerable effort and loyalty from both groups in meeting its exacting control standards such as zero defects, even if, at the beginning, a certain amount of lead time would be needed to learn the company's work procedures. This was especially true for parts suppliers that had serviced Detroit's Big Three companies in the past and wanted business from the new plants. Because they lacked experience with specifications that Honda imposed on its suppliers, the car firm, when first coming to Ohio, turned to the seasoned suppliers it had developed back in Japan for imports and investment in immigrant parts plants that would be near enough to deliver on a JIT basis. Even with these sources, Honda realized, especially as it was rapidly expanding output, that it would have to rely more on U.S. parts companies and resolved to aggressively work with domestic suppliers to bridge "the gulf that existed between American and Japanese managers on correct practices of business management, production organization, and relations with the partner firm" (Mair 1994, 144). In this regard, the newcomer came under increased pressure from critics to produce "American" cars and not assemble products primarily of Japanese imported components with minimal domestic content. More succinctly, American workers should make the parts, and U.S. firms should get more of Honda's parts business. Understanding that such complaints could mushroom into onerous government regulations like the voluntary export restraints of 1981, Honda set a 75% domestic content goal, and to achieve it, "Honda sought exclusively long-term relations with its domestic parts makers where possible, and became prepared to invest a determined organizational effort if necessary to bring them up to required standards" (Mair 1994, 143). The modus operandi even entailed working with companies not engaged in the auto parts business, especially since firms that had supplied the Detroit carmakers were frequently unwilling or incapable of meeting Honda's requirements. Some two-thirds of the domestic parts makers that dealt with Honda fell in this category and were cut from its network of suppliers. They became the core of critics supporting domestic content legislation pressuring the main auto assembler to buy their products. By the time their campaign peaked in the early 1990s, however, Honda's efforts at building a parallel supply system that could meet its strict objectives were established, and it comprised such diverse elements as:

1. Transplants built in the United States by Japanese parts suppliers.

2. Non-auto domestic companies that, with considerable help from Honda, became exclusive parts makers for the auto company.

3. Joint ventures or equity stakes in domestic firms with engineering and managerial assistance imparted by Honda (Mair 1994, Chapter 5).

Adding impetus to the purchase of U.S.-made parts was the appreciable strengthening of the yen against the dollar on foreign exchange markets. Paradoxically, this weakening of its own currency had been advocated by Washington as a means of assisting U.S. exporters and reducing the sizable deficits in the merchandise trade accounts. For Honda, the high costs of operating in Japan caused by the strong yen further justified the massive investments it and other Japanese makers made abroad, particularly since the migration to North America allowed them to be firmly embedded in the world's biggest and wealthiest consumer market. In the final decade of the twentieth century, moreover, the U.S. economy experienced its longest period of expansion while, conversely, Japan was plunged into prolonged recession. The geoeconomic circumstances not only made Honda a global player but a very profitable one as well.

FALTERING UNIONS

By the 1980s international business as advanced by trade and direct foreign investments together with the information revolution centering on the personal computer (PC) and, later, the Internet, dealt body blows to organized labor in the United States as more menial tasks were done abroad, and computerized automation reduced workforce needs in high-cost operating areas. In addition, the advent of the highly educated, knowledgeable employee in expanding fields like computer engineering and programming stigmatized unions as old-fashioned, antibusiness, and violence-prone in a new economic era mesmerized by Silicon Valley, Bill Gates and the company he founded, Microsoft, and the high-finance fireworks of booming Wall Street. Television and the PC carried the message to all areas of the United States and in Ohio, where Honda was madly building capacity, the media's message handicapped any organizing goals set by the United Automobile Workers union. Even Douglas Fraser, president of the UAW while these momentous events were occurring, cited globalization as having the most profound effect on U.S. labor–management relations (White and Warner 1999, A8).

Honda was also assisted in resisting UAW efforts by upheavals taking place in the industry. For one thing, American auto companies were busily establishing plants abroad and closing facilities at home, which led to thinning union membership rolls. In addition, Detroit's operations were becoming profitable again, and the UAW was actively working to have its existing members share in the prosperity. For Honda's nonunionized employees, the dynamic nature of its growth in Ohio provided meaningful and challenging job opportunities at the firm as well as advancement into managerial and supervisory positions. International travel was also possible to Honda's far-flung facilities, and employees who worked on the assembly line could readily share in the company's growing reputation for making high-quality, well-designed vehicles. Throughout the 1980s, moreover, their wages continued to advance against U.S. pay averages for manufacturing workers from a 9% premium in 1980 to a 35% above-average level in 1990 (Mair 1994, Table 6.3). Honda also used some of its North American profits to diversify its base of operations with investments in Canada, Mexico, and, recently, the deep southern state of Alabama. Such extensions would become alternatives to its Ohio complex should the latter turn into an unproductive facility because of aging equipment or confrontations with labor.

NISSAN GOES SOUTH

Once Honda decided to locate in the United States, it was inevitable that all major Japanese automakers would make similar moves in order to remain competitive. This was especially true for Toyota and Nissan, which occupied top spots in the home market and had no wish to be upended by the upstart Honda. The situation, however, posed difficult choices for the two leading firms because they were so ingrained in Japanese business society and had developed a parochial way of conducting operations that tolerated no dissent from labor unions, workers, and the community. Their rise, moreover, was achieved in the aftermath of World War II, when a poor and docile populace was content just to get hired. Now, each was being forced into the rough-and-tumble milieu of the very loud superpower that had crushed Japan in the war. Shouts of "Japs go home!" and "remember Pearl Harbor!" and the Bataan death march were sure to be heard, even though Honda's move into Ohio had been a relatively smooth undertaking. For one thing, Honda was not around during the Pacific conflict (and carried no wartime baggage), and for another, it was a much smaller company than Toyota or Nissan, and hence its arrival in the United States was treated like a novelty. Nissan's move to Tennessee, in comparison, was a much bigger event, and sure to be noticed by organized labor were the state's right-to-work laws which permitted and even encouraged a nonunionized workforce. Other possible Nissan sites included the deep southern states of South Carolina and Georgia, where "governors and mayors recruited foreign investors with the promise that the area is union-free" (Perrucci 1994, 56). Tennessee was also known for its Appalachia-poor and rural folk, mainly dependent on agriculture and mining for a livelihood in an area bereft of high-paying industrial jobs— especially automaking—which had congregated farther north around the Great Lakes.

In the aftermath of the civil rights revolution in America's South, moreover, a new breed of elected officials supplanted the archsegregationist who had controlled the area's politics since the Civil War, and these more progressive individuals, like Governor Lamar Alexander of Tennessee, openly courted outside investors to the state. To get the Nissan and other factories, "Alexander made six promotional trips to Japan between 1980 and 1986 and met with the Japanese prime minister three times," offering a $66 million package of incentives to Nissan, thus matching what the richer state (Ohio) had given Honda (Perrucci 1994, 54–55). Nissan's initial investment of $660 million for a truck-making plant in Smyrna, Tennessee, however, dwarfed the smaller Honda commitment of $250 million and $35 million for an auto and motorcycle plant, respectively, in Marysville, with both Honda and Nissan sites located in small towns with rural characteristics.

With many more financial resources to draw upon for its huge Smyrna project, Nissan was further able to recruit a Ford vice president in charge of assembly plants, Marvin T. Runyon, to start up and oversee its new operations. Runyon had thirty eight years of automotive experience at Ford and was furthermore willing to learn and incorporate Japanese technical and managerial procedures to enhance the Smyrna undertaking. He also favored the antiunion stance of Nissan and welcomed the flexibility of making swift changes. Union–management negotiated work rules and contracts would only bog things down, as Runyon had experienced at Ford. A major shift came on May 11, 1984, when Runyon as president of Nissan's production in the United States announced that the Smyrna facility would increase truck output from 120,000 to 140,000 units per year and, more significantly, begin the annual assembly of 100,000 Sentra cars as well. Furthermore, both types of vehicles would be built on the same assembly line, "a technique the company says is helped by strong teamwork and a lack of restrictive work rules" that the UAW tends to negotiate at organized facilities (Levin 1989). The move to dual production was further necessitated by Washington's 1981 voluntary export quota, which had curbed Nissan's car exports to the United States. Its U.S. market share had consequently fallen from 5.7%, to 4.2%, while Honda's, whose output at Marysville was not affected by the quota, had risen from 4.3%, to 5%. Furthermore, with Honda constructing more capacity in Ohio and Canada, Nissan realized that if it did not quickly move into carmaking in the United States, its market would be eviscerated by the Honda charge. Dual product capability at Smyrna was accomplished with a $85 million retooling allocation, which Nissan's top management in Japan readily supported, especially since it had already judged the plant a success based on its early financial returns and on the high-quality trucks it was producing ("Nissan to Start" 1984, 35). Moreover, a year after start-up, *Fortune* magazine named it "one of the ten best-managed factories in America" (Halberstam 1986, 622). The plant's flexibility was again demonstrated in 1988, when the product mix between cars and trucks was shifted in favor of the former, raising the car's output percentage from 30%, to 60% in two weeks. The following year, bolstered by strong sales and profits, management announced a $490 million expansion, which would increase annual output from 265,000, to 440,000 trucks and cars, making Smyrna the largest such production plant in the United States (Levin 1989).

UAW Campaign

In 1986 the United Auto Workers made a tepid effort to organize Honda's booming Marysville facility, only to twice cancel its election bid to represent workers. To compensate for the halfhearted effort, the union, two years later, launched a concerted effort at Nissan's Tennessee plant, which was in the midst of a furious expansion. It was not a propitious time for labor because Nissan contrasted its busy operations against unionized plant closings concurrently being carried out by Detroit. This forced the UAW on the defensive since union membership had failed to prevent the job losses and indeed may have contributed to management's decision to close the facilities. The union attempted to override the issue by emphasizing better wages and working conditions, but the plant closing concern was reinforced on the day of the Nissan election by GM's announcement to close its Framingham, Massachusetts, Buick and Oldsmobile plant because of faltering car sales. GM "sent its 1,300 workers home with little hope that the plant will ever reopen" ("G.M. Plant Closes" 1989). In Smyrna, the election tally went as expected, with the union being outvoted by 1,622 to 718. The UAW realized that the odds in Tennessee were against them especially since the governor, legislature, press, and business community were strongly behind Nissan from the beginning, and the company had certainly delivered in terms of a massive investment and well-paying jobs. The union, in the face of dwindling membership rolls, had to make a stand, however, if only to show workers that it still remained a viable alternative.

Inevitably, bad economic times will come to the Smyrna facility, and the UAW will be able to conduct a stronger campaign provided it remains in the community and serves the interests of the workers.

A PLANT IN ENGLAND

Unfortunately for the union, however, Nissan was already preparing to strengthen its bargaining hand by constructing a $650 million immigrant plant in northern England that would complement the company's global business and steer it clear of the UAW. Its entrance into the United Kingdom, moreover, was fully supported by the Conservative government of Prime Minister Margaret Thatcher as well as the northeastern community of Sunderland, where the plant was to be built and where, far from the prosperous southern end around London, unemployment was rampant. The British auto industry had declined to such an extent that the country could look only to foreign investors like Nissan for rejuvenation. Organized labor, once infamous for its militancy, had also accepted the reality of the situation, and Nissan decided that, unlike the nonunion Smyrna plant, it would cooperate with the local union at Sunderland. Besides bringing employment at high wages to a job-starved region, Nissan fully expected that the egalitarian practices that it had perfected in Japan would similarly help to reduce the labor–management division that had plagued working relations in England. An absence of titles, executive dining rooms, and time clocks for workers would distinguish its way of producing automobiles. In rejecting these irritants, management made clear that it expected labor's full cooperation in implementing its just-in-time auto parts delivery system, its state-of-the-art robotic and computerized welding machinery, and the firm's specific attention to productivity improvement, cleanliness in the work area, and exacting quality control standards. These endeavors would permit the firm to export much of the plant's output to the Continent where it would engage in fierce competition with existing manufacturers. The U.K.'s relatively small consumer population necessitated the export policy, and the country's membership in the European Union made it feasible by removing tariffs on the cars. There would certainly be reluctance by France, Italy, and even Germany in accepting these "Japanese" imports, but the British prime minister—affectionately known as the Iron Lady—convinced them that the vehicles were bona fide, English manufactures. France's reluctance further crumbled when its carmaker Renault—partially owned by the state—took a large stake in the faltering Nissan Motor Company.

TOYOTA MOVES

Back in Toyota City—the company's shogunate castle town, comprising row houses and dormitories, a 30,000-seat stadium, baseball diamonds, gyms, swimming pools, tennis courts, and sumo rings for 35,000 employees and their families as well as its manufacturing empire ringed by *keiretsu* suppliers—an apprehensive giant was contemplating a break from its industrial cocoon (Lohr 1982, F1). Already, Honda and Nissan were well into plans that would inaugurate their manufacturing in North America, but the largest automaker, reined in by the huge investments in its home city and the usual conservative nature of Japan's leading business enterprises, was still weighing the costs of an American venture, even though it had accumulated Mt. Fuji-size profits from the auto trade. Indeed, the specter of a Nissan-type stumble from which it would be rescued by a *gaigin* (foreign) company like Renault was especially troubling in a society where losing face is tantamount to committing ritualistic suicide (*seppuku*) as a means of exiting from a hell on earth. Even a minor stumble for Japan's foremost manufacturing firm would be highly troubling. Toyota consequently hedged its bets by first producing in California, where it already had a small facility, in a joint venture with the General Motors Corporation, a bigger target to blame in case the gambit failed. After all, GM was already being held responsible for everything wrong in U.S. business. Conversely, GM could temper such criticism by placing responsibility for its small-car development with Toyota and oversee work on bigger cars, in which it was still dominant. Furthermore, the existing Fremont, California, plant, which was to be used to make the subcompact Corolla model, represented a sunk cost for GM that could be put to productive use following its retooling and start-up by Toyota. To complement Fremont production, the world's largest automaker also contracted with its Japanese affiliates to import the Suzuki Alto and an Isuzu subcompact, both of which were smaller than the Corolla. This would give it a full lineup in small cars. Any problems with a unionized workforce would be left for Toyota, since the latter would be in charge of operations and responsible for recruitment and training in its lean production techniques (Holusha 1983).

A Unionized Workforce

Toyota's legendary process for manufacturing motor vehicles had been perfected at home, surrounded by its intercorporate *keiretsu* group of suppliers. During the austere times following World War II, militant unions were cowed into submission by a combative management, and workers were won over by the solicitous perquisites given them by a benevolent firm. These included lifetime employment, which for this rural community was quite a concern since there was really only one viable employer in Toyota City. Under such circumstances, the auto firm could readily develop its *kanban* or inventory card-regulating system that coordinated the just-in-time delivery of parts to workstations when needed. Other practices included the continuous inspection by workers as the vehicle is assembled, resulting in a low incidence of defective products, and a company-wide suggestion system that resulted in a phenomenal 1.3 million responses in 1981 alone, with costs being cut by $45 million upon implementation of those suggestions judged to be the most worthwhile. Such an outpouring of productivity-enhancing ideas is, of course, abetted by the employment security covered by Toyota's social contract guaranteeing employment. The labor force is similarly not intimidated by the use of automation and computerized equipment to replace manual work (Lohr 1982, F26). These attitudes, of course, could not be expected in Fremont, particularly since GM had laid off the entire force upon closing the plant in 1982.

While the Japanese automaker knew that recalcitrant workers in California could shatter its finely tuned production system, the company had little choice, after Honda and Nissan had successfully begun operations, but to make a minimal commitment in the United States. The business risk would be shared with GM, investment outlays would be small since the plant was available, and the joint venture could be terminated if unproductive. Toyota, in hindsight, was also using this opportunity as a trial run to see if it could transplant its operating system to the United States as well as work with the United Automobile Workers union. On both counts, the Fremont venture yielded valuable answers.

In 1985 Toyota's primary U.S. investment plan was announced: an $800 million stamping and car assembly plant in Georgetown, Kentucky, that was geared to make 200,000 vehicles per year and have 3,000 nonunionized workers. The decision to avoid the UAW in Kentucky was probably made not because of clashes with the Fremont workers, which were few, but in order to keep up with its archrival Nissan, which had fought off the union in neighboring Tennessee. Toyota had already proven to the world and itself that it could work effectively with both GM and the UAW, especially after convincing them of its superior operating paradigm. The success at Fremont was again demonstrated as Toyota ventured farther east into territory where it had never been before. This time, however, the reception accorded its Kentucky investment by local officials stood in stark contrast to the voluntary export restraints slapped on its exports by the Reagan administration in 1981. Working with GM had brought a powerful ally, and bringing thousands of jobs to a small community would help pacify labor and encourage the state to offer a generous incentive package of $150 million to attract the Japanese firm. By then, Kentucky officials were apprehensive about getting such a prime investment as neighboring states (Ohio, Tennessee, Illinois) had. Invidious comparisons arose prompting questions of official sloth, insularity, and ineptitude in the Bluegrass State. For its part, Toyota was fully aware of financial concessions given other automakers and bargained hard to have the state purchase the large tract of land it needed, along with site preparation such as new roads and utility connections. Worker training was also offered by the governor through the state's human resources department.

Kentucky Showcase

Because of Toyota's reputation as Japan's largest manufacturer-exporting company, the Georgetown plant quickly became a celebrity facility, even a shrine, where pilgrims visited to imbibe the secrets of the Far East's lean-production strictures. No less than the Massachusetts Institute of Technology proclaimed the primacy of this new operating paradigm and demise of Henry Ford's mass production methods in a best-selling book by Womack, Jones, and Roos (1990). Moreover, "In the four years that Toyota has been making engines and cars here, tens of thousands of manufacturing executives and production engineers journeyed here. Indeed, 20,000 came last year alone, convinced that what is happening here can change the American way of mass production" (Levin 1992). Thus, the Georgetown plant disseminated decades of research and development by Toyota and Japanese competitors. This followed the common practice in Japan under the administrative guidance of the Ministry of International Trade & Industry, which deemed that important breakthroughs—particularly those that were financed or suggested by the government—should become available throughout the sector and not monopolized by one or two firms. After all, Japan at the time was poor and had only a limited budget for research and development (R & D) expenditures. In the United States international joint ventures between GM and Toyota, Ford and Mazda in Michigan, and Chrysler and Mitsubishi in Illinois guaranteed the rapid spread of the foreign manufacturing paradigm. In addition, some U.S. supplier firms received business from the transplants, and they were expected to adhere to such practices as zero defects and just-in-time parts delivery. New car designs and specifications were shared with the suppliers so "that they would be expected to have the dies and castings they needed for mass production available when Toyota was still building prototypes." This enabled the parts firms to eliminate defective procedures and materials by the time the new models were set to be mass-produced (Sanger 1990, D8).

With all transplants requiring similar quality standards and partially dependent on American parts suppliers, the spread of Japanese work methods occurred rapidly in the 1980s, overthrowing the older Ford-Taylor paradigm as contrasted in Table 3.4. The latter was based on Henry Ford's mass-production, division-of-labor techniques as well as the scientific management concepts of Frederick Winslow Taylor, which featured the time measurement of discrete work elements. In this "survival of the fittest" setting, workers who did not meet minimum job standards were dismissed, and management never solicited suggestions from employees, who were perceived as being too ignorant and lazy to be of much assistance. On the other hand, the Japanese work rules, especially when examined in their new American setting, were highly convincing because, although simple, many actually improved worker efficiency and reduced product defects. For Toyota, business vindication of its manufacturing approach as well as its investment came when the Camry model assembled at Georgetown became the best-selling passenger car in the United States for the years 1997 to 1999.

Indiana SUV Plant

By the late 1990s, however, the dynamic motor vehicle industry had made a major detour that would dethrone the Japanese carmakers from their pacesetting role. With fuel prices low and economic growth fueling U.S. prosperity, the attention of American drivers became focused on light trucks, which were deemed safer than the small cars made by the Japanese. Light trucks, namely, sport utility vehicles (SUVs), pickup trucks, and minivans,

Table 3.4
The Japanese versus the Ford–Taylor Paradigm

Japanese	Ford-Taylor
Highly competitive industry fosters considerable innovation and cost cutting	Oligopoly of Big 3 producers with little price competition.
Enterprise labor unions work closely with management to foster respect and good faith.	Industry-wide UAW union with history of confrontation and strikes.
Heavy export orientation and considerable investments abroad.	Principal concern is the U.S. domestic market; protectionist measures used to keep the Japanese out.
Participative management. Egalitarian work atmosphere. Division between labor and management minimized. Greater responsibility assigned to, and suggestions solicited from, operators.	Pyramidal management hierarchy with top-down decision making. Large salaries and highly visible perquisites for top management.
Production emphasizes economies of scope; small lot sizes; flexible manufacturing systems; demand control with JIT, *kanban*.	Economies of scale: large lot sizes and inventories; dedicated machinery with heavy automation; computerized "push" production control system.
Lifetime employment system. Layoffs a last resort. Productivity gains used to contain costs. Employees considered a valuable resource built up through job rotation, work teams, multiskill training.	Employee layoffs frequently used with capital substitution to reduce operating costs. Labor thus expendable and interchangeable under job fragmentation and division of labor, poor training, myriad work rules and job classifications, perfunctory recruiting.
Close cooperation between design and process engineers, engineering and plant personnel, company and suppliers effect continuous product and process innovations.	Little interaction between functional groups; between labor and management. Scientific achievements often not commercialized. Competitive bidding and changing of suppliers over far-flung network.
Quality, cost, and production control generally assigned to plant engineers and personnel and integrated with operations.	Scientific management control (Taylorism). Discrete functional areas such as quality control, engineering, scheduling. Toleration of high defect rates.

Source: Leslie S. Hiraoka, "Paradigmatic Shifts in Automobile Manufacturing," *Engineering Management Journal*, 1(2) (June 1989): 13, exhibit 3. Copyright date 1989 by the American Society for Engineering Management.

moreover, were the specialty of Detroit manufacturers, and as this category of motor vehicles reached sales parity with cars, pickups made by Ford and GM's Chevrolet division became the nation's top-selling vehicles, outpacing sales of the Camry, Ford Taurus, and Honda Accord. The foreign producers, now including BMW in Spartanburg, South Carolina, and Mercedes-Benz in Alabama, made concerted efforts to catch up with the American makers, with BMW committing $600 million to build its SUV plant and Honda and Toyota putting up facilities on what had been green fields in Indiana and Alabama, respectively, costing $400–$500 million apiece. The Americans, however, maintained their lead as GM began planning a $450 million plant in Michigan, Ford expanded facilities in Missouri and Michigan, and DaimlerChrysler enlarged its pickup truck-making factory in Fenton, Missouri, with capital expenditures of $450 million. The Big Three, moreover, were mainly building at sites where they already had sizable production complexes, using technology that they had pioneered. This was not true for Toyota, which was completing construction of a pickup truck facility in Princeton, Indiana (Meredith 1999).

Toyota's Indiana Reception. Unlike the welcome mat extended by Kentucky, Toyota's reception by the small town of Princeton was somewhat strained. For one thing, the unemployment rate in the area stood at a low 3.6%, caused by other blue-chip companies like General Electric expanding operations. For its new plant, Toyota consequently had to raid local businesses by paying workers a wage premium that the smaller firms could not match. The situation became severe when Toyota, having hired 1,250 employees to assemble its Tundra pickup truck, decided to recruit 1,000 more workers to produce a sport utility vehicle at the same site. This would clearly alter the small-town ambience of Princeton, which Toyota had wanted in order to undercut any organizing effort by the United Auto Workers union. Thus, the chapter on the Japanese transplants remains fluid as the milieu shifts again. The remarkable point of their successful move to the United States, however, remains the start of the industry's globalization, even though community leaders are no longer as eager to welcome these giant facilities as they once were (Aeppel 1999, A1).

NICHE TRANSPLANT

Indiana had been the last state around the Great Lakes to get a Japanese transplant, and its selection by a joint venture between Fuji Heavy Industries, which made Subaru vehicles, and Isuzu Motors was predicated on the absence of other Japanese carmakers in the state. Both partners were niche players in world markets, and as small cars went out of favor in the United States, the commitment of $500 million to produce in Lafayette, Indiana, became a heavy financial burden. The plant, which was expected to make as many as 240,000 vehicles per year, reached an annual capacity of 170,000 in 1991, with sales so slow that output had to be cut to 37% of the lower operating rate. The production slowdown was subsequently used by the Hoosier State's governor to renege on $34 million in training funds that it had used to lure the immigrant plant to Indiana. The former Rust Belt State, having turned the corner and seeing jobless rates decline, decided that public tax funds for profit-making enterprises were no longer needed.

With their fortunes ebbing, it would be expected that the two lightweight manufacturers would attempt to sell or even abandon their Indiana venture and concentrate on Asian, particularly Japanese markets. Unfortunately, both markets were experiencing severe economic downturns, leaving Fuji and Isuzu the sole option of persevering in the booming U.S. economy. Each firm, moreover, had certain strengths that could be relied on in the event that losses reached unmanageable levels. Isuzu, the weaker of the two, had a strong financial backer in General Motors, which already held a 37.5% stake in the company. Moreover, in December 1998 GM said that it would increase its ownership share to 49% with the purchase of $437.5 million of new Isuzu stock. Cooperation between the two companies would also be increased by the simultaneous announcement of a $320 million joint venture to produce diesel engines in Ohio for GM's pickup trucks, with Isuzu taking "over development of diesel engines as part of a global reorganization of GM's power-train operations" (Reuters 1998).

GM–FUJI ALLIANCE

GM's Asian thrust continued in 1999 when it announced that it would invest $1.4 billion for a 20% share of Fuji Heavy Industries without taking management control of the small but highly profitable maker of the Subaru Outback sport utility wagon. Fuji had developed the all-wheel-drive vehicle in 1994 specifically for the American market, and it became an instant success, with sales tripling and production spurred at the Indiana plant, where the Outback was assembled. Under such circumstances, Fuji (Subaru) contrasted considerably with its joint venture partner, Isuzu, where GM's cash infusion was needed to finance its losses mainly in Asian markets. In the new alliance, Fuji will use the funds to expand its operating capacity because it will now have access to GM's vast marketing and distribution systems in the United States and Europe. For the giant company, its investment gives it the opportunity of tapping Fuji's technical expertise in small vehicles as well as a larger presence in Japan and the rest of Asia. It thus will use its substantial North American profits to fund its global strategy (Hyde 1999).

REFERENCES

Aeppel, Timothy. "Toyota Plant Roils the Hiring Hierarchy of an Indiana Town." *New York Times*, April 6, 1999, pp. A1, A8.

"G.M. Plant Closes." *New York Times*, July 28, 2989, p. A26.

Halberstam, David. *The Reckoning*. New York: William Morrow, 1986.

Hiraoka, Leslie S. "Paradigmatic Shifts in Automobile Manufacturing." *Engineering Management Journal*, 1(2) (June 1989): 7-15.

Holusha, John. "G.M.-Toyota Pact Held Near." *New York Times*, February 11, 1983,

p. D1.

Hyde, Justin. Associated Press business headlines via Yahoo.com/ "GM Buys 20% Percent Stake in Subaru," December 10, 1999.

Ingrassia, Paul, and Joseph B. White. *Comeback: The Fall and Rise of the American Automobile Industry.* New York: Touchstone, 1994.

Levin, Doron P. "U.A.W. Bid to Organize Nissan Plant Is Rejected." *New York Times,* July 28, 1985, p. A1.

———. "Toyota Plant in Kentucky Is Font of Ideas for U.S." *New York Times,* May 5, 1992, p. A1.

Lohr, Steve. "The Company That Stopped Detroit." *New York Times,* March 21, 1982, pp. F1, F26.

Mair, Andrew. *Honda's Global Local Corporation.* New York: St. Martin's Press, 1994.

Meredith, Robyn. "A Boom on Big Wheels." *New York Times,* June 3, 1999, p. C1.

"Nissan to Start Building Cars in U.S. Next Year." *New York Times,* May 12, 1984, p. 35.

Perrucci, Robert. *Japanese Auto Transplants in the Heartland.* New York: Aldine de Gruyter, 1994.

Reuters press release via Yahoo.com/ "GM says to boost stake in Isuzu to 49% in March," Tokyo, December 18, 1998.

Rubenstein, James M. *The Changing US Auto Industry.* New York: Routledge, 1992.

Sanger, David E. "U.S. Suppliers Get a Toyota Lecture." *New York Times,* November 1, 1990, pp. D1, D8.

U.S. Trade Representative press release, "Impact of America's Car Companies on the U.S. Economy," Fax document number 40102. Washington, DC: Office of Public Affairs, May 10, 1995.

White, Joseph B., and Fara Warner. "Why Labor Unions Have Grown Reluctant to Use the 'S' Word." *Wall Street Journal,* December 16, 1999, p. A1.

Womack, James P., Daniel T. Jones, and Daniel Roos. *The Machine That Changed the World.* New York: Rawson Associates, 1990.

Chapter 4

U.S. Recovery

The Iranian revolution of 1979 not only devastated the American economy with
gasoline shortages, recession, and an inflationary spiral but also brought an end
to the presidency of Jimmy Carter with his ineffective handling of severe
stagflation at home and the 444-day hostage situation in Tehran. These led to the
landslide election of Ronald Reagan after Carter made a failed and fatal attempt
to free the hostages held by militant revolutionaries in the U.S. Embassy in Iran.
Eight U.S. servicemen were killed in the abortive rescue mission six months
before the November 1980 elections. Fifty-two hostages, held captive since
November 1979, were released by Iran's leader, the Ayatollah Khomeini, but
only after Reagan was inaugurated as the fortieth president of the United States
on January 20, 1981.

Campaigning strongly on a conservative platform that stressed the removal
of big government from the backs of the American people, Reagan, as described
in this chapter, became one of the most proactive presidents of modern history
with a record of government intervention and excess that could readily be
compared to the highly liberal New Deal administration of Franklin Delano
Roosevelt. Both presidents worked to get the American economy growing again,
with Reagan acting with a strong bias promoting industry and Roosevelt relying
heavily on the government's curbing and regulatory action of irregular business
activity and excesses that had precipitated the Great Depression. In favoring the
private sector, the Reagan presidency had considerable positive impact on the
U.S. motor vehicle industry, then under attack from foreign, particularly
Japanese firms, with the realization that without the revival of this vital
manufacturing sector, there would be no recovery in the economy. Facing such a
challenge, the new president adopted a wide range of administrative programs to
increase consumer and business spending in addition to enacting specific
measures that would assist and even protect major industries like motor vehicles.
Somewhat incorrectly touted as conservative, Reagan's moves were, in the end,

more pragmatic, as in his desire to increase spending by enacting the largest tax cuts in the nation's history, even though this would go counter to conservative fiscal policy, which preferred to balance (and not bust) the federal budget. The consumer-dependent auto industry, of course, was a prime beneficiary of the resulting increased disposable income.

Detroit's recovery during the 1980s must therefore be juxtaposed against the economic policies of Reagan's eight-year presidential tenure, beginning with his desire to implement an agenda that included:

1.   Massive tax cuts.

2.   Increased expenditures for a strong military defense program.

3.   Reduced spending on social welfare and allied programs.

4.   A streamlined bureaucracy that called for the elimination of the Departments of Education and Energy (not attained).

5.   A balanced federal government budget.

The popular and consequently easy-to-enact parts like tax cuts of the preceding agenda were quickly implemented, but not the difficult measures like reduced government spending, so that budget deficits reached record levels that shocked fiscal conservatives in Reagan's own Republican party. He simply left the budgetary balancing to his successors, and the issue was effectively used by presidential challenger Bill Clinton of the opposing Democratic Party in his 1992 campaign against the profligate spending of Republican administrations.

Two specific interventions by Reagan that, like his signature deficits, could hardly qualify as conservative or free-market included his protectionist measures that placed a quota on cars from Japan imported into the United States and the Plaza accord of 1985, which increased the value of the Japanese yen on foreign exchange markets. The quota had a negligible impact, while, in contrast, the stronger yen and weakened dollar increased the price competitiveness of the beleaguered U.S. motor vehicle industry and greatly injured its Japanese rivals. Both measures promoted the globalization of industries as Japanese firms built factories in the United States to get around the quota and be cost-effective by operating in a dollar-based environment; Detroit similarly engaged in international moves to effectively meet the competition by moving to low-cost areas. Considerable technology transfer consequently occurred on American soil, especially in joint ventures between Detroit's Big Three firms (General Motors, Ford, and Chrysler) and Japanese transplants. The productivity-enhancing measures, however, were of secondary importance to U.S. government programs that increased consumer spending and, in turn, industrial production and employment. An ancillary result that also greatly assisted the Detroit recovery was the dampening of gasoline prices, although little of this can be credited to the federal government. The prolonged recession in Japan reduced the need for foreign oil by the Asian industrial giant, leading inexorably to price decreases in world oil markets.

REAGANOMICS

One of Reagan's first presidential acts was the elimination of the Council of Wage and Price Stability, which had been set up by Richard Nixon to counteract the explosion of gasoline prices during the energy crisis of the Arab oil embargo. By 1981, however, the abrogation was largely symbolic because wage and price controls—anathema to big business—proved unworkable in the complex U.S. economy, and, at any rate, price increases from the 1979 Iranian revolution had already peaked. Leaded regular gasoline, for example, cost 62.6¢ per gallon in 1978, nearly doubled to 119.1¢ in 1980, peaked at 131.1¢ in 1981, and fell to 122.2¢ in 1982. Price controls, at the time of their demise, were also on a voluntary basis and largely overlooked in business transactions. Their elimination further meant that market forces could now work to curb the inflationary excesses unleashed by the energy crises and they were sufficiently powerful to cause U.S. oil imports to peak at 8.4 million barrels in 1979 and fall to 5.1 million barrels in 1985, well below the 6.1 million barrels imported in 1975 (*The World Almanac 1999*, 164–165). The higher gasoline prices themselves would assist in naturally curbing demand and the problem of its availability (unhappily remembered during the frustrating experience of waiting in long gasoline lines), with these prompting drivers to replace their gas-guzzling vehicles made by Detroit with fuel-efficient, small cars made in Japan. By 1980, moreover, the imported, fuel-efficient cars had captured a sizable share of the U.S. market, causing fuel imports to drop until 1985, when the return of prosperity increased the popularity of large American trucks and cars and spurred the consumption of foreign oil. Market forces thus broke the stranglehold held by the Organization of Petroleum Exporting Countries on the important oil patch and automobile industry, and Americans resumed their "love affair" with big vehicles, with impetus for the resumption given by the development of the minivan and tanklike sport utility vehicle.

At the beginning of his tenure, President Reagan's biggest problem was the lack of consumer and business confidence, which translated into unemployment rates of 9.6%–9.7%, as shown in Table 4.1, statistics not seen since the ending of the Great Depression and the beginning of World War II in the 1940s. Reagan knew that such politically charged numbers, together with interest rates at a staggering 21.5%, could easily end his White House occupancy, and he immediately prepared a highly stimulative fiscal policy by revising the 1982 budget prepared by former president Carter. "The major changes in the budget included a large increase in defense spending, reduced spending for nearly 300 other programs, and a major reduction in tax rates" (Niskanen 1988, 9). These changes were codified in the Economic Recovery Tax Act (ERTA), of 1981 which not only reduced personal income tax rates but increased substantially the deduction that could be taken for contributions to individual retirement accounts (IRAs) and Keogh pension plans. In addition to these, reduced business taxes

Table 4.1
U.S. Economic Statistics

	1979	1980	1981	1982	1983	1984
Gross National Product in constant 1972 $ billions	1483	1481	1510	1485	1534	1637
% Unemployment Rate	5.8	7.1	7.6	9.7	9.6	7.5
% Increase in Consumer Price Index	11.3	13.6	10.4	6.1	3.2	4.2
Federal Government Budget Deficit in $ billions	40.2	73.8	78.9	127.9	207.8	185.3
Defense Department Expenditures in $ billions		136.1		185.8	207.9	223.9

Sources: 1986 Information Please Almanac (Boston: Houghton Mifflin); *The World Almanac 1999*, (Mahway, NJ: World Almanac Books).

through accelerated depreciation methods were major provisions of this, the largest tax reduction act in the nation's history. Revenues were expected to fall by $37.6 billion for fiscal 1982, with revenue losses amounting to $750 billion over ERTA's first five years. The budget deficit subsequently ballooned from $40 billion in 1979, to $127.9 billion in 1982, and to an even more startling $207.7 billion the following fiscal year (see Table 4.1). A significant cause of the mounting red ink could be attributed to increased military expenditures, although some of this had been initiated during the final years of the Carter administration. In 1986 the deficit reached $221 billion, prodding the U.S. Congress to pass the Tax Reform Act, which, among other measures, eliminated the $2,000 IRA tax deduction for most taxpayers. The dramatic stock market crash of October 1987 further highlighted the seriousness of the government's deficits, which peaked in 1992. The mounting deficits, however, were of little concern to Reagan, already reelected to his second term and prevented by the Constitution from seeking a third term. They had furthermore stimulated growth in the U.S. economy, which was what Reaganomics was really after since real gross national income, as shown in Table 4.1, had dipped from 1981 to 1982. With growth resuming in the economy, unemployment receded but still remained at the troublesome level of 7.5% in 1984. This was due to strong imports of Japanese small cars that eased gasoline consumption but, together with their transplanted factories, caused extensive plant shutdowns and worker layoffs among American automakers.

Voluntary Export Restraints

The growing car imports also caused another deficit to mushroom in the American economy as the merchandise trade deficit—previously spearheaded by foreign oil imports—jumped from $25.5 billion in 1980, to $112.5 billion in 1984. Organized labor and big business, excluding GM, which believed that government should not intervene, petitioned Washington for protection against the imports, which were bankrupting American firms (especially Chrysler under Iacocca) and taking American jobs. Both Congress and the president responded with presumed indignation, even though the latter professed a conservative, laissez-faire ideology. Within two months of his inauguration, President Reagan asked the Japanese foreign minister to seek restraints on auto shipments from his country to the United States. A month later, the U.S. trade representative was dispatched to Japan to negotiate a "voluntary" export restraint on automobiles of 1.68 million cars per year. The artifice of having the Japanese government unilaterally restrict its industry's exports was needed to evade U.S. trade law, which included the General Agreement on Tariffs and Trade, which the United States had ratified. It was also needed to meld, in his pragmatic way, the blatantly protectionist measure with Reagan's free-market principles. Toward this end, the subterfuge did not work: the Reagan presidency went down as the most protectionist since Herbert Hoover's, with the latter infamously known for signing the Smoot-Hawley tariff bill, which helped precipitate the Great Depression. Reagan's deficits led to stock market crashes and a recession that extinguished the reelection hopes of George Bush.

The reasons that Japan acquiesced in promulgating the quota are varied, but essentially it was a harmless (even profitable) way of placating its most important trading partner. The export blitz had already turned Japan into an economic superpower with billions of dollars going into its trade accounts and corporate profits. Moreover, many of these firms were intent on investing huge sums in U.S.-based facilities, making it foolhardy to risk the ire of Washington, which would have jurisdiction over these operations. The transplants also were a profitable way of circumventing the quota since output would be labeled as "USA-made" and not subject to the trade restraint. A second quota circumvention was the move to luxury nameplates of bigger, more expensive cars like the Acura and Lexus, and these would be exported, while the cheaper models would be made in North America, and the reduced number of exports, with its luxury component, would never breach the quota limit. It was furthermore an opportune time to move upscale because consumer demand for luxury goods had returned, and gasoline shortages had been forgotten.

The automobile voluntary restraint agreement (VRA) was also used to increase prices on less expensive models, which both American and Japanese firms discovered was easy to do because the quota had crimped the supply of popular, small cars from Japan before their U.S. plants were fully operational. Consumer spending, meanwhile, had picked up smartly with the huge tax cuts and government deficits spurring demand. The altered situation with gas prices receding further meant that big, American cars benefited, and this became the foundation of Detroit's recovery, which continued into the next millennium. The preceding industrial benefits, of course, came with ancillary costs, most of which were passed on to the American car buyer: "The annual cost to consumers of the auto VRA was more than $1.1 billion, about $240,000 per job saved in the domestic auto industry. The long-term cost of the VRA may also be substantial, because it increased the cost of the domestic industry labor contracts negotiated in 1984 and 1985, probably preventing the domestic industry from being competitive in the production of small cars" (Niskanen 1988, 140). These concerns were of minor significance to the Reagan administration, which was prepared to incur a $207.8 billion deficit for fiscal year 1983 in order to get the economy moving again in time for the November 1984 elections. Reagan was reelected by a second landslide margin, after which the huge deficit problem that he had created was left to others to solve. His immediate successor, George Bush (vice president under Reagan), bore the heaviest part of the burden when the deficits impelled him to increase taxes, which precipitated a recession and his demise in the 1992 elections. His painful attempts to balance the budget and the stock market crashes of 1987 and 1989 went a long way toward convincing the American voter and the succeeding Bill Clinton presidency of the critical need for paring spending and balancing the federal deficit and indeed paved the way for budget *surpluses* in Clinton's second term.

DETROIT'S COMEBACK

For its recovery, Detroit met the competition with different strategies and realized divergent results. Ford and Chrysler marshaled their limited resources in effective ways and essentially waited for the Reagan turnaround of the national economy. Economic growth, consumer spending, and falling gas prices brought the market back for big, full-size cars and enriched the coffers of companies, like Ford and Chrysler, that had distinctive and attractive cars to sell. After all, Japanese compact cars all had a small, boxy look, which the U.S. auto buyer would readily perceive after higher income levels allowed him or her to become choosy again. Ford noticed this in 1979, the depths of its corporate recession, when annual losses approached $1.6 billion, but its truck division was still profitable. The company felt that a distinctive new family sedan would also excite customer interest and initiated a six-year, three-billion-dollar investment program—part of it debt-financed in the absence of retained earnings—not to meet the Japanese small car head-on but for the design and development of the Taurus sedan, a family car that had always been the workhorse of Detroit. The considerable risk for Ford can be seen in comparing its losses for 1980–1982 which totaled $3.3 billion, to the $3 billion it would invest in the Taurus, which would not debut until 1986. The risk was further increased when top management decided to give it a radical, aerodynamically sleek, "jelly-bean" look to distinguish the Taurus from the dull, boxy cars offered during austere times of the gas shortages. The go-ahead was given after the new design had been successfully tested on the 1983 Thunderbird and the 1984 Ford Tempo and Mercury Topaz compact models. More auspicious for Ford, however, was the turnaround in the national economy, which even before the introduction of the Taurus had helped propel the company's earnings to a record $1.9 billion in 1983 and $2.9 billion in 1984. In the new prosperity, management decided to make the Taurus bigger, a full, four-door family sedan that would be Ford's "Chevrolet," the car that had made General Motors the world's largest manufacturing company. It worked as planned when, in 1986, the leading entrants in the midsize sedan market were the Ford Taurus and its twin, the Mercury Sable, with the former becoming the best-selling car in the United States, surpassing the Honda Accord. Ford's profits for the year at $3.3 billion surged ahead of GM's $2.9 billion, giving it the lead for the first time since the Great Depression. The turnaround also boosted sales at Chrysler, as it sailed out of bankruptcy under its new chairman, Lee Iacocca, who had already introduced the minivan in 1983 to receptive customers and who bought the Jeep sport utility vehicle in 1987 (Ingrassia and White 1994, Chapter 5).

GM-10 Development

General Motors had also gambled heavily for the industry's new age with a massive GM-10 development program costing $7 billion and taking six years which was planned to answer all challenges from both the Organization of Petroleum Exporting Countries (OPEC) oil cartel and the Japanese small-car firms. Ironically, GM was the single firm that could afford such a huge gamble, but it failed to stop the erosion of its market share because the move to downsize its big cars (Cadillac, Buick, Oldsmobile, Pontiac) to compete against small, foreign ones was undermined by the Reagan turnaround of the U.S. economy. GM's basic idea was quite sound, given the market share that it had lost to the Japanese since the 1973 Arab oil embargo, and the strategy even tempted Ford's president, Don Peterson, to follow suit, except that Ford had meager financial resources that could cover only the Taurus development. No such constraint marred the GM-10 program, which affected four factories and four models made with its new "flexible technology" based on lean production and product technologies learned from the Japanese. The industrial restructuring entailed common platforms for its 100 different nameplates, new dies and parts for downsized models, and considerable plant retooling and automation to make the smaller cars. The economizing steps, in GM oxymoron fashion, entailed the spending of huge sums that could never be recouped even with the use of Toyota's leanest production methods. More important, the resulting GM-10 cars all looked alike and, introduced two years after the Taurus and Sable, had little chance of dislodging the Ford front-runners of the U.S. family sedan market. The $3.5 billion Saturn project, which was also under way, similarly failed to turn back the Japanese small-car challenge, and the lackluster results from these expensive programs caused GM's market share to drop from 43% in 1985, to 35% in 1992. This turn of events produced a $4.45 billion loss for GM in 1991, resulting in a wrenching change in the company's executive suite, with a new chairman appointed with a mandate from the board of directors to immediately stem the hemorrhaging of red ink that was pushing the giant company to financial ruin (Ingrassia and White 1994, Chapter 6).

Ford's Big Cars

Ford was consequently left to spearhead the American auto industry to record sales of 16.3 million cars and trucks in 1986, but it was not the Taurus that was bringing in the money: "The car had cost too much to develop. The real money came from a gaggle of aging behemoths: the Ford Crown Victoria, Mercury Grand Marquis, and the Lincoln Continental, Town Car, and Mark VII" (Ingrassia and White 1994, 133). These were the only big cars available because Ford had no money to downsize its fleet during the energy crises as General Motors had done. The austere times also forced Ford to rationalize operations ten years before GM, when, from 1979 to 1983, it closed thirteen plants and cut close to 90,000 employees from its payroll. Stringent measures were applied in the development of the Taurus that made it much cheaper to assemble than comparable GM, but not Japanese, cars. In assembly time, the Taurus could be built in twenty hours, while the Pontiac Grand Prix needed thirty five. Such economies and the new sales environment favoring its big cars made in fully depreciated factories earned Ford $5.3 billion in profits for 1987, a record amount for an industrial business. The profits allowed the company to:

1.   Begin construction of its $500 million plant in Mexico, thus diversifying operations away from the American Midwest to a foreign locale.

2.   Form a production arrangement with Mazda such that Ford models would be assembled at Mazda's new plant in Michigan, thus quickly obtaining additional capacity when demand for its cars was increasing.

3.   Purchase Britain's Jaguar luxury carmaker in 1989 for close to $2.5 billion.

4.   Undertake development of the Explorer sport utility vehicle, which was introduced in 1990 and greatly enhanced the company's profit-making ability.

JAPAN'S ECONOMY STUMBLES

Similar to its U.S. counterpart, Japan's auto industry rested on the strength of its powerful domestic economy, including its commercial banking and real estate sectors and equity markets such as the Tokyo Stock Exchange, which, according to capitalization measures, had become the largest in the world. While better known abroad, its export companies and their earnings were of secondary importance to the sales and profits in the domestic economy. Various intercorporate arrangements were also thought to undergird Japanese industry, of which the *keiretsu* grouping of companies was the principal type. The center of the *keiretsu* was generally a large commercial bank, trading company, or large manufacturer like Toyota surrounded by its supplier firms. The Nissan *keiretsu* proved highly vulnerable in the late 1990s, when falling sales at home and abroad resulted in huge losses for the main motor company and bankruptcy for its suppliers because Nissan was their only customer. Other *keiretsus* surrounded a large bank like the three best-known ones—Mitsubishi, Mitsui, and Sumitomo—and this arrangement was popular because it helped ease financial liquidity problems, with the banks offering low-interest loans to member firms and making large, long-term purchases of their stock. Insurance and other financial institutions similarly held large portfolios of member company shares, and these long-term holdings helped shield corporate management from the vicissitudes of the stock market that appeared to plague corporate executives in the United States. It was also thought that such stable holdings were responsible for the sustained rise of the Tokyo Stock Exchange (TSE), which had seen its index climb from 1,000 in 1960 to near 50,000 by the late 1980s. However, when the TSE began to crack in 1989, no amount of intercorporate alliances proved effective in stemming the fury of a burst speculative bubble that saw its stock index nose-dive to 15,000, from which it did not recover for much of the 1990s. Falling equity prices wreaked havoc with bank balance sheets, thus spreading the crash throughout the "impregnable" bank-centered *keiretsus* and the rest of the economy. Government policy provided by the Ministry of Finance and the Ministry of International Trade & Industry was also found to be wanting, with both inert bureaucracies incapable of forming an effective strategy for bringing the economy out of its recession. Both ministries had successfully guided Japan's postwar recovery, as outlined in Chapter 2, but as the corporate sector internationalized and thus moved beyond the jurisdiction of Tokyo's regulatory reach, the government was left with an outmoded plan for dealing with economic downturns by prodding its industrial sector to invest in new plant and equipment for greater productivity and increased output. The approach was suitable for a nation emerging from the ruins of World War II, when increased demand in domestic and even export markets could be taken as a given. By 1989, however, Japan's aging population was no longer hell-bent on consumption, turning the economy into a mature, replacement one with workers more interested in saving for their retirement than in buying the latest sports coupe from Honda. The U.S. market for Japanese small cars was also slowing, and many of the factories for most of Japan's export industries were relocating in the New World closer to the huge overseas market, leaving behind a "hollowed-out" country with rising unemployment and falling business investment. In the United States the Reagan administration had jump-started the national economy with huge tax cuts and government deficits, but these approaches were too radical and foreign for a timid Japanese government, and prime ministers rose and fell in quick succession, with all promising a recovery that never came. Some of these leaders were undone by scandal either in their personal lives or in government work, but these were a sideshow to the economic slowdown that gripped the country for all of the 1990s. Some action as on foreign exchange rates, simply exacerbated the problem and further disillusioned the electorate about the credibility of the economic bureaucracy, especially the Ministry of Finance, where lax regulation of the failing banking industry was uncovered, with high officials receiving payoffs and bribes. The Finance Ministry also proved incapable of handling the huge overhang of bank loans that had gone into default because of the failing economy. Bank officials were lectured but rarely dismissed, and few banks were closed or taken over by stronger ones. The government's prevailing hope was akin to Herbert Hoover's statement at the beginning of the Great Depression justifying government inaction because "prosperity was right around the corner." As with Hoover's approach, Japan's cautious muddling through until better times simply prolonged the economic downturn.

Rising Yen

The Ministry of Finance also possessed regulatory jurisdiction of the nation's central bank, the Bank of Japan, and therefore had considerable influence over monetary policy, the level of interest rates, and the foreign exchange rate of its currency, the yen. Following the Bretton Woods Agreement of 1944, the yen was pegged to the U.S. dollar at 360 yen to the dollar, with the dollar tied to gold at the official government rate of $35 per ounce of gold. As a defeated Axis member of World War II, Japan was forced to subscribe to the new gold-exchange standard. With recovery and strong industrial growth, the yen–dollar exchange rate proved beneficial in Japan's export drives, because the yen was at too low a level, giving its exports a considerable price advantage in U.S. markets. This led to large bilateral trade surpluses, and in the early 1970s, President Richard Nixon—frustrated by corresponding deficits in his country's trade accounts—let the dollar as well as all other major currencies like the yen float on foreign exchange markets. The yen rose to 238 to the dollar in 1985 but had little effect on Japan's growing current account surplus, which stood at $49.2 billion, while the U.S. deficit for the same year continued its steep decline to $117.7 billion from surpluses earned in 1980–1981. The deterioration in the current account from 1980 to 1985 could be ascribed to "the multilateral trade-weighted value of the dollar [which] increased 74% in real terms!" (Niskanen 1988, 175). Fearing that the Reagan deficits would fuel inflation, the Federal Reserve increased U.S. interest rates relative to rates in other industrialized nations, and this attracted sizable inflows of "hot" foreign funds seeking the higher returns with the purchases of dollar-denominated securities, causing the dollar to appreciate on foreign exchange markets. The rise in the dollar with respect to the yen because of high U.S. interest rates further exacerbated the trade imbalances in both countries as well as in Europe, where government ministers were hardly overjoyed with Japan's trade successes in the region. International efforts were thus afoot to undermine Japanese industry by altering the value of the yen. Interestingly enough, Japan's Finance Ministry and central bank acquiesced to such a move, probably because they could not fathom the extent of damage that a strong yen would have and certainly had no strategy for counteracting the damage. Moreover, these officials had habitually succumbed to foreign pressure—buying peace in their time—in the hope that nothing major would change.

Plaza Accord of 1985. Having energized the U.S. economy with its massive budget deficits and adopted specific trade policies like the voluntary export restraints on Japanese cars, the Reagan administration set out to depreciate the value of the dollar in order to stem the current account deficits caused by an excess of imports over exports. A lower dollar would make American goods cheaper abroad—and therefore more competitive—and, at the same time, make foreign imports more expensive—and therefore less competitive—in the United States. Intervention in international money markets thus appeared to be too good a weapon *not* to be used by an energetic Reagan presidency, and indeed it had already been wielded by Richard Nixon when he earlier cut the dollar's tie to gold and established the flexible exchange rate regime, which still prevails. Nixon could unilaterally move because, at the time, the United States was the superpower of the free world, and the dollar was a pivotal currency. By 1985 other economic superpowers like West Germany and Japan had evolved with their own strong currencies, and in this environment the Reagan administration knew that it would have to act in concert with them if the dollar were to depreciate. In a secret meeting of the G-5 meeting of finance ministers and central bankers from the five largest industrialized nations (US, U.K., West Germany, France, Japan) held on Sunday, September 22, 1985, at the Plaza Hotel in New York, an accord was reached on a U.S. proposal for "orderly appreciation" of nondollar currencies against the dollar. The appreciation would be effected through coordinated purchases of nondollar currencies, using dollars held by governments in their official reserve accounts. As shown in Table 4.2, the yen appreciated quickly from 238 yen to the dollar, to 145 in 1987, to 128 in 1988, before falling back in 1990. The U.S. trade deficit fell with the dollar from $159.5 billion in 1987, to $108.8 billion in 1990, while Japan's trade surplus shrank from $96.4 billion in 1987, to $63.5 billion in 1990. The rising yen further convinced large manufacturers to forsake production in the home islands and move facilities to low-cost, developing countries, mainly in Asia. This exodus is also tabulated in Table 4.2, where direct foreign investments leaving Japan rose from $12.2 billion in the year of the Plaza accord, to $56.9 billion in 1990. Old plants were subsequently closed, and workers were laid off just as they were in the United States during the turbulent years of the gasoline shortages and inflationary spiral. The yen crisis (or *endaka*) hit Japan particularly hard because it had a smaller economy than the United States, and, in addition, it depended to a much greater extent on its export markets. Simple calculations show how a Japanese exporter would be affected at two exchange rate levels: 200 yen versus 100 yen to the dollar. At the 200-yen rate, a dollar of profit made by selling in the United States a product made in Japan, would mean a 200-yen profit. At the 100-yen rate, a dollar of profit made in the same manner would be worth only 100 yen, resulting in a 50% reduction in profit. The drop in profits from the export trade would be further exacerbated by the strong yen, making Japanese products more expensive on foreign markets, and the profit shortfall would cause domestic stock and real estate markets to tumble in a vicious downward spiral that abruptly ended the country's economic growth.

Table 4.2
U.S. and Japanese International Economic Statistics (in $ billions except for exchange rate)

	1982	1985	1987	1988	1990
Yen to $ Exchange Rate	249	238	145	128	145
U.S. Balance of Trade	-36.4	-122.2	-159.6	-127.0	-108.8
Japan's Balance of Trade	20.1	61.6	96.4	95.0	63.5
Japan's Direct Overseas Investments	7.7	12.2	33.4	47.0	56.9

Sources: Keizai Koho Center, *Japan 1992 An International Comparison* (Tokyo: 1992), Table 6.4; Keizai Koho Center, *Japan 1995 An International Comparison* (Tokyo: 1995), Tables 4.3, 5.6, 6.2.

Economic Decline

No one in Japan's central bureaucracies or large export companies could imagine that an agreement to raise the foreign exchange value of its currency would undermine the nation's economy, which had experienced nearly continuous growth since the 1950s. Even the oil crises of the 1970s barely touched the country because, at the time, the huge U.S. market for Japanese small cars and appliances added to the demand that was coming from its own domestic economy. But by 1990, as shown in Table 4.3, car production in Japan peaked (indicating a mature market), as did exports to the American market, which was renewing its preference for big U.S. cars and briskly purchasing the new and bigger sport utility vehicles. Such vehicles were not a specialty of Japanese carmakers simply because fuel prices had always been high and parking space at a premium, making large vehicles unaffordable to the average buyer. The percent change in real gross domestic product, which had grown at a robust 4.8% rate in 1990, turned negative in 1993, with anemic changes (up or down) occurring throughout the 1990s, undoubtedly due to the strong yen which stood at 120 to the dollar in 1999. Real estate markets also plummeted as businesses closed their doors. Failing enterprises saddled commercial banks with $800 billion worth of bad loans, which banking executives would keep on their books as productive assets to maintain the facade that they were still solvent. Savvy account holders sensed trouble and withdrew their holdings, in the process beginning a run on the banks' dwindling assets. Not wishing to add to their trove of bad loans, bank officers adopted stringent loan procedures, and credit needed for business transactions and growth became increasingly difficult to obtain. Japan thus became enmeshed in a liquidity crisis, common in less-developed countries but highly unusual in an "advanced," industrialized nation.

Table 4.3
Japan's GDP Growth, Car Production, and Exports

Year	Car Production*	Car Exports*	% Real GDP Growth
1985	7.6	4.4	5.0
1990	9.9	4.5	4.8
1991	9.8	4.8	4.3
1993	8.5	4.1	-0.2
1994	7.8	3.4	0.5
1995	7.6	2.9	0.9
	* in million units		

Sources: Keizai Koho Center, *Japan 1987 An International Comparison* (Tokyo: 1987), Table 3.5; Keizai Koho Center, *Japan 1992 An International Comparison* (Tokyo: 1992), Table 4.7; Keizai Koho Center, *Japan 1993 An International Comparison* (Tokyo: 1993), Table 4.7; Keizai Koho Center, *Japan 1995 An International Comparison* (Tokyo: 1995), Tables 1.10, 4.6; Keizai Koho Center, *Japan 1997 An International Comparison* (Tokyo: 1997), Tables 2.6, 3.14.

Asian Financial Crisis. With Asia's premier economy stuck in severe recession, it was to be expected that smaller, developing countries that had patterned their own economies on Japan's economic regimen would suffer similar devastation but with a major difference. Japan's economy was hurt by the strengthening of its currency; because their currencies were weak, Thailand, South Korea, and Indonesia had to support their currencies—the baht, won, and rupiah, respectively—on foreign exchange markets in order to attract foreign direct investments. The support was effected by the purchase of the local currency, using hard currencies from official government reserves. A financial crisis ensued whenever foreign investors sensed an impending devaluation of the local currency, which occurred as governments exhausted their hard currency reserves in supporting (buying) their weakening currencies. Thailand was the first to cave in, in July 1997, when its government let the baht float with the currency, losing a considerable amount of its value against the yen and dollar. South Korea and Indonesia followed, and money continued to flee these and nearby countries like Malaysia and the Philippines from 1997 to 1998 as their banks and businesses failed and billion-dollar bailouts were sought from the International Monetary Fund as well as large foreign commercial banks and rich nations like the United States and Japan. In the new international financial age, foreign exchange markets came to have powerful impacts on contrasting economies and in the process affected the globalization trend in the motor vehicle industry that began with the export of Japanese cars to the United States. Some important consequences are:

1.   For Japan, a strengthening yen disrupted export markets and reverberated back to undermine the domestic economy, forcing major automakers like Nissan and Mazda to seek cash infusions from foreign sources.

2.   Japanese facilities that were transplanted to lower-cost nations in Asia succumbed to a second crisis as weakening currencies devalued their foreign investments.

3.   The falling currencies resulted in business failures, curbing domestic consumer demand for autos made at the new facilities.

4.   The United States became the nation of choice for foreign investors as billions of dollars from domestic and foreign sources spurred the New York Stock Exchange to record levels and brought such economic prosperity that the federal government balanced its budget. Record profits were earned by the huge U.S. motor vehicle industry. The DaimlerChrysler merger, discussed in the next chapter, was a manifestation of the U.S. attractiveness for foreign money.

GM RESTRUCTURING

In the early years of the Japanese recession, the downturn went virtually unnoticed by Detroit because its stalwart firms were going through their own retrenchment phases, with GM announcing a $1.98 billion quarterly loss on October 31, 1990: "The General Motors Corporation, acknowledging that it would not soon recapture lost ground in a glutted market and wary of harder times in the industry, moved today to close up to nine factories that employ tens of thousands of workers. The closings which will cost G.M. billions of dollars, resulted in its biggest quarterly loss ever" (Levin 1990). The company and its new chairman, Robert Stempel, were at long last facing its eroding financial and business situation, but, characteristic of Detroit's once-premier firm, GM was moving too slowly and, in important cases, going in the wrong direction. Stempel realized that the company's labor costs were simply too high in the new competitive milieu and looked to early retirement as an accommodating way of paring his highly paid, unionized workforce. Under the delusion that GM still possessed a financial treasury of earnings from prior years, Stempel convinced the union to agree to his labor reduction plan by establishing a $3.35 billion fund for employees who elected his early retirement program. In tandem with the closing of plants and a national recession that emptied more facilities, GM workers briskly availed themselves of the fund, causing it to be drained in two years even as the giant firm was writing off hefty plant closing costs and losing sales because of the recession.

The recession also spelled the political demise of George Bush, who had followed Ronald Reagan as U.S. president in 1988, the year between the stock market crashes of October 1987 and 1989, caused in large measure, by the Reagan budget deficits. In an effort to calm a jittery market and dispel the specter of the great stock market crash of 1929, which began the Great Depression, Bush, at the end of 1990, signed a $500 billion spending reduction and tax increase bill, effectively removing the fiscal stimulus that had fueled the Reagan boom years. In the ensuing recession, GM lost $1 billion on its new

Saturn compact car, and the slowdown knocked the wind out of Ford's profit-making big cars and trucks, causing the smaller firm to record a $3.2 billion loss for 1991.

Executive Shifts

General Motors posted a $4.45 billion loss for the same year, the largest for any U.S. corporation, and GM's Robert Stempel—admitting that "current events worldwide and the unusually deep automotive slump in the United States" were responsible for the disastrous loss—announced the eventual closing of 21 plants and elimination of 74,000 jobs (Levin 1992, A1, D6). Twelve facilities were picked for immediate retrenchment, with five of them in the home state of Michigan (two of the five in Detroit), two in Ontario, Canada, between Lakes Eire and Ontario, and the North Tarrytown plant north of New York City and the farthest away from GM headquarters. The move away from the Great Lakes region of North America had begun in earnest for General Motors. Its global perspective was enhanced within a few months of the record-shattering loss, when the company's board of directors named Jack Smith, head of GM Europe, as the new president and chief operating officer. Smith, in turn, immediately brought in Jose Ignacio Lopez de Arriortua from GM Europe to be the executive in charge of GM's worldwide purchasing activities, who in his new capacity set out to reduce costs by $4 billion by "ripping up GM's components contracts and demanding new bids, with price cuts of 10 percent or more" (Ingrassia and White 1994, 303). The drastic steps convinced GM's board that new leadership was needed at the highest level to stem the company's severe losses, and within six months of making Jack Smith president, it dismissed Robert Stempel and appointed Smith to the position of chief executive officer (CEO). For his senior staff, Smith again turned to GM Europe, now headed by Louis Hughes, and appointed him to be executive vice president of international operations. G. Richard Wagoner, in charge of GM do Brasil, was made the new chief financial officer.

GM's new executive suite signaled a seismic shift in corporate governance from the days when the CEO imperially ruled with an iron fist and singlehandedly appointed his successor with little input from a passive board. Still, the GM change was not as momentous as the bigger one at another corporate giant, IBM, where the board not only dismissed a sitting chief executive officer but went outside the company to find a successor. At General Motors, Smith was already being groomed for the executive post, and the board's intervention simply accelerated his move upward. Lopez was the principal outsider who got a senior position in May 1992, but the mercurial Lopez abruptly quit within a year to take charge of both purchasing (his specialty) and production at Volkswagen. His departure was not an amicable one. GM began legal action against Lopez for stealing corporate secrets, and the peripatetic executive also came under criminal investigation for industrial espionage by German prosecutors and the U.S. Department of Justice (Ingrassio and White 1994, Chapter 17).

A Leaner GM

While the departure of Lopez proved highly irritating, it did not daunt GM's efforts at turning the company around by implementing stringent cost-cutting plans (some initiated by Lopez) and lean operating methods used in its joint ventures with the Japanese. Most of these changes had been initiated by Jack Smith's predecessors: Roger Smith (no relation to the other Smith) and Robert Stempel, who were unfortunately occupying the CEO office when GM announced its billion-dollar losses, consequently bearing the brunt of the blame and calls for change. "Three harshly critical books and a wickedly satirical movie called *Roger and Me* had made [Roger] Smith the poster boy for American industrial decline" (Ingrassia and White 1994, 20). In reality, Roger Smith, from the beginning of his tenure as GM's chairman in 1981, moved quickly to solidify alliances with Japanese carmakers and learn their efficient production techniques. In 1981, for example, GM took a 3.3% equity stake in Japan's Suzuki Motor Corporation, a small-car manufacturer, and this led to a joint venture in Canada, the Canadian Auto Manufacturing, Inc. (CAMI), where the American firm participated in operating a plant run by the Japanese. A GM executive became vice president of manufacturing at CAMI and subsequently used the CAMI plant design and process as the basis for GM's highly efficient Adam Opel plant in Eisenach, Germany. Roger Smith's most publicized alliance, however, began on March 1, 1982, when he secretly met his Toyota counterpart in New York to begin negotiations on the New United Motor Manufacturing, Inc. (NUMMI) joint venture, which would assemble compact cars at an abandoned GM plant in Fremont, California, under Toyota supervision. Smith furthermore remained aloof of the voluntary export restraints instituted by President Reagan and advocated by Ford and Chrysler, to demonstrate that GM was willing to work with foreign competitors and not embrace protectionist measures that would keep them out. For the NUMMI deal, Roger Smith appointed Jack Smith as his principal negotiator, a move that would set the younger Smith on a path that would make him head of GM Europe as the Eisenach plant was being planned and then on to become CEO of General Motors.

Eisenach. The circumstances surrounding the Eisenach plant put it at the center of GM's global attention during its darkest days, when plants around the Great Lakes were being closed. It was furthermore located on East German soil, giving Adam Opel, the GM wholly owned German subsidiary, access to the site only after the fall of the Berlin Wall in 1989 and reunification of the two Germanys. The new plant was designed to satisfy the emerging demand from democratized nations of Eastern Europe provided a suitable workforce could be hired from a former communist population known for its slovenly work habits. All German workers were also being motivated to increase labor productivity up to U.S. and Japanese standards because protectionist barriers keeping out foreign motor vehicles were being eliminated in 1999. With such challenges and being one of the few major construction projects in the early 1990s, it was not surprising to see the Eisenach project attract the attention of GM's most aggressive planners and design engineers, who were eager to implement what they had learned and adapted from the CAMI joint venture with Suzuki and the NUMMI joint venture with Toyota to Eisenach and make it the prototype for all future GM facilities. This would help turn around the world's largest manufacturing company and possibly save it from financial ruin. Naturally, it had the full attention of the board and corporate headquarters as well as Robert J. Eaton, the president of GM Europe, who went on to succeed Lee Iacocca as chairman of Chrysler (Miller and Kerwin 1993, 67–68).

The Eisenach plant used or adopted most, if not all, of the operating and design principles practiced by the Japanese in their U.S. transplants, including:

1. Twelve weeks of intensive training and motivation of new workers hired from a former communist system.

2. Organization into teams, with job rotation among team members such that work done by the team could be performed by any member.

3. Suggestion solicitation from line workers to implement continuous improvement and zero-defect goals.

4. Just-in-time delivery systems enhanced by computer networks of suppliers with the assembly plant.

5. Round-the-clock operations for lower per unit operating costs as well as faster amortization of capital costs.

The new plant also began experimenting with modular manufacturing in which subassembly is done at supplier sites, with final assembly of the modules done at Eisenach. This became the basis for GM's Blue Macaw facility in Brazil as well as the Delta small-car program, which was conditionally approved in 1999 and strenuously objected to by the American labor union because Delta facilities would utilize far less unionized workers. The CAMI plant, manned by the Canadian autoworkers union, was designated for conversion to modular assembly, making it the lead plant for the Delta program. The CAMI plant would furthermore cut manufacturing and investment costs by placing all car, minivan, and sport utility vehicles on a common platform (Akre, 1999). Obviously pleased with the results of the CAMI alliance with Suzuki, GM in September 1998 paid $315 million from its now highly profitable business to purchase additional shares in Suzuki Motor, increasing its stake in the Japanese company from 3.3% to 10%. The following April, Suzuki reciprocated by purchasing $37 million of GM stock, thus strengthening its global partnership with the giant firm, in which the smaller company would have primary responsibility for minivehicle development, especially in Asia, and General Motors would handle larger vehicles in the rest of the world (AP press release 1999). GM was also utilizing its expanded financial resources to purchase 52.5 billion yen worth of shares in Isuzu Motors Ltd., another Japanese affiliate that was floundering in the long Japanese recession. Its tenuous position could be compared to Suzuki's in terms of GM's increased ownership in each. The Isuzu stake rose to 49%, while GM's share of Suzuki remained small at 10%. The cash infusion helped Isuzu in its new joint venture with GM "to build a $320 million plant in Ohio to make diesel engines for GM pickup trucks. GM and Isuzu agreed last year that Isuzu would take over development of diesel engines as part of a global reorganization of GM's power-train developments" (Reuters press release 1998).

FORD'S NEW CAR DEVELOPMENT

With its financial future secured by profits from its large trucks and automobiles, the Ford Motor Company sought to streamline and integrate its $85 billion multinational enterprise such that it could tap managerial and engineering expertise from anywhere in the world as well as steer clear of mistaken approaches made by the industry in the new global competition. Effectively curbing excessive development and operating costs as in the Saturn and Taurus cases, was becoming essential because Japanese makers were introducing redesigned models at a brisk pace and using this ability to hold onto the 20%–30% market share that they had gained in the United States. In developing countries, the Japanese edge in small-car development was also paying off as economic growth in such markets spurred the demand for reasonably priced passenger vehicles. Ford's expertise and profits, moreover, were derived from the large-car, affluent U.S. market, prompting top management's decision to broaden the company's product base by the development of a small car that could be sold in all areas of the world from North and South America, to Europe, the Middle East, and Asia. It would be Ford's answer to the Japanese challenge and even use Mazda's engineering and the same car platform as the Mazda Familia, since the latter was in the process of becoming a Ford affiliate.

The Escort (and its twin, the Mercury Tracer) was Ford's entrant in the small-car competition, and even with technical assistance from Mazda, its development costs came to $2 billion. Together with its low market price, the Escort was a money loser in 1990, but it did have an important redeeming feature. It was a low emitter of air pollutants, and this allowed Ford to sell more of its heavily polluting, but very profitable, large cars and still remain within government environmental quality guidelines. The development of the European Escort ran along a different engineering track from the one used by its American counterpart of the same name, with product development shared by teams in Germany and England with no overriding authority. Product testing and quality control fell through the cracks, with huge defects such as its destabilizing tendency to sway when driven on the highway discovered only after the car went on sale. A market disaster, the European Escort did allow Ford to experiment with an international supplier system, with parts coming from twelve European countries as well as Canada, the United States, and Japan. Moreover, some of the suppliers were independent subcontractors, with Ford interested in getting low-cost, good-quality parts from anyone and the signing of proven parts suppliers into long-term relationships. "The company was also prepared to integrate product development and total quality management (TQM) with the network of suppliers (Chen 1996, 220).

Under its future chairman, Alex Trotman, who would be head of worldwide operations in 1992, Ford vigorously pursued its globalization plans despite the setbacks in the Escort. A midsize global car became the next goal, and it occupied the compact car niche vacated by the Taurus when it was enlarged to meet domestic demand for family sedans. The new car had three different badges, with Mondeo used in Europe, Contour in the United States, and Mystique for the more expensive Mercury line of cars. Planned for fifty nine countries, development costs soared to $6 billion, even with platform engineering and using a common platform employed to cut costs in important invisible parts (underbody, chassis, engine, transmission) and different styling, seats, and options used to distinguish the car and cater to various tastes. Because the Mondeo car was designed new from the ground up, considerable time and money were expended on developing an engine and transmission and rededicating plants on two continents to make parts and assemble the vehicle. "Mondeo was introduced in Europe in March 1993 and in Asian Pacific markets (Taiwan, Hong Kong, Thailand, Singapore) in the fall of 1993. The Contour and Mystique were introduced in North America during September 1994," with the American models made in Cuautitlan, Mexico, and Kansas City, Missouri (Czinkota, Ronkainen, Moffett, and Moynihan 1998, 13). Prior to the U.S. introduction, Alex Trotman—who was born in England and possessing work experience on four continents—became chairman of Ford and launched a massive reorganization of the firm to make it a truly global enterprise by the year 2000.

FORD 2000

In his Ford 2000 plan, Trotman remembered the cost overruns for Escort, Taurus, and Mondeo and combined North American and European auto operations into a single group. Asia-Pacific and Latin American operations, the two big emerging market areas, were also combined into the International Automotive unit, which itself was eventually combined with North America-Europe into one auto unit for the entire world. The combinations dampened regional, country, or other geographical distinctions at the top of Ford's managerial hierarchy and thereby increased cooperation worldwide and eliminated redundancy and regional fiefdoms. In multinational enterprises, regional or country managers have had a tendency to become "kings" of their particular areas, resisting calls for change even from headquarters. "We know what is best" and "we can do it better" are frequent replies to memos from above. For a global car, such comments coming in from various parts of the organization could easily torpedo a new project before the first blueprint was drawn. Having one automotive operations unit therefore streamlined decision making by giving it the responsibility and authority of melding the disparate parts of the organization and implementing those plans set by the chairman's office and approved by the board. Veto power would also be removed from a regional group once all regions had been placed under the authority of one automotive unit.

In the Ford 2000 reorganization, product development was centralized by vehicle platform into five centers: "one in Europe for small cars like the Escort, and four in Dearborn for large front-wheel-drive cars like Taurus, large rear-wheel-drive cars like the Crown Victoria, light trucks including the F-series and Explorer, and commercial trucks" (Walton 1997, 222). Each vehicle center had a center director as well as line directors for specific vehicles being developed. Functional managers for vehicle, body, chassis and power-train engineering were also part of the center, with technical personnel reporting to both a line director and engineering functional manager. The rationale behind the new setup was, of course, to reduce product development times and costs by using fewer platforms (sixteen instead of twenty four) and building more vehicles sharing the reduced number of platforms. The emphasis on common centers and platforms would reduce time and costs for new platform development and enable the reuse of existing factories and tools. Toward this end, the five vehicle centers were reduced to three in 1997 with the merging of the two large car centers and the two truck centers. "This restructuring reflects Ford's attempt to reduce the amount of redundant engineering work in the different centers and share more components in different product lines. Through these changes, Ford expects to reduce engineering costs per vehicle, material costs, servicing costs, and manufacturing equipment investment" (Cusumano and Nobeoka 1998, 97–98).

Similar to GM's efforts under Lopez, Ford 2000 planned to get the most cash savings by streamlining its $37 billion a year program for purchasing parts and raw materials. By combining its two big North American and European units, the company sees considerable savings in both product development and purchasing, and "Ford will scour the world looking to buy more common parts from fewer suppliers at lower prices" (Templin 1994, A3).

FORD'S LIGHT TRUCKS

While Ford attempted to wring more profit from its automotive units, its bottom line in the 1990s was handsomely bolstered by the popularity of its pickup trucks and sport utility vehicles (SUVs). In the United States, light trucks, which include pickup, SUVs, and minivans, reached sales parity with cars in 1998, with both cars and trucks each selling about 8 million units for the year. The light trucks, however, are more expensive than cars and thus contribute more to corporate profits. Their sales popularity compared to cars is clearly indicated in Table 4.4, showing six of the ten best-selling vehicles in 1996 as light trucks, with the Taurus being the only auto in the top five. The absence of a Japanese light truck in the table further establishes the recovery mode of the U.S. industry as one dependent on large, gas-guzzling vehicles with considerable space for goods, children, and pets and suitability for long-distance travel. Heavier and higher, most light trucks are considered safer than smaller cars, with the laws of physics favoring the bigger vehicle in a collision. This

Table 4.4
Best-Selling Vehicles of 1996

1. Ford F-series pickup	780,838
2. Chevrolet C/K pickup	550,594
3. Ford Explorer SUV	402,663
4. Ford Taurus	401,049
5. Dodge Ram pickup	383,960
6. Honda Accord	382,298
7. Toyota Camry	359,433
8. Dodge Caravan minivan	300,117
9. Ford Ranger pickup	288,393
10. Ford Escort	284,644

Source: *Automotive News*, January 13, 1997. Automotive News DATA CENTER. Copyright 1997.

feature has endeared them to the American parent transporting young children around town. The availability and low prices for fuel, together with an extensive highway system, also support the popularity of light trucks in the United States and the trend toward bigger, more expensive models, with the American firms in the vanguard of this movement.

Michigan Truck Plant

The nuts-and-bolts aspect of the sport utility vehicle business can be illustrated by Ford's Michigan Truck Plant in Wayne, which works around the clock, six days a week, producing full-size SUVs. About 245,000 Expeditions, selling for $36,000, and 48,000 Navigators, selling for $45,000, are produced per year, with profit margins coming to $12,000 for the former and $15,000 for the latter. Margins are high because development and retooling costs have been recovered at the truck plant that formerly made full-sized pickup trucks before converting to SUV production. The conversion was completed with minimal retooling and SUV development expense because sport utility vehicles are mainly covered pickup trucks, with the cabin containing the attributes and comfort of a passenger car. The low outlay of investment funds and high production rates, profit margins, and retail prices all translate into annual sales of $11 billion for this single plant's output, bringing to Ford $3.7 billion in pretax profits. "While Ford has 53 assembly plants worldwide, the one here accounted for a third of the company's total profits last year" (Bradsher 1999, 14). Such profits have swelled the coffers of the company, allowing it to purchase the automotive operations of Volvo at the beginning of 1999 for $6.5 billion to further advance its globalization program.

REFERENCES

Akre, Brian S. "GM Mulls Small-Car Assembly Plants." AP Headlines via Yahoo.com/ Detroit, January 7, 1999.

AP press release via Yahoo.com/ "Suzuki Buys into General Motors." Tokyo, April 17, 1999.

Bradsher, Keith. "Making Tons of Money and Fords, Too." *New York Times*, February 14, 1999, section 4, p.14.

Chen, Min. *International Technology Transfer*. London: International Thomson Business Press, 1996.

Cusumano, Michael, and Kentaro Nobeoka. *Thinking beyond Lean*. New York: Free Press, 1998.

Czinkota, Michael R., Ilkka A. Ronkainen, Michael H. Moffett, and Eugene O. Moynihan. *Global Business*. 2d ed. Fort Worth: Dryden Press, 1998.

Ingrassia, Paul, and Joseph B. White. *Comeback: The Fall and Rise of the American Automobile Industry*. New York: Touchstone, 1994.

Levin, Doron P. "G.M. Plans to Shut up to 9 Factories; Loses $1.98 Billion." *New York Times*, November 1, 1990, p. A1.

———. "G.M. Picks Plants to Be Shut as It Reports a Record U.S. Loss." *New York Times*, February 25, 1992, pp. A1, D6.

Miller, Karen Lowry, and Kathleen Kerwin. "GM's German Lesson." *Business Week*, December 20, 1993, pp. 67–68.

Niskanen, William A. *Reaganomics*. New York: Oxford University Press, 1988.

Reuters press release via Yahoo.com/ "GM Says to Boost Stake in Isuzu to 49% in March." Tokyo, December 18, 1998.

Templin, Neal. "Ford's Trotman Gambles on Global Restructuring Plan." *Wall Street Journal*, April 22, 1994, p. A3.

The World Almanac 1999. Mahwah, NJ: World Almanac Books.

Walton, Mary. *Car*. New York: W. W. Norton, 1997.

Chapter 5

The DaimlerChrysler Merger

On May 6, 1998, the world's motor vehicle industry was profoundly altered by the megamerger of Daimler-Benz AG of Stuttgart, Germany, and Chrysler Corporation of Auburn Hills, Michigan. The resulting company, DaimlerChrysler AG, would have worldwide sales of $180 billion with combined 1997 motor vehicle sales of 4 million units and a 7.4% market share. The new giant was still smaller than General Motors, Ford, Toyota, and Volkswagen, whose 1997 world market percentages came to 16.2% and 12.9% for the Detroit leaders and 9% and 7.4% for Toyota and VW. More important than the combined numbers were the possible synergies involved between two distinctive companies—one European and the other American—with few overlapping areas. Daimler-Benz is known for its luxury car Mercedes-Benz nameplate and although it has a very successful niche in the U.S. market, 63% of its sales come from Europe. Chrysler's sales, on the other hand, are 93% derived from the American market, where its best-sellers include the Ram pickup truck, Caravan minivan, and Jeep Grand Cherokee, a sport utility vehicle whose Jeep brand was acquired in the takeover of American Motors Corporation.

The partners are strong financially, and therefore the merger did not entail a bailout of a floundering company as in the Ford takeover of Mazda or the equity stake extended by Renault to Nissan. Nevertheless, the two vehicle manufacturers are not front-runners in their domestic markets, and Chrysler nearly collapsed in the 1970s from Japanese inroads in the United States. Mercedes-Benz was also in for a jolt when Toyota, Honda, and Nissan moved to upscale nameplates (Lexus, Acura, Infiniti) and when a 1993 recession slowed sales of luxury cars in a reunited Germany. Rising labor costs and benefits, together with a strong deutsche mark on foreign exchanges, began to erode export sales, as even luxury cars proved price-elastic in the affluent American market. This prompted Daimler-Benz to adopt a workforce reduction in 1992–1993 of 40,000 employees, most of them at the Mercedes-Benz truck and auto group and at its smaller aerospace division. The company, in a diversification/globalization move, announced plans in September 1993 to build a $300 million assembly plant in Alabama following a similar move in 1992 by Bayerische Motoren Werke AG (BMW) to open a plant in South Carolina. Both German luxury vehicle companies intentionally chose southern states as manufacturing sites, learning from the bitter experience encountered by Volkswagen in 1988 as it closed its sole U.S. plant in Pennsylvania (a strongly unionized, northern state) after continuous labor disputes with the powerful United Auto Workers union. The South, lacking the militant unionism found in the industrialized North, has become the U.S. area of choice for both Detroit and foreign auto companies, which are even willing to locate in underdeveloped countries to escape the high costs and labor troubles of industrialized nations.

GLOBALIZATION

The corporate urge to survive and prosper in rapidly evolving global markets is the sine qua non behind the DaimlerChrysler merger of two very successful companies, whose sales areas are becoming mature and diluted as markets internationalize. Chrysler's 1997 market share was only 5.3% of total worldwide vehicle sales, while Daimler-Benz with its predominantly luxury cars was a smaller 2.1%. The combination resulted in more impressive numbers, with 1997 sales reaching $130 billion and pretax earnings climbing to $7 billion. The monetary amounts made DaimlerChrysler the third largest motor vehicle manufacturer, enabling it to keep up with global leaders in the following ways:

1. Expansion of product lines with highly recognizable brand names in important American and European markets.

2. Economies of scale in purchasing parts, production runs, and product development and distribution.

3. Sufficient financial strength to underwrite capital projects globally, especially in fast-growing, emerging markets.

4. Diversification of markets, removing undue reliance on large, domestic ones that may be maturing.

5. Protection against foreign exchange fluctuations by having corporate assets denominated in numerous hard currencies, permitting losses in one to be offset by gains in another.

6. Greater global depth in management and technical expertise as well as training opportunities in foreign environments.

Several of these pro-merger points became evident to the new partners as front runners General Motors, Ford, and Volkswagen undertook major investments in China, India, Latin America, and East European states that were liberated in the 1989 fall of the Berlin Wall. These moved Daimler-Benz to strengthen its presence in the huge American market with its 1993 investment in Alabama, becoming the first German company to list its stock on the New York Stock Exchange (the world's largest equity market) and culminating in the megamerger with Chrysler under U.S. accounting rules. Growth through internal corporate investments and external acquisitions has been a mainstay of the motor vehicle industry, beginning with moves by Japanese firms across the Pacific Ocean. It became a high priority for Daimler in the mid-1980s under its former chairman Edzard Reuter, who began a $5 billion acquisition program that included nontruck and auto companies like the Dutch aircraft maker Fokker NV. The large investment in Fokker, however, became problematic with the ending of the East–West Cold War and attendant reduction in defense expenditures. As sales slumped, Fokker became a candidate for divestiture by Juergen E. Schrempp, who had become chairman of Daimler-Benz in 1994, even though he had supported the acquisition a few years earlier. The flip-flop cost Daimler-Benz over $3 billion in write-off losses, but it was integral in refocusing it on its traditionally strong truck and auto business. The failed Fokker deal impressed Schrempp with the importance of having a good fit in future combinations as well as a keen understanding of major problems that could surface in international alliances. Such skepticism arose in earlier negotiations with Chrysler where the objective included possible joint ventures in Latin America or Asia, where each side was lagging. The talks broke down because the firms had little experience with each other, and thus investments at foreign sites carried a large amount of risk, even though they were highly desirable. Daimler-Benz also vetoed a controlling stake in Nissan Motor Company when the floundering Japanese firm approached it for a cash infusion in 1999. Daimler indicated that it was already too busy ironing out the details in its huge merger with Chrysler and, in addition, had not received a satisfactory accounting of Nissan's liabilities. Comparison of the two potential merger partners clearly shows that Chrysler's strong profits in a robust U.S. economy easily beat out a money-losing Nissan in a recession-plagued Japan.

CORPORATE BACKGROUND

In 1997, prior to the merger, Daimler-Benz had pretax earnings of $2.4 billion on sales of $71 billion, making it slightly bigger than Chrysler's sales of $61 billion. The latter, however, had nearly twice the earnings ($4.6 billion) of the German firm, attributable to the booming U.S. market for its minivans and light trucks and its lean workforce, which produced and marketed 2.9 million vehicles with 121,000 employees. Vehicle sales for Daimler-Benz were lower at 1.1 million units, but its large payroll had 300,000 employees, many in less-profitable business lines like aerospace and information services (Coleman and White 1998). Such numbers made it apparent to Daimler-Benz that Chrysler was the sole feasible American merger partner because union with General Motors or Ford would be tantamount to a takeover of the German company and elimination of its independence. Chrysler was thus Daimler's last chance to be a major player in American markets. Its industry sales ranking was also significantly raised because, alone, it sold fewer motor vehicles than such small Asian companies as Suzuki and Hyundai and was furthermore below its archrival BMW. The combined company was a leader in sales, putting it in fifth place on the strength of Chrysler's sales, which moved up a single notch from sixth place (by itself) to fifth with Daimler-Benz.

In light of Chrysler's stronger sales and profit positions, why would the Michigan company acquiesce to merge? Greater business clout and the prestige status of the Mercedes-Benz nameplate are ready explanations. By itself, Chrysler would remain the weakling of Detroit's Big Three automakers, with a history of close encounters with the financial abyss that claimed similarly small firms like Studebaker and Packard. The possibility of internal growth to the size of General Motors or Ford also looked bleak, particularly since GM's 1997 sales at $178 billion towered over Chrysler's $61 billion. Moreover, GM had already established an immense network of global alliances, some going back to 1925, when it took over Germany's Opel car firm. For Chrysler, therefore, merger with Germany's largest industrial enterprise would at least lessen the unequal footing that Chrysler was in vis-à-vis its American competitors. Daimler-Benz was also willing to pay a premium to Chrysler's shareholders for their votes approving the merger. As these details were announced, Chrysler's stock responded, rising 17.8% in price. The two chairmen, Juergen Schrempp of Daimler and Robert Eaton of Chrysler, also held a common understanding of the future of their industry, and this facilitated merger talks: "The two men shared the view that the industry was heading rapidly into a period of brutal competition and consolidation that could leave fewer than a dozen independent auto makers on the world stage in ten years, compared with the 20 or so there are now" (Ingrassia and Mitchener 1998).

IACOCCA, THEN EATON

For the Kansas-born Robert Eaton, the wretched downsizing of Detroit's imperial auto industry was experienced firsthand as a rising executive at General Motors who jumped ship in 1992 after the battleship GM suffered some direct hits from Japanese exports and their American transplants. The Chrysler Corporation was listing badly, too, under the flamboyant, but aging, Lee Iacocca, who had brought the company back from the brink in 1980 and was gamely attempting to rescue it a second time. More importantly, Iacocca, sensing that the curtain was soon to fall on his tenure, was very intent on leaving in grand style with munificent stock grants and options, $95,000 more in pension benefits, a half-million-dollar consulting contract, and use of the corporate jet, to which he had become closely attached. These "baubles" failed to assuage the "emperor's" lust for the trappings of office, but when they became public in the annual report, their extravagant dimensions assured the end of Iacocca's reign. The denouement was closely watched by Robert Eaton, president of GM Europe since 1988, whose own path to GM's top spot had already been blocked by John Smith, only two years older than Eaton and expected to be the next chairman. With a well-placed Chrysler executive pushing Eaton's candidacy and with a short, but genial, relationship developed with the mercurial Iacocca, Eaton in 1992 was made vice chairman of Chrysler in a move that would make him the chief executive officer at the beginning of 1993 (Ingrassia and White 1994, Chapter 11).

Eaton's ascendancy was a fortuitous one because Iacocca had toiled not only at lining his pockets but at successful attempts to put Chrysler on a solid, profit-making foundation. In the 1980s, for example, he commercially launched the Plymouth and Dodge minivans that became immediate successes for suburban "soccer moms"—parents who needed a large passenger vehicle for transporting their kids to and from school or to soccer practice after school. For the next ten years, these minivans would best all competition, with their peak sales coming in 1994 as soccer moms began turning to the sport utility vehicle in hopes of inculcating their mundane domestic chores with a more rugged vehicle image. Another coup occurred in March 1987, when Chrysler agreed to purchase American Motors Corporation (AMC) from the hapless Renault and independent shareholders for about $1.5 billion. Chrysler thereby came to own the Jeep light truck maker, and it became the basis for the buyer's highly profitable sport utility line of vehicles. Had either company stalled until after the October 1987 stock market crash, it is doubtful that Chrysler, always hard up for cash, would have been able to add the Jeep jewel to Iacocca's crown. Even before the crash, Standard & Poor's Corporation was examining Chrysler's financial circumstances for a possible downward revision of its credit rating (Holusha 1987, D8).

The payoff for Chrysler is easy to glimpse in the company's best-selling models for 1997, headed by the Dodge Ram pickup truck at 350,257 units sold in Europe and the United States, the Dodge Caravan with sales of 285,736 vehicles, and the Jeep Grand Cherokee with 278,381 units sold. In addition to this type of contribution to Chrysler's bottom line, the Jeep technology, purchased from AMC, must have attracted the attention of top management at Mercedes-Benz who were planning to assemble its M-class sport utility vehicle at its new U.S. plant in Alabama (Andrews and Holson 1998, A1).

International Moves Falter

Chrysler's success in these new motor vehicles was, however, confined to its domestic borders even as the AMC acquisition brought with it the Beijing Jeep joint venture in the capital of China. One of the first entrants in the potentially huge Chinese passenger vehicle market, Beijing Jeep lost its front-runner position to aggressive moves by the bigger Volkswagen and General Motors, which wooed Chinese officials with considerable transfer of much-needed technology and capital to the impoverished country (see Chapter 8). In order to remedy its lagging international operations, Chrysler's Iacocca approached Fiat, Italy's largest industrial group, for a possible merger. If consummated, the deal would have advanced the industry's move toward globalization by eight years, the amount of time Chrysler would wait for Daimler-Benz to make its offer. In the talks with Fiat, Chrysler's financial situation appeared too shaky and the times too tenuous, with stock market crashes in 1987 and 1989, for union to occur with the hesitant Italian company.

Much of the blame for the falling stock markets could be ascribed to massive budgetary deficits incurred under President Ronald Reagan, who succeeded in cutting taxes with his individual retirement account program while increasing expenditures for military defense. Deficits in the federal government budget approached $300 billion, causing Wall Street to react in a one-day record plunge in the Dow Jones stock index of over 500 points in the 1987 crash. The smaller crash in 1989—during the Fiat merger talks—dropped Chrysler to less than $10 a share, persuading a stunned Fiat that times were too chaotic for any reasonable assessment of Chrysler's value. Ever the salesman, Iacocca attempted negotiations with his old employer, Ford, only to be quickly rebuffed. The megamerger that was to be a capstone of his career would therefore have to wait for calmer times and the arrival of Robert Eaton, Iacocca's handpicked successor (Ingrassia and White 1994, 204–206). The destabilizing U.S. budget deficits were reduced by a Bill Clinton presidency (starting in 1992), with tax increases and moderate expenditure growth in defense spending coinciding with the ending of the Cold War. Interest rates, inflation, and unemployment fell sending U.S. equity markets to new highs, and the better times brought considerable tax revenues to government coffers. Recession in Asia was also beneficial by reducing world demand for oil and bringing gasoline prices down. This then prompted record sales of sport utility vehicles, minivans, and pickup trucks, especially for Chrysler, whose newly won profits attracted Daimler-Benz to the merger table.

The luxury carmaker was not totally out of place at Chrysler's headquarters because Iacocca had earlier proceeded to upgrade the company's humdrum product image through alliances with such European fashion plates as Lamborghini and Maserati of Italy. In 1984, with money coming in following his turnaround of the company, Iacocca agreed to the development by Maserati of the Chrysler Touring Coupe. This was followed in 1987 by his purchase of American Motors as well as the luxury sports car maker Lamborghini, only to have the latter jettisoned by Robert Eaton in one of his first acts as chairman. Lamborghini was sold to a son of President Suharto of Indonesia, who then sold it to Volkswagen when the Suharto presidency and empire dissolved in the aftermath of the Asian financial crises. VW, like Iacocca, is interested in sprucing up its staid product image and has added Rolls Royce to its lineup after a strenuous bidding war with BMW. The Maserati development of a luxury sports coupe came to naught, like the Lamborghini purchase, forcing Iacocca to terminate this costly, but worthless, program in 1989. Shortly after his resignation, the mercurial Iacocca attempted to take operating control of Chrysler in concert with the billionaire financier Kirk Kekorian, who acquired 13.75% of the company's outstanding stock. In 1996 Kekorian, but not Iacocca, was offered a seat on the board of directors in exchange for a five-year moratorium on any accumulation of Chrysler's shares. The new board member proceeded to pressure the company's executives to increase shareholder (and his) stock value, making them amenable to the Daimler offer and in the end giving Kekorian billions of dollars worth of capital gains on his Chrysler investment. In cashing out, Kekorian relinquished any role in the new company. Eaton, too, surrendered his chair after three years for a monetary sum exceeding $40 million, leaving the younger Schrempp in sole charge (Binkley 1998).

Cultural Shifts. The international merger may thus have removed unwanted powerful interlopers, but the streamlining of the executive suite with Eaton's early retirement makes the melding of disparate corporate cultures and manufacturing paradigms somewhat problematic. The national bias of top executives has already tilted toward Stuttgart with the departure of two senior vice presidents from Chrysler to Ford and the retirement of Chrysler's executive vice president of manufacturing. This leaves nine of the eleven managers who report to the cochairmen from Daimler-Benz. In the past, interaction of each side with activities across the Atlantic has been minimal, with Daimler-Benz conducting most of its business in Europe and Chrysler staying in the United States. Market niches and product design engineering remained distinct and foreign to the other side, resulting in little mutual experience and understanding acquired by managers at all levels. As a prime example of this, Germany's protected market, together with the luxury status of Mercedes-Benz sedans, never encountered the onslaught of cheap, well-made imports that Chrysler faced as it struggled to survive the competition from Japan on its home turf. Then, Dennis Pawley was a pivotal manager who brought many of the lean production techniques learned at the Mazda assembly plant in Flat Rock, Michigan, to Chrysler when he was appointed head of manufacturing. This experience will be muted when Pawley retires. Throughout the 1980s, moreover, Chrysler under Lee Iacocca willingly experimented with state-of-the-art manufacturing, which even entailed a joint venture with Mitsubishi Motor Company formed to build a new plant in Normal, Illinois. Chrysler dispatched its top engineers to observe firsthand the production, quality, and cost control methods of the Japanese. These were brought back and adapted at Chrysler, with the technology transfer significantly improving its plant productivity. Little of such cross-pollination occurred in Europe as firms generally worked behind protectionist barriers stymieing competition from foreign imports and investments.

INTERNATIONAL COMPARISONS

The different experiences surfaced in labor productivity studies conducted by the McKinsey Global Institute of Washington, D.C., and published in 1993. A productivity index, in terms of value-added per hour worked, showed that auto assembly labor productivity had narrowed between U.S. and Japanese facilities—100 for the U.S. and 116 for Japan—and both performances were considerably ahead of the German index at 66. The institute study concluded that "integration, continuous improvement and supplier management" methods are ways in which the Japanese raise worker productivity and also cited their American transplants as conduits for their dissemination in the United States. Germany's lagging index was attributed to the lack of competitive exposure and incentives that would streamline a "complex, highly specialized and inflexible job classification system." Workers performed highly specialized operations and had some difficulty in making suggestions for process improvement because they lacked an overall view of the factory. When repairs are needed, the line worker must call a maintenance specialist as mandated by work rules even if the employee could have fixed the problem without assistance. Downtimes are consequently longer. Quality control also suffers because line workers are not authorized to stop production for problems or defects and must call a supervisor. "Many American and German plants have large rework areas" to correct defective vehicles, requiring more "investment in plant space and tools for rework" (McKinsey Global Institute 1996, 8). The work environment in Germany derived from a closed, booming home market with low unemployment that strengthened the bargaining hand of the powerful IG Metall labor union. As instituted by German law, holding nearly half of the seats of a company's supervisory board, the union's power was enhanced with access to important corporate information like profits and costs, which it could effectively use against management in a tight labor market. Moreover, as an industry-wide union, it could use gains won at other companies to wring concessions from management in a process that continually ratcheted up benefits and pay increases with each bargaining round.

Heinous Legacy

The limits placed on management by labor's strong position—exact opposites to postwar developments in Japan—can be traced back to Hitler's embrace of the auto industry and its complicity in using slave labor for the fuhrer's armaments production. While such action defied the Geneva and most other moral conventions governing prisoners of wars, their more heinous aspect was the release of mainly Jewish workers, after replacements had been trained to keep up production lines, to their deaths at Auschwitz and other concentration camps. Principal automakers—Daimler-Benz, Volkswagen, Porsche— implicated in the use of slave labor pleaded innocent of Third Reich atrocities even as their plants "churned out jeep-type vehicles, Tiger tanks, airplane engines and parts for the V-1 flying bomb" (Kandell 1998). With the ending of the war, the car companies returned to their original line of business, with Volkswagen becoming independent of Porsche by government action. In 1998 VW recognized, under pressure of a lawsuit and from the state government of Lower Saxony where it is headquartered, its "historical and moral obligations" and established a compensation fund for slave workers used in its World War II factories (Andrews 1998).

Labor Power

While VW's corporate recognition came over fifty years after the war's end, German society and its democratically elected government took swifter action to curb industry and management's power as a result of their startling abuses. Conglomerates like I.G. Farben were dissolved, VW was separated from Porsche, and organized labor was given oversight responsibilities on the corporation's supervisory board but not on the firm's management board. Daimler-Benz's 1997 supervisory board, for example, had ten of twenty seats occupied by employee representatives. These have resulted in considerable gains for labor, not won in the United States, such as shorter, thirty five-hour workweeks, annual six-week vacations, and the world's highest compensation rates paid to labor. Such concessions have forced even luxury carmakers like Daimler-Benz to invest in other industries and foreign countries in order to become more competitive. Unfortunately, the firm's diversification moves under its former chairman (Reuter) have largely been counterproductive, and the merger with Chrysler could be problematic once the U.S. economy begins to slow. High labor costs and low manufacturing productivity may then force management to close excess capacity, forcing a bitter showdown with labor. Already, 1996 average hourly wage rates, including fringe benefits, showed German workers, at $31.87, way ahead of their counterparts in Japan ($21.04) and the United States ($17.74) (Ball and McCulloch 1999, 213). Compensation, furthermore, is still paid when workers are laid off. Under the terms of the merger, labor's powerful position at the board level will continue because Chrysler will be taken over by Daimler-Benz, with the resulting combination classified as a German firm and subject to German regulations. This begs the questions: Will the American labor union, which is already interested, serve on the new organization's supervisory board? How will management implement cuts in labor in lieu of the great productivity differences in the two countries? Will a basis of understanding form between the powerful German and American labor unions, whose views have heretofore been narrowly nationalistic and protectionist?

Shorter Work Times

Labor's power on the board could also slow efforts to implement cost-cutting practices like shorter changeover times in stamping operations, which were first observed in the Japanese transplants. In stamping out body parts from sheet metal, downtime can be extensive (up to three hours) when dies have to be changed for a different shape. Using various productivity-enhancing methods, the Japanese transplants could make the changeover in five to twenty minutes. Downtime is also considerable when a car model is redesigned, necessitating retooling of assembly lines. Honda's plant in Ohio was so efficient in this type of changeover that it could retool without stopping the assembly line (McKinsey Global Institute 1996, 7). In the competitive U.S. milieu, many of these techniques spread quickly to American firms.

Manufacturing efficiencies to keep costs down were also found to be incorporated during the design stages of a new truck or car. Such efforts have increased in importance as car buyers have demanded reasonably priced, durable, and attractively designed products, with competition making older models stale in a short period of time. Rising incomes mean a more sophisticated consumer class in countries throughout the world, particularly in emerging markets where industrialization and trade are lifting the economy, prompting a strong demand for a durable, inexpensive global car that is smaller and cheaper than Chrysler's Neon compact model. DaimlerChrysler currently lacks such a car, and this will definitely be a big drawback in its efforts to become a major player in global markets. With such cars already being produced by Ford and Fiat, the merged company will not have the luxury of designing new models in the usual time-consuming linear fashion where design, engineering, and manufacturing do their work sequentially without regard to functions and problems—like ease of manufacturability—outside their areas of concern. If cost constraints weren't met or if management was dissatisfied with the results, the various areas would simply redo their work, and the project would be delayed. Such slovenly practices made Chrysler a weak player in the past, and the company again faced tenuous times at the beginning of the 1990s, when its K-line of passenger cars could not attract much consumer attention, and the car company needed a new design for the important family sedan market. The competitive environment further demanded that the new models had to have eye-catching styling and features to distinguish it from a crowded field of popular models like the Ford Taurus and the Honda Accord. To contain costs and make the cars price-competitive, Chrysler's new LH models, as they were designated, had to be designed for efficient production whereby a common platform would undergird different models such as the Dodge Intrepid, Eagle Vision, and Chrysler Concorde. Lee Iacocca, furthermore, demanded that the design cycle for the LH line be completed in record time, and to assist in satisfying the chairman's wishes, Chrysler engineers again focused on its joint venture operations with Mitsubishi in Normal, Illinois. There it found that "Mitsubishi organized itself for simultaneous decisions, instead of sequential ones, by using product-development teams that cut across departmental lines" (Ingrassia and White 1994, 437). This matrix organization for multiple product development at the Japanese transplant was adopted by Chrysler, where it became the basis for its platform teams that were formed to spearhead the development of all new cars that shared a common platform.

Platform Engineering. The vehicle platform includes the chassis and underbody parts and, in terms of cost and complexity, rivals the engine as one of the most important parts of the vehicle. It furthermore has a tremendous impact on the car's appearance. Its common use in different models, moreover, spreads considerable design and developmental costs over greater production volumes, reducing per unit costs and permitting lower prices. Platforms can also be reused for newer models, and this further cuts costs and shortens both product and process development times since machinery for the assembly of older models can be salvaged to work on newer ones. In such ways, Chrysler's platform engineering has used the developed LH platforms for newer models like the 300M and LHS. A new platform team has been formed to develop the JR platform by 2001, which will be used for the redesigned Chrysler Cirrus, Dodge Stratus, and Plymouth Reliant models, whose popularity has fallen off. The three are grouped together because they currently share the JA platform. In a similar progression, the old PL platform for the Neon cars, first introduced in 1994, was replaced by a new 2000 Neon platform designed for the new millennium. To take advantage of the car's success, DaimlerChrysler is planning to use the 2000 Neon for a whole new set of vehicles from sedans, to sport utility vehicles and maybe small pickup trucks. In addition, new RS minivan platforms will replace older NS ones. For its best-selling sport utility vehicles, the company assembled the Jeep Grand Cherokee on a new WJ platform in 1998 and will do the same with the Jeep Wrangler on the VJ platform in 2002. The same year will see a redesigned Ram pickup truck on a new BE platform. The closeness of these platform introductions implies that many of them are not really new but instead were built on elements of older ones that could be effectively reused. Development times and costs are considerably reduced and engineering expertise can be transferred from old to new designs (EIU 1999a).

Platform Teams. The preceding types of platform engineering and reuse should be distinguished from the platform teams that were first formed by Chrysler and Iacocca to cut down on development times for the LH and PL platforms (the latter used for the Neon). They are based on new car development projects at Mitsubishi (and Honda), where all product development is overseen by a general manager. Individual projects have their own managers and a few engineers who can draw additional expertise from the company's functional divisions such as body design, material engineering, engine research, and vehicle testing. The engineers from the functional divisions are temporarily assigned to specific projects and return to their permanent division upon completion of their work. This keeps the project staff lean, while simultaneously it can draw from all functional divisions for its decision-making process. Comprehensive consultation of the functional areas further ensures that important manufacturing and styling features are efficiently incorporated at the project's beginning rather than at its middle or end which would then entail considerable reworking of completed details. The lean project staffs also allow multiple projects to proceed simultaneously since any one project is unlikely to completely tie up a functional division. This problem is inherent in sequential, linear development processes where a major job stalls all work behind it (Cusumano and Nobeoka 1998, 64–65).

When Iacocca was presented the platform team concept for speeding up development of the much-needed LH cars, the former chairman shrewdly remembered how a GM reorganization had failed because of confusing lines of management authority. This could also prove inherent for his teams because a typical member would have two bosses: the project manager and the functional division manager where he originated. Iacocca's solution to the potential problem was to appoint company "big shots" to oversee major projects. The vice president of engineering was thus in charge of Jeep and truck development; the vice president of purchasing oversaw the LH project; the vice president of design managed minivan development, while the vice president of regulatory affairs led small cars. With such overall corporate oversight provided by Iacocca himself, the LH project was completed in record time—thirty nine months compared to fifty four months for the preceding K-car development. In spite of its fast-paced schedule, LH had a lean staff of 740 engineers compared to 2,000 used for the K-cars. Manufacturing efficiencies were also effectively designed in, with the LH cars requiring 3,000 assembly line workers, while for a similar production schedule, the K-car lines required 5,300.

For the PL team coordinating the development of Chrysler's compact cars, the cost constraints were more stringent because the selling price of the smaller car would be $10,000–$19,000 below that of the LH line of sedans. To stay within a saleprice of $9,000 per vehicle and development costs of $1.3 billion, PL engineers were forced to use an existing plant to produce the Neon car, which was launched in September 1993. Its commercial success ensured that the concepts of platform teams (to reduce development time) and platform engineering using common platforms and the reuse of machinery would become permanent fixtures of the automotive industry. Platform development teams would also grow to include marketing as well as engineering expertise to make product decision making more inclusive of important business functions (Ingrassia and White 1994, 437–449).

SMALL-CAR SHORTCOMINGS

The use of the new design and manufacturing efficiencies propelled Chrysler to record profits and brought Daimler-Benz to the merger table. What they failed to do is give Chrysler a global small car that could compete in emerging markets like Brazil, China, and India. Chrysler, after all, had developed the Neon compact car as a means of getting back market share lost to the Japanese in its affluent home market. All corporate strategy and investments were thus made in the United States without much regard for the foreign environment. At any rate, Chrysler perennially ran short of cash and therefore had to husband scarce resources for its most important market. This occurred in 1991, when it was forced to sell its 50% share of the Normal, Illinois, joint venture to its partner, Mitsubishi Motors. Small-car development expertise also exited the firm with the departure of Lee Iacocca and the retirement of Dennis Pawley in 1999, who was head of manufacturing while the PL line was developed and who was expected to go on DaimlerChrysler's management board.

Robert Eaton has acknowledged the need for a small global car needed for emerging markets, and to reduce development time and costs, the global car would have to be developed in partnership with another firm or through acquisition of outside expertise. It would then be a replay of the Mitsubishi joint venture, and indeed the Japanese company still makes the Dodge Avenger and Chrysler coupe models for its erstwhile partner. Eaton's comments also imply that the Neon car is too big and expensive for the global, small-car market since "it is only 145 millimeters shorter than the Mercedes-Benz C-class and . . . its engines are comparable in displacement with many cars classed as large and luxury in Europe" (EIU 1999a, 92). The Neon, furthermore, is an American-built car, dedicated to the affluent U.S. market—hardly amenable to conditions in third-world countries. In the first quarter of 1999, following the successful completion of the megamerger, Eaton stated: "I am absolutely certain that we will have one of these vehicles . . . a single 800 cc to 1200 cc vehicle that could be sold in South America and throughout Asia. It is the big thing missing in our worldwide product line-up" (EIU 1999b, 8). Eaton, however, will not be around long to bring the preceding outcome to fruition since he will be relinquishing his cochairmanship in the year 2001.

Moreover, experience in subcompact car development is even leaner at Daimler-Benz, a name synonymous with top-of-the-line sedans sold in the industrialized nations. To diversify its product line, the company in 1998 launched a small car for city driving named the Smart in association with the Swatch watch company. A new firm, the Micro Compact Car GmbH, was formed to build the two-seater in a factory erected in France in a radical move to broaden Daimler's staid image. Unfortunately, the company's lagging experience surfaced when major problems were discovered, delaying the introduction of the Swatchmobile. One was the car's tendency to skid out of control on icy roads. In inevitable comparisons with competing models in its price range of $9,000, the Smart was also found to be too expensive, considering its attributes and untested nature. With sales slumping, the Swatchmobile has become "a billion-dollar headache for DaimlerChrysler," with its operations expected to be scaled back and perhaps terminated if the situation does not improve (Andrews, May 19, 1999). There is also the option of transferring small-car development to Chrysler since that is where the expertise is in the merged company. Mercedes could then concentrate on upscale cars in affluent markets like Europe, the United States, and Japan.

CORPORATE SYNERGIES

While lack of a global car may be a shortcoming in DaimlerChrysler's product line, it can also be seen as an opportunity in which the new company can benefit by critically observing how Ford, General Motors, Volkswagen, and Fiat are doing as they sink sizable development sums in an area that has yet to become profitable. Significant overcapacity has resulted from these various attempts in emerging markets, particularly with the advent of global financial crises, which have curbed demand in once-booming markets. The downturn, moreover, has had relatively little impact on DaimlerChrysler, with its main business positions in affluent markets of the United States and Europe. Since little overlap exists, top management does not have to close redundant facilities and lay off workers, with unamortized costs written off against current income possibly producing negative earnings. Instead, each side can focus on realizing potential growth on the other side of the Atlantic Ocean by utilizing the marketing expertise of its new partner. At merger time, estimates of such gains from increased sales or cost savings were expected to be $1.4 billion in 1999, the first year of the union, and $3 billion three to five years later. About half of the latter amount comes from streamlining the purchasing of parts in the consolidated purchasing budget of $60 billion, using Chrysler's considerable experience at cost reduction in the area. The American firm came up with its innovative strategy during difficult business cycles when the smallest U.S. auto company lacked the clout to demand cost reductions from its numerous independent suppliers. To attain its objectives, the company instead proposed a sharing of cost savings with its suppliers on a 50–50 basis, giving them significant incentive to unearth and implement cost-cutting ideas in their dealings with Chrysler. The system, named SCORE for "supplier cost reduction effort," does require suppliers to come up with cuts amounting to at least 5% of its annual business with Chrysler. It was developed by Thomas Stallkamp while he was head of purchasing at the old company, and it will be implemented at the new company because it has already been deemed superior to Daimler's own supplier cost-saving system. Stallkamp was a project manager of the platform team that oversaw development of the LH cars under Iacocca.

Merger Fallout

Some of the partners' main suppliers are forming their own alliances to keep up with the merger. Arvin, a large U.S. exhaust supplier that supplied 75%–80% of Chrysler's needs, has bought a 49% equity stake in Zeuna Starker, a major German supplier to Mercedes-Benz. Other supplier firms will similarly have to grow through mergers, acquisitions, or joint ventures in order to meet the expanded requirements of DaimlerChrysler. The greater scale of operations is necessitated by the SCORE strategy of devolving considerable technical development of parts on supplier firms whenever there are design changes made by the main assembler. Such participation in the development work of new parts further enables the supplier to uncover ways of cutting costs. The cost reduction is rewarded by Chrysler not only with 50% of the savings as described earlier but with continued business over the long term. In terms of SCORE's impact on Chrysler's bottom line, it is estimated that savings reached $6 billion in the 1990s, with $2 billion coming in 1998, the year of the merger (Simison 1998, B1).

The melding of supply systems is a natural step in the merger process, and consolidation of management cultures, product lines, and distribution networks must likewise ensue for the union to be a success. As the Chrysler background has shown, turbulent economic times have frequently called for difficult management decisions requiring bold experimentation in engineering, design, and manufacturing that paid off in the company's showroom. Will Chrysler, which is being taken over by Daimler, "be able to infuse the larger organization with the same type of brash optimism, fun, entrepreneurship and cost-cutting that made Chrysler the envy of the industry?" (EIU 1999b, 3–4). Several reasons mitigate against this outcome:

1. The merger will put the resulting company in the league of a General Motors, whose bureaucratic organization and enormous size made it difficult to respond quickly in a competitive environment.

2. Daimler-Benz has been "known for decades as a ponderous, slow-moving and intensely conservative corporation" and will be incessant about maintaining the "carefully cultivated upscale-image of its Mercedes-Benz brand" (Andrews and Holsom 1998, D4).

3. With the departure of key American executives and Chrysler subsumed by Daimler, it is possible that the former's product image will become blurred and begin to mimic the luxury carmaker. This happened to GM when its divisions all began producing similar-looking, big, gas-guzzling cars, leaving no small car to compete against foreign imports.

4. Different cultures can also lead to managerial stalemate, as in the Renault takeover of American Motors Corporation, when disagreements caused sales to plunge just as the Japanese transplants were coming onstream to intensify competition in the United States.

5. In melding different managerial pay scales, it is expected that U.S. remuneration will be cut to effect salary parity with German counterparts. "Some estimates suggested that former Chrysler managers at DaimlerChrysler at the end of 1998 earned two to eight times as much as former Daimler-Benz executives who had similar job functions" (EIU 1999a, 80). Pay cuts could lead to the departure of experienced personnel at a time when profitable operations at Ford and GM have encouraged them to hire such talent. Two senior vice presidents have thus gone to Ford, and a vice president of communications, to GM.

Impact of Capital Markets

Some U.S. shareholders are also deserting the company, even though sales and profits at the combined company have remained strong. In November 1998, when the merger took effect, 44% of the shareholders were from the United States, with the percentage dropping sharply to 25% by March 1999. This caused the stock price to fall to 89 after reaching a high of 108. Some of the selling occurred when Standard & Poor's, the financial rating agency, removed the company from its closely watched S & P 500 stock index because it no longer considered DaimlerChrysler an American firm. Mutual fund managers of index funds who buy and sell according to the makeup of the S & P index consequently sold their considerable holdings. Of course, other fund managers could have bought if they expected the stock to rise in price, but given the uncertainties of the merger, these managers instead turned to more exciting areas like the booming Internet stocks.

As indicated, the evaluation of a company's stock by international financial institutions like the New York Stock Exchange is fairly critical when mergers or acquisitions cross national boundaries and when not much information is known about the foreign side. For the takeover of Chrysler, Daimler-Benz had to switch its corporate accounting from German to U.S. practices to effect the transaction as a pooling of interests, all-stock deal. This had to be done because German rules insist that pooling transactions can occur only in a merger of equals. Since the market valuation of Daimler exceeded that of Chrysler's by $20 billion, it was decided to use U.S. pooling rules, which were more flexible in such financial circumstances. The stock value is also important whenever a company is planning a major acquisition such as the type DaimlerChrysler is contemplating with respect to filling out its lagging expertise in developing a small global vehicle. The higher stock price means that less cash need be expended, and in many situations, a low stock price can even inhibit a takeover by encouraging a competing bid from a more attractive suitor. In Chrysler's 1987 purchase of American Motors Corporation from Renault SA, the Detroit firm nearly lost the bid because of its falling share price. It finally was forced to pay Renault $200 million *in cash* for the latter's 46% holdings in AMC. The remaining AMC shares were exchanged for $600 million of Chrysler stock, with Chrysler also issuing $600–$800 million of new securities to retire AMC debt (MacDonald 1998; Holusha, 1987, A1).

Nissan Talks Abandoned

Following a smooth beginning in the transatlantic merger, speculation focused on the Far East, where a financially troubled Nissan Motor Company was searching for a major alliance to keep operating. Daimler's chairman, Juergen Schrempp, was again expected to be on the prowl; after all, Germany's largest industrial empire now had a powerful American presence and wished to diversify its revenue base by doubling the tiny 10% share in ten years that it got from Asia. The large continent also had the greatest market potential for motor vehicles even if business had stalled because of Japan's lengthy recession and attendant financial crises in emerging markets. The product fit in the tripartite union of automakers was also good, and the idea was given a boost by Schrempp himself, who declared that an equity stake in Nissan was not out of the question.

In truth, an alliance with Nissan had already been preempted by the Chrysler merger, and Schrempp, who had supported and then unraveled the failed acquisition of Fokker, was certainly in a position to understand this. In terminating talks with Nissan in Tokyo, Schrempp acknowledged "that the opportunities that a close relationship with Nissan offer are not achievable as quickly and smoothly as initially expected" (Andrews, March 11, 1999, C1). The risks, however, were well known to Schrempp from the beginning, the salient ones being:

1.   Daimler and Chrysler were in the midst of their own complicated merger process, which could have been derailed by a Nissan deal.

2.   Japan's decade-long recession showed no hint of ending, with losses at Nissan expected to continue.

3.   Management at Nissan had no game plan for ending the losses that entailed

difficult choices like selling assets, closing facilities, and laying off employees and managers.

4.   Debt at the company had already reached a staggering $21.2 billion, with unrealized liabilities possibly doubling the amount.

Despite the enormous risks, Nissan's value to a European carmaker interested in expanding its base was readily apparent. As Daimler exited the scene, the smaller Renault of France quickly stepped forward with a cash infusion that kept Nissan viable. The French firm, in the aftermath of the megamerger, had concluded that it, too, would have to diversify its geographical sales area and product offerings in order to be an effective player in the global competition and before all smaller firms were absorbed by the likes of Ford and GM. Indeed, at about the same time, Ford—even though it stood at the forefront of globalization—saw fit to spend $6.5 billion to acquire the auto division of Volvo SA. The American giant, along with GM and Volkswagen, had been steadily adding strong positions in such huge emerging markets as Mexico, Brazil, Argentina, China, and India, as detailed in the following chapters of this volume. Even if a heavyweight like GM was not expressly in a large country like India, it was still well represented by the smaller Suzuki, with which GM had an equity relationship and which has a sizable majority share of the Indian passenger car market.

MERGER MANAGEMENT

From a global perspective, the success of the merger depends mainly on continued strong growth of American and European markets. This will give the partners time and profits to pool corporate operations and invest in important markets like Asia and Latin America, where they have little presence. If the U.S. economy falls into recession, chances of a favorable outcome will be greatly diminished, as Nissan's troubled times currently indicate. Rising oil prices or an energy crisis could also be a significant threat, especially for Chrysler's large trucks and sport utility vehicles, which are not fuel-efficient. These threats, however, are not on the immediate horizon and most forecasts indicate slower, but not negative, growth in the United States as interest rates go up slowly, and more inflation pushes up oil and gasoline prices.

At the corporate level, much will depend on Juergen Schrempp in effecting a smooth merger. Otherwise, Chrysler executives will exit the company, and shareholders will sell their stock. Billions of dollars of merger savings will not materialize, and lackluster profits will further dampen the price of the stock. Does Schrempp have the capabilities for preventing such a negative scenario from unraveling his megamerger? An analysis in the *New York Times* answers affirmatively: "Orchestrating complex mergers across borders and cultural divides takes a lot more than management skills—it takes the political knack to win over a wide range of people, often with sharply conflicting agendas. And Mr. Schrempp, the intense German chief executive who last year brought about the world's largest completed industrial merger, may best exemplify this blending of skills" (Ibrahim 1999, C1).

Prior action by the chairman also indicates that he can react quickly when profits are jeopardized. This type of threat greeted him at the time he assumed the top spot at Daimler-Benz in 1995, and he aggressively cut money-losing assets like Fokker, removed 200 managers at corporate headquarters, and laid off 40,000 workers in the ensuing two years. These moves, together with a shift in corporate priorities back to its traditional motor vehicle business in luxury cars and industrial trucks, succeeded in turning the company around with substantial growth in earnings. Schrempp also understands the power of Wall Street and the U.S. media with their abilities to influence the course of his merger. Days before the announcement of the DaimlerChrysler deal, Schrempp went to New York to practice his presentation before investment bankers and lawyers from Wall Street and New York media and public relations experts (Ibrahim 1999, C1).

Since the announcement and consummation of the merger, financial and operational results have been released to show that the union is proceeding smoothly. In February 1999 DaimlerChrysler reported that 1998 earnings rose a fairly healthy 28% over 1997 numbers. For its first annual meeting in May as a combined company, the sales for the first four months in 1999 had grown by 9%, and sales for the full year will probably be $148 billion, $3 billion more that earlier forecasts.

If, in the long run, the merger succeeds, Schrempp's largest contribution will probably be his move ending the cochairmanship with Robert Eaton in a short period of time and in an amiable manner such that the Chrysler side was not offended. The scenario was probably planned from the beginning, when Schrempp grabbed the initiative by diplomatically going to Chrysler headquarters to present his startling proposal to Eaton himself. The latter's passive agreement signaled that Schrempp would be steering the deal and, not surprisingly, end as the sole chief. To keep Chrysler's managers and shareholders on board, however, the facade had to be maintained that DaimlerChrysler would be a "merger of equals" and did not represent a takeover by the German firm. In this endeavor, Eaton had to play a crucial role to reassure his constituents that the merger was in their best interests. No setbacks could be tolerated during this precarious period, when a new global corporation was being created with product and plant decisions to be made, with computer, financial, and supplier systems to be integrated, and with employees from each side equitably fitted into the new organization. The initial steps have gone smoothly, with Eaton successful in at least getting his side to accept the leadership of Juergen Schrempp.

REFERENCES

Andrews, Edmund L. "Volkswagen in Shift, Will Set Up Fund for Slave Workers." *New York Times*, July 8, 1998, p. A3.

————. "DaimlerChrysler Abandons Talks About Buying Control of Nissan." *New York Times*, March 11, 1999, pp. C1, C4.

————. "DaimlerChrysler's Smart Car Is Lone Sore Spot at Meeting." *New York Times*, May 19, 1999, p. C8.

Andrews, Edmund L., and Laura M. Holson. "Daimler-Benz Will Acquire Chrysler in $36 Billion Deal That Will Reshape Industry." *New York Times*, May 7, 1998, pp. A1, D4.

Ball, Don, and Wendell McCulloch. *International Business*. 7th ed. New York: Irwin McGraw-Hill, 1999.

Binkley, Christina. "Kerkorian Is Emerging as a Winner." *Wall Street Journal*, May 7, 1998, p. A10.

Coleman, Brian, and Gregory L. White. "In High-Tech War Rooms, Giant Is Born." *Wall Street Journal*, November 13, 1998, p. B1.

Cusumano, Michael A., and Kentaro Nobeoka. *Thinking beyond Lean*. New York: Free Press, 1998.

EIU. first quarter 1999a, *Motor Business Europe*, "DaimlerChrysler: An Initial Profile of the New Company," Chapter 4.

EIU. first quarter 1999b, *Motor Business International*, "Face to Face: With Bob Eaton of DaimlerChrysler." Chapter 1.

Holusha, John. "Chrysler Is Buying American Motors; Cost is $1.5 Billion." *New York Times*, March 10, 1987, pp. A1, D8.

Ibrahim, Youssef M. "Importance of Being Persuasive." *New York Times*, May 20, 1999, pp. C1, C7.

Ingrassia, Lawrence, and Brandon Mitchener. "I Was Thinking That, Too, Said Mr. Eaton—And the Talks Were On." *Wall Street Journal*, May 8, 1998, p. A1.

Ingrassia, Paul, and Joseph B. White. *Comeback: The Fall and Rise of the American Automobile Industry*. New York: Touchstone, 1994.

Kandell, Jonathan. "Ferdinand Porsche, Creator of the Sports Car That Bore His Name, Is Dead at 88." *New York Times*, March 28, 1998, p. A11.

MacDonald, Elizabeth. "Proposed Deal Faces Rocky Road Due to Different Accounting Rules." *Wall Street Journal*, May 7, 1998, p. A10.

McKinsey Global Institute. "Auto Assembly Case Study Summary." *Manufacturing Productivity*. Washington, DC, October 1993.

————. "Automotive Case Study." *Capital Productivity*. Washington, DC, June 1996.

Simison, Robert L. "A Cost-Cutter's Charge: Save $1.5 Billion." *Wall Street Journal*, November 13, 1998, pp. B1, B4.

Chapter 6

Mexico: *Maquiladora* Plants and NAFTA

The proximity of California and Texas, with their extraordinary agricultural and industrial sectors' growth during and after World War II, had profound consequences south of the Rio Grande River, where a burgeoning poor population became a legal source of seasonal migrant labor for U.S. farms and orchards. The Bracero Program, operating since 1945 and driven by the economic disparity between the two nations, grew into millions of "temporary" Mexican farmworkers by the mid-1960s and in 1964, in an attempt to control the vast migration, was terminated by the U.S. government.

By this time, however, interaction between the two countries gave the Mexican government a blueprint for accelerating the country's economic development and spurred job creation to ameliorate the effects of its northern border closing. In a major move, automobile imports were banned in 1962, forcing foreign makers to produce in Mexico, bringing with them much-needed jobs, technology, capital, and management expertise. Much of the output of the new operations would be exported north to earn U.S. dollars, and, at any rate, the poor Mexican economy had limited ability to absorb expensive durable items like automobile sedans. The emphasis on trade was learned from successful reconstruction programs in Asia and Europe, where Japan and West Germany had begun massive export drives to markets as far away as North America. In international commerce, moreover, large U.S. companies like General Motors exemplified an insularity built up after the war from engaging in its primary mission of supplying pent-up demand for a reviving, very large domestic market. Growth in Asian and European markets would eventually attract investment dollars from U.S. multinational corporations, and it is these funds as well as the accompanying technology that the Mexican government set out to secure in an effort to stem the unemployment crisis arising from the closed border crossing and its growing poor population.

THE *MAQUILADORA* PROGRAM

The Border Industrialization Program (BIP), set up by Mexico's Ministry of Industry and Commerce, permitted designated *maquiladora* plants to import parts, raw materials, subassemblies, and machinery duty-free provided all output from the *maquilas* was exported. Other incentives of the BIP included proximity to the huge U.S. market and access to cheap Mexican labor. Foreign companies, furthermore, could own 100% of the Mexican operations, whereas nondesignated *maquilas* of foreign firms had to have Mexican partners who held majority ownership.

U.S. tariff schedules also permitted those components and subassemblies made in the United States and exported for use in a *maquila* plant to be reimported to the United States duty-free. Any tariffs would thus be assessed only on the value-added assembly operations in Mexico and not on the much larger value of the final product. In 1976 U.S. duties on Mexican imports made in certain *maquila* plants were lifted entirely provided 35% of the value of the manufactures was of Mexican origin (Wilson 1992, 38). In this free-trade move, the United States was responding to the growth and influence of *maquila* operations formed by multinational American firms that were still producing for the U.S. market. By 1978 the number of such plants had grown to 457 with over 90,000 employees, and more remarkable growth was in store for the 1980s (Fatemi 1990, 4). In addition, the tariff preference measure was a tangible gesture of goodwill extended in the Cold War to noncommunist developing countries in general and to its southern neighbor in particular. In the same vein, the United States along with its two neighbors Canada and Mexico—all firm believers in the economic benefits of regional trade—had begun negotiations that would lead to the North American Free Trade Agreement.

THE ARAB OIL EMBARGO

In the 1970s severe inflation and recession gripped the U.S. economy, beginning with the Arab oil embargo of 1973–1974. The embargo had the sponsorship of the Organization of Petroleum Exporting Countries (OPEC) with its self-serving agenda of restricting oil output to boost prices. While Mexico and Canada remained out of OPEC, Venezuela and Ecuador (two large producers in South America) fully backed the oil cartel, hardly endearing themselves to the United States, the world's largest oil-importing nation.

As gasoline shortages spread in the United States, its Big Three automakers (General Motors, Ford, and Chrysler) came under considerable siege from an export blitz of small, fuel-efficient cars from Japan and, as indicated in Chapter 4, were appealing to Washington for protectionist or preferential treatment that would assist the industry at home or abroad. In the new milieu, the automakers were forced to adopt stringent cost-saving measures in order to remain competitive with the foreigners, leading to plant closings in the United States and their relocation to Mexico and other Third World countries. In the migration, the first to move was General Motors when a Mexican subsidiary of its electrical parts division began making wire harnesses in 1978 in Ciudad Juarez, across the border from El Paso, Texas (see Figure 6.1). A second GM division, Inland, began to make wire seat covers and interior trim in the same city and in 1979 initiated production of brake-hose assemblies, dashboards, and steering wheels in Matamoros, Mexico, across the Rio Grande River from the southern tip of Texas (Rubenstein 1992, 243). These were exploratory operations by the giant automaker, as employment statistics in the still-small *maquila* industry indicate: at the end of the 1970s, transportation equipment accounted for only 4.5% of employment in these facilities, way behind electric and electronic equipment and materials makers with 56.9% (Wilson 1992, 45). Moreover, the quintessential American company, General Motors, undoubtedly held considerable reservations about producing in a foreign locale, particularly in Mexico, where expressions of "Yankee, go home!" were still heard. Mexican politicians preyed on such sentiments and were reluctant to be seen as overtly solicitous of U.S. ownership of Mexican resources, especially since Washington had ended the Bracero Program and was now fortifying the border to prevent illegal immigration.

Any apprehension felt by the Big Three over moving to Latin America was shattered in 1980, when business nose-dived at home under the onslaught of Japanese small-car imports, resulting in annual losses totaling $4 billion. GM's share of this amount came to $763 million, constituting its worst financial performance since 1921. Ford added to its red ink when losses in 1981 and 1982 reached $1.6 billion. Chrysler—the smallest and therefore most vulnerable firm—had already appealed to the U.S. government, seeking an additional $400 million in loan guarantees to keep it out of bankruptcy (Salpukas 1981, A1). All three companies were in the same financial bind, which included not only falling sales but huge retooling and other investment costs needed to shift to the production of small cars now being demanded by the American consumer. The oil crisis of the 1970s consequently forced the Big Three to abandon a business-as-usual, xenophobic, arrogant mentality and begin serious restructuring in order to survive.

THIRD WORLD DEBT CRISIS

The industrial turmoil in North America initiated by rising oil prices in the 1970s extended to Mexico in the 1980s, when falling oil prices choked off revenues to its most important industry, petroleum, and the government subsequently defaulted on the enormous debt it had incurred in capitalizing its young petroleum-producing sector. The major foreign oil companies had not been invited to participate in development of this capital-intensive business because of the presumed exploitation that Mexicans had experienced in their prior dealings with the Standard Oil trust. This led to the nationalization of the petroleum sector and forced exodus of foreign oil giants. Without capital assistance from these multinational firms, Mexico's external debt ballooned, when the nation found it impossible to keep up with interest payments and when oil prices collapsed, sending the peso currency into free fall and the country into

Figure 6.1
Location of Motor Vehicle and Supplier Factories

severe recession. Mexico was not the only Third World, industrializing nation whose foreign debt payments were in limbo. Almost all countries in Latin America, Asia, and Africa were deleteriously affected by falling prices for their export products, bloated government payrolls, and costly social welfare and military-defense programs. The Mexican crisis, however, had the greatest impact on the globalization plans of the world's motor vehicle industry.

The inauguration of President Miguel de la Madrid in 1982, when his government was defaulting on foreign loans from large commercial banks like Citicorp of New York, was followed by drastic measures to quell the crisis and capital flight north to U.S. dollar havens. The proverbial "seven lean years" were now descending on the Mexican economy as they followed "seven fat years" induced by the discovery of massive oil reserves, coinciding with the quadrupling of world prices for "black gold" during the Arab oil embargo and Iranian revolution of 1979. Billions of petrodollars flowed into Mexican coffers from America's insatiable demand for oil and from huge loans proffered by multinational banks operating under the delusion that an oil-rich, sovereign state like Mexico could never go bankrupt.

Countervailing forces were already at work, however, to upend the Mexican economy. The U.S. recession and Japanese imports of fuel-efficient cars dampened America's "insatiable demand" for petroleum, and world prices were cut in half. The downturn had also reduced the prices of other Mexican exports like silver and farm produce, moving the country's balance of payments into the red. An overvalued peso, wrought by 60% annual inflation and interest payments on foreign debt exceeding $100 billion, sent money fleeing the country in anticipation of the peso's devaluation by both the government and foreign exchange markets. In response, President Madrid turned to the automobile industry—making it the country's priority industry—as well as the moribund *maquiladora* program to attract dollar investments back into Mexico and assuage rising unemployment rates. The peso was also wrenchingly devalued, which in no small way encouraged direct foreign investments by further reducing capital costs and wage rates in Mexico vis-à-vis the United States. In like manner, it raised the price of imports from America—already prohibitive—in the Mexican market, forcing U.S. exporters to set up operations in the country if they wanted any local business.

RISE OF THE AUTO INDUSTRY

During Mexico's boom years of the 1970s, U.S. automakers, mired in their recession at home, looked south for export markets in Mexico, now flush with petrodollars. In total national vehicle sales for 1981, Chrysler, the most depressed of Detroit's Big Three, had a market share of 20%, followed by Ford with 19.5% and General Motors with 10.5%. The oil boom had also attracted Volkswagen, which led the others with a 22.8% market share and, together with Nissan, was assembling vehicles for sale not only in Mexico but for the export market as well, with VW's output headed for West Germany and Nissan's to other markets in Latin America. The depressed state of the American economy, marred by plant closings and 250,000 autoworkers on indefinite layoff in 1982, generally discouraged, until the recession lifted, Mexican-made vehicles from entering the United States. The industry's export bias, however, had already been laid in the early days of the *maquila* program. Even after domestic sales had risen 19% per year during the oil boom of 1978 to 1981, the number of vehicles sold in the country was only 14,428 compared to the sizable 44,113 vehicles that were exported (Fatemi 1990, 119–120).

With the abrupt ending of the boom coinciding with default on the country's massive foreign debt, President Madrid issued the 1983 Auto Decree, designed to turn the Mexican motor vehicle industry into "Detroit South." The plan focused on luring the U.S. Big Three across the border, where they would still supply their home market but now would have distinct manufacturing cost advantages against Japanese transplants that were being rapidly constructed on U.S. greenfield sites. In capturing 50% of the country's sales, the Big Three had already demonstrated that Mexico could be a locale for business success. Ford consequently formed a 1983 venture with Japan's Mazda to build a $500 million automobile assembly and body stamping plant in the Mexican border town of Hermosillo. The winning site beat out two others in Portugal and Taiwan, with Mexico's 1983 Auto Decree helping to tip the Ford decision, especially since the decree "stated unequivocally that the producers had to match every dollar of imports with an equal amount of exports" (Fatemi 1990, 118). Heretofore, Ford had been importing parts and assembled vehicles into Mexico because of the strong economy. If such shipments were curtailed by the government decree, the company's operations would be crippled, and it would fall behind competitors in this important developing market. Hermosillo, in effect, would be Ford's answer to the new regulations since the output from the new plant would be dedicated to the export market, in particular the United States, which was showing recovery signs under President Ronald Reagan.

Exports Climb

As U.S. market conditions improved, the *maquila* factories established themselves as low-cost, volume suppliers to the American export trade, especially in motor vehicles. This, in turn, accelerated investment moves by Detroit south of the border to combat Japanese imports and their output from U.S. transplants in the "car wars" of the 1980s. To foster this migration, President Madrid's decree of 1983 streamlined government procedures for establishing *maquila* operations, and auto assembly and component plants grew from 51 in 1984, to 129 in 1988. These led to similarly large increases in employment from 29,378 workers in 1984, to 77,502 in 1989. Recession and peso devaluation helped mitigate the cost of increased hiring: for autoworkers, hourly wage rates denominated in dollars actually declined from $2.56 in 1983, to $1.48 in 1986, prompting not only Ford's new project in Hermosillo but major investments by Chrysler and General Motors as well. By 1988 the Big Three had captured 88.4% of Mexico's total exports. Ford's leading share of

37.8% was supplied by the opening of the Hermosillo plant, which began production in 1987. Chrysler's exports to the United States involved a large 43% of pickup trucks in addition to the usual small car like the Mercury Tracer compact model, made at the new Ford facility (Fatemi 1990, 121–126).

In the second half of the 1980s, strong international currents further enhanced the importance of Mexico's motor vehicle industry. The Japanese yen had begun its inexorable climb on foreign exchange markets, necessitating the move by their manufacturers to lower-cost sites overseas. In 1989 Nissan Motor Company announced a $1 billion expansion of its plant in Aguascalientes in concert with plans to double production in Mexico by 1992. In this respect, the American companies had been ahead of Nissan: in 1987 Chrysler decided to close its K-car plant in Kenosha, Wisconsin, and move production of its Plymouth Reliant and Dodge Aries models—compact cars that had helped rescue the company from bankruptcy during the oil shortages—to its Toluca plant outside Mexico City. Ford was building the Hermosillo plant while GM started to close eleven U.S. factories in 1986. Even Volkswagen shut its sole U.S. facility in New Stanton, Pennsylvania. Moving in the opposite direction were Japan's big three automakers—Toyota, Nissan, and Honda—as they expanded production in the United States when the surging yen made exports from the home islands commercially prohibitive for most low- and midpriced models. Both profits from the U.S. export trade along with the rising yen helped to finance large dollar investments that were either wholly owned or joint ventures with U.S. partners.

AUTOMOBILE TRANSPLANTS

In addition to the appreciating yen, protectionist measures adopted by the U.S. government and financial incentives extended by the states such as tax abatements encouraged Japanese firms to come to the United States. In February 1981 a voluntary restraint agreement (VRA) was agreed to by Japan and the United States, limiting car exports from the former to the latter to 1.68 million units per year. In 1982 Honda's new assembly plant in Marysville, Ohio, began production of its "American-built" Accord model, helping the company to circumvent the VRA quota and high-yen problem at the same time. Start-ups were subsequently announced by Nissan in Smyrna, Tennessee, and by Toyota in Lexington, Kentucky. Joint ventures evolved between Toyota and General Motors in Fremont, California; Mazda and Ford in Flat Rock, Michigan; and Mitsubishi and Chrysler in Normal, Illinois.

These international alliances were executed simultaneously with the closing of U.S. factories by Detroit's Big Three and their movement to Mexico. President Madrid's Auto Decree of 1983 and the falling peso consequently had the same effect on the American car companies as the rising yen and President Reagan's VRA quota of 1982 were having on their counterparts in Japan. Globalization of the motor vehicle industry thus began with a multinational vengeance, and it spilled over into communist and socialist countries like China and India and reached the southern tip of the Americas as well as former communist countries in Eastern Europe. The thrust abroad, moreover, was not reversed even with the return to profitability by the Big Three, which in these trying times learned how to operate competitively on the world stage. In contrast, the Japanese industry—that had initiated the global contest with exports and investments to the United States—was not able to sustain its momentum as the home market plunged into severe recession precipitated by the fall of the Tokyo Stock Exchange and real estate markets in 1989. Corporate losses reached billions of dollars, forcing Mazda to succumb to a takeover by Ford. In 1999 Nissan and Mitsubishi Motors also sought infusions of funds from foreigners (DaimlerChrysler and Renault) in order to continue operating.

Ford and Mazda in North America

The management takeover by Ford Motor Company of Mazda Motor Corporation represents the culmination of its cooperative ventures in the United States and Mexico, during which each side experienced success and adversity in efforts to remain internationally competitive. Ford, always the bigger and financially stronger of the two, first attempted in 1971 to buy Mazda stock, undoubtedly with the view of taking control of the smaller company. The latter —under the paternalistic protection of Japan's Ministry of International Trade & Industry—successfully resisted the move, and the two auto firms marched separately into the maelstrom of the Arab oil embargo of 1973. Mazda's sales fell because its cars used the Wankel rotary engine, a German invention not characterized for being fuel-efficient. In the United States sales of Ford's gas-guzzling, large cars were heavily impacted by shortages and rising prices of gasoline, just as the company was losing market share to the subcompact imports from Japan. Mazda's duress caused it to turn to Ford, hoping to get a much-needed capital infusion, but Ford's own weakened position undermined the effort, a mere two years since its offer to buy shares in Mazda had been rejected.

Mazda subsequently survived with support from its principal lender Sumitomo Bank. The company jettisoned the Wankel engine and began manufacturing the same box-shaped, fuel-efficient subcompact models that had become popular in the United States. It further adopted Toyota's lean production system, with the moves returning the company to profitability. Eager to examine the causes of Mazda's revival, Ford in 1979 bought a 25% stake in the Hiroshima-based auto company for $130 million. Together, the firms proceeded to construct assembly plants in Hermosillo, Mexico, and Flat Rock, Michigan, even as Ford was closing six U.S. auto plants in the early 1980s.

Ford's Maquiladora Factory. Mazda's Michigan facility proved to be a minor part of the massive Japanese–U.S. transplant migration, but its design, engineering, and managerial oversight of Ford's Hermosillo operation became an international milestone for the giant motor vehicle industry. The plant's significant dimensions included:

1.   A profound recognition by Ford that it needed outside, even foreign assistance during these trying times for its moves abroad.

2.   The plant's location in a developing country without much of an established motor vehicle industry and limited infrastructural development.

3.   An inexperienced workforce that would assemble finished automobile and auto engines—the most complex and important part of the vehicle.

4.   Quality control problems on output destined for the hotly competitive U.S. small-car market, where Japanese transplants were already operational.

5.   Problematic worker productivity, including high absentee and turnover rates endemic in the Mexican labor force.

6.   Considerable opposition by the United Auto Workers union, which was lobbying Washington for protectionist legislation requiring foreign cars sold in the United States to have 90% U.S.-made parts and labor, commonly referred to as "domestic content."

7.   A heavy-handed Mexican central government, generally antagonistic to foreign, especially American multinational corporations and characterized by slothful bureaucratic procedures and official bribery.

Clearly, the risks for Ford would have been higher if it lacked the cooperation of Mazda with its technical expertise in small-car production. In its partnership with the Japanese firm, Ford was heavily influenced by the California joint venture between GM and Toyota as well as the interaction that transpired between Ford and Mazda after the 25% equity stake had been made. Ford management was impressed with Mazda's operations in Japan, and this made it willing to cede technical and managerial authority over the project to the smaller partner just as GM was doing in Fremont, California. Ford's learning experience in Hermosillo, however, was more extensive than GM's because it extended to low-cost, *foreign* manufacturing whose output was dedicated to the export trade.

Neither an industrial standard-bearer like Ford nor planning to invest in Mexico, Mazda's objectives were more mundane and included licensing and management fees for its car design and production technology. They also involved the potential for considerable business as a supplier of knockdown kits and car parts to the Ford plant. Mazda's risk was also decidedly minimal since it did not have an equity stake in the venture, probably because the smaller Japanese firm was short of cash from the plant project it had begun in Flat Rock, Michigan. In the endeavor, Mazda was playing catch-up with front-running Japanese firms that were confidently building huge facilities, by themselves, at the following rural sites: Honda in Marysville, Ohio; Nissan in Smyrna, Tennessee; and Toyota in Lexington, Kentucky. The leaders were fully intent on maintaining their market shares in the United States, which had provided each with substantial profits from the export trade. In contrast, Mazda, already partly owned by Ford, located its U.S. facility at an abandoned Ford plant in urban

Michigan, bastion of the United Auto Workers union. This was done because it lacked the marketing prowess of the other Japanese leaders and fully depended on consigning half of the new plant's output to Ford's retail marketing unit.

Flat Rock versus Hermosillo. Underlying both capital projects was Mazda's small-car production expertise, shrewdly and correctly perceived by Ford as a surefire way of supplying the rising demand for sporty subcompact and compact cars in the United States. The American car company had already attempted to make a cost-effective vehicle, the Mercury Topaz, at its plant in Cuatitlan outside Mexico City. Its assembly line there—described as "primitive"—lacked suitable automation equipment and a just-in-time delivery system that would reduce inventory costs for parts. Quality control was especially vexing: vehicle decorative stripes were applied by workers in a parking lot "with brushes soaked in old Coca-Cola cans" (Nag and Frazier 1984, 25). Such operating techniques together with the incessant need to correct defective production problems made costs at Cuatitlan 30% higher than at a comparable plant in the United States (Nag and Frazier 1984, 25). These results convinced Ford to leave most of the production aspects to Mazda at both Flat Rock and Hermosillo and instead concentrate on design decisions for its vehicles since the company had significant expertise in making cars that catered to the preferred tastes of American buyers. This capability was clearly demonstrated in 1985 when Ford introduced the aerodynamically designed Taurus, the midsize sedan that became the best-selling car in the United States in 1988 and in the five consecutive years from 1992 to 1996.

Even with profits coming in from the redesigned Taurus, Ford initially did not have an equity stake in Mazda's new Michigan plant. The project remained under Mazda's ownership despite the considerable cooperation engaged in by the two companies, which commenced planning and construction of their Mexican and U.S. facilities at about the same time. Ford capitalized its plant at $500 million and confirmed its investment plans to the media in January 1984. The Mazda facility called for an investment of $550 million and was announced at the end of the year. Initial operating rates were 100,000 for the Ford facility and 240,000 vehicles at the Michigan unit, with the smaller rate probably due to the less-developed, foreign circumstances of the Hermosillo location, including formidable logistical problems such as the lack of export and marketing channels of distribution. No such production or marketing constraints affected Mazda's assembly of the Ford Probe model at Flat Rock, where it could tap the vast materials supply system extant in Michigan and the American Midwest. Sales of the Probe proved so successful that a second shift was added in 1988, one year after start-up, at which time the Probe hatchback would constitute as much as 70% of total output of Mazda's plant.

Other cars assembled at Flat Rock included the sporty Mazda MX two-door coupe and the popular 626 compact model, with Ford and Mazda vehicles built on the same 626 chassis. No Mazda cars were assembled in Mexico, with Ford selecting the Mercury Tracer to be built on a Mazda 323 chassis. The comparative lack of sales and brand recognition for Mazda cars in North America, of course, became a tremendous liability for the Japanese company since the New World represented the company's major effort at internationalizing its operations. The fabled lean production system that Mazda used consequently proved incapable of compensating for the pronounced marketing deficit. Ford, meanwhile, took advantage of Mazda's considerable manufacturing and tooling expertise by licensing its technology, which included buying equipment designed and constructed in Japan by suppliers recommended by Mazda. The latter's *keiretsu* partner, Sumitomo Trading Company, was also brought in as a procurement and exporting intermediary to assist in the bulky transpacific shipments of equipment and tools, in which the large trading house already had considerable experience. In addition to this, Sumitomo Trading facilitated the flow of Japanese-made auto parts to the Hermosillo assembly site. These parts constituted about 70% of the car's final value. The high-yen cost for the imported parts made the Mercury Tracer too expensive for the Mexican consumer, and, at any rate, Ford had already earmarked the bulk of the output for the U.S. export market (Haigh 1992, 65–66).

Various training and work practices prevalent at Mazda's Hiroshima plant in Japan were also adopted by Ford, and these included quality circles, just-in-time supply systems, and employee teams of fifteen workers, called technicians. Ford engineers even videotaped Mazda's Quality Deployment System in Hiroshima. Hundreds of employees were sent to Japan and other Ford plants in Valencia, Spain, and Genk, Belgium, for extensive training (Haigh 1992, 67–68). Trainees were lectured on Mazda's definitive work principle, centered on everlasting improvement or *kaizen* and a constant effort at eliminating waste and inefficiency. The term was ubiquitous at the Flat Rock plant, where it was used unceasingly by new hires. "Later, when it became obvious to the workers that their suggestions were only increasing their own workloads, enthusiasm for *kaizen* all but disappeared" (Fucini and Fucini 1990, 161).

Kaizen fell further in usage, especially in the business press, as Mazda's financial fortunes nose-dived with the beginning of severe recession in Japan. This time, Ford acted decisively: in 1992 it purchased a 50% interest in the Michigan plant, and in 1996, after taking a controlling interest in the Japanese auto company, Ford installed its own man as Mazda's new president. At corporate headquarters in Hiroshima, *kaizen* gave way to *gaigin*, the Japanese word for foreigner, an apt description of the new executive, who could neither read nor write Japanese and proceeded to manage Mazda "the Ford way!"

The success of Ford's Hermosillo, wholly owned subsidiary, using Japanese design and engineering, was evident after start-up in 1986. Product quality and plant productivity were both high, with the latter predicated on low-wage rates of $3.40 an hour compared to $18.50 in Detroit. Unfortunately for the American firm, its skilled Mexican workers became aware of their outstanding labor performance for puny remuneration, and the site—despite its worker organization by a pliable Mexican union—was visited by three major strikes from its inception to 1995, as well as mass firings, including the dismissal of leaders of a militant union slate that won election in 1987, and an employee turnover rate of 20%–40% per year. Ford's turnover, however, was still below the 100% rate at Nissan's *maquiladora* plant in Aguascalientes.

Nevertheless, labor's case was advanced by the Ford success because it inspired other foreign firms to launch major projects south of the U.S.–Mexican border, and the newcomers enticed experienced workers away with better pay and working conditions (Shaiken 1995, 254–256.

In time, Ford drastically altered the Mazda system at Hermosillo, spending $300 million for "a complete transformation of the plant's product line, supplier system, and work organization" (Shaiken 1995, 256). Japanese suppliers were replaced by closer American ones, and Mazda's team concept, soliciting suggestions for improvement from workers on the plant floor, gave way to greater top-down line supervision. With high turnover in its workforce, it was inevitable that Ford would return to the operating principles established by its founder in which mass production performed by malleable foreign or immigrant laborers would be a centerpiece, along with complete control by top management in its effort to meet burgeoning consumer demand in the American car market.

ADVENT OF NAFTA

The start-up of the Hermosillo plant accelerated production numbers in the Mexican industry for the last half of the 1980s, when output of passenger cars, light commercial vehicles, trucks, and buses soared from 341,052 in 1986, to 820,591 in 1990 (EIU second quarter 1997, 37). The new Mexican industrial force under American corporate ownership helped accelerate negotiations by President George Bush of the United States on the formation of the North American Free Trade Agreement (NAFTA) with border partners Canada and Mexico. In 1992 Bill Clinton was elected U.S. president and, with the support of all four preceding presidents from the two leading political parties, obtained congressional ratification of the treaty in the face of strong opposition by organized labor, especially the United Auto Workers (UAW) union. Its membership had fallen as Detroit's Big Three closed plants in the United States. While many of these closings were replaced by Japanese transplants, the UAW had little success in organizing workers at the new sites; its attempts at solidarity with the Mexican autoworkers union were similarly brushed aside.

NAFTA's passage in 1992, however, did not usher in another sizable jump in Mexican motor vehicle production. It grew from 820,591 units in 1990, to 1,219,259 in 1996, and at this rate it would fall far short of the 2 million mark in 2000 jubilantly forecast by auto industry executives. The main reason that the growth rate fell off can be attributed to the peso crisis in 1994–1995, which quashed Mexican domestic demand for motor vehicles. On the northern side of the Rio Grande River, in contrast, prosperous times attracted a surge of imports from Mexico, with the figures more than tripling from 276,869 units in 1990, to 978,145 in 1996 (EIU second quarter 1997, 37). The movement north, moreover, was not prompted by NAFTA because favorable treatment of Mexican-produced goods had already (prior to NAFTA) been added to the U.S. tariff schedule, and auto executives had invested in Mexican facilities knowing that a sizable percentage of their output would be exported. Instead, the momentum north was sustained by the U.S. demand as well as the concurrent 70% downturn in Mexican domestic sales as peso devaluation, capital flight, and recession gripped the nation's economy. The peso crisis, however, proved short-lived, ameliorated in large measure by the surging U.S. economy in the north and the significant amount of aid secured from world agencies like the International Monetary Fund and the U.S. foreign exchange stabilization fund. In the Mexican rebound, domestic sales of motor vehicles surged 78% in 1996 (over the prior year), encouraging foreign investors to once again consider billion-dollar projects there. As indicated in Table 6.1, such plans were under review by Chrysler, Volkswagen, and Ford for the last years of the twentieth century.

The economic rebound, moreover, increased U.S. automotive exports (both vehicles and parts) to Mexico, rising from $7.9 billion in 1993, to $8.3 billion in 1996. The trade was also aided by the NAFTA requirement that cut Mexican tariffs on U.S. cars and light trucks in half, from 20%, to 10% in 1994, with phaseout of the duties on light trucks to occur by January 1, 1998, and on cars and parts at the beginning of 2003. The tariff reductions and related reforms resulted in the growth of U.S. exports of motor vehicles from a small 17,000 in 1993—mainly due to Mexico's protectionist barriers—to a more robust 91,000 vehicles in 1996. Nontariff barriers were also eliminated or reduced, such as the trade balancing requirement that had forced Ford to export most of output from the Hermosillo plant. Local content restrictions were similarly lifted. As a consequence, "Ford decided to consolidate all production of Ford Thunderbirds and Mercury Cougars at its Lorrain, Ohio assembly plant, discontinuing low-volume production of these two models at its Cuatitlan plant in Mexico" (Clinton 1997, 46), the same plant with the "primitive" operations. Nissan relocated production of its Altima engines from Mexico to Tennessee, closer to its huge assembly plant in Smyrna and, in return, shifted all Sentra car production to Aguascalientes, Mexico. The trade balancing and domestic content restrictions had, prior to NAFTA, resulted in small production runs at Mexican facilities, and with their full or partial elimination, the foreign manufacturers moved quickly to better optimize operations at their various North American facilities.

MEXICO'S FOREIGN "BIG FIVE"

Table 6.1 details the leadership positions of the U.S. Big Three and Volkswagen in Mexico as the new millennium approached, with Nissan lagging and Honda establishing a beachhead. The listing somewhat masks the globalization in the industry because the leading producer, Chrysler, has merged with Daimler-Benz to form DaimlerChrysler and is therefore no longer independent, and Renault, in 1999, took a 34% equity stake in Nissan. Unlike the earlier takeover of Mazda by Ford, the Renault–Nissan alliance does not entail any subordination of Nissan's identity because the former is not much of a factor in the exceedingly important North American market, which it will try to alter by using the extensive production and marketing network of the latter. A

Table 6.1
Motor Vehicle Production, Exports, and Investments

	1996			1995-2000
	Production	Exports	Vehicle Sales	Investments
Chrysler	361,212	325,408	54,499	$ 1,000 million
General Motors	267,090	202,593	89,202	400
Volkswagen	231,078	176,662	51,508	1,000
Ford	213,391	179,788	66,048	1,500
Nissan	135,637	90,957	59,620	100
Honda	1,194	0	1,998	900

Sources: EIU second quarter 1998, Tables 3.7, 3.10, 3.14; EIU second quarter 1997, Tables 3.5, 3.7.

production laggard in Mexico, Nissan is still close to the leaders in domestic sales, and its comparatively small investment budget may get a boost from Renault's equity cash infusion.

An Export Boom in Trucks

In 1997 output of Mexican-built vehicles surged to 1.32 million units, induced largely by the huge U.S. demand for sport utility vehicles and physically bigger pickup trucks like the newly introduced GM Silverado. Of total truck output, 78.3% was earmarked for the export market compared to 69% for passenger cars produced in Mexico. The data show that NAFTA and corporate rationalization plans were having their intended effect, with Chrysler and Ford exporting over 83% of their Mexican vehicle production. The movement north was led in particular by Chrysler's Ram and Ford's F-series pickup trucks. Other leading exported nameplates were the Volkswagen Jetta (117,798), the Ford Escort (104,914), and the GM Cavalier (84,516). The VW numbers do not include the new Beetle, which was introduced in the United States only in 1998 to considerable consumer acclaim (EIU second quarter 1998, 44–45).

The Old "Bug"

Advocated by Adolf Hitler in 1934 and designed by Ferdinand Porsche (who would establish the sports car company bearing his name), the

Volkswagen Beetle was always meant to be a small "people's car" afffordable to the working class. The low price tag and its rugged durability made it a favorite not only in post–World War II Europe but in the United States of the 1950s and 1960s and in emerging markets like Mexico, where it was manufactured and sold as a low-cost sedan. The toylike Beetle was introduced in the affluent American market in 1949 as an export from West Germany, where it found a market niche that set it apart from bigger, more expensive, American-built cars that increased in price with each model changeover. Keeping its original design and economical price, the old Bug attained a 6% market share in the United States in 1968, its high-water mark, with sales of 400,000 cars. In the interim, VW's profits soared and, together with the booming economy and export trade, lifted the West German standard of living in a manner similar to Detroit's early effect on the United States. Rising labor costs—generally passed on to the consumer—were a consequence in both countries that would have dire circumstances when the Arab oil embargo of 1973–1974 devastated the industry. Cheaper, higher-quality Japanese imports torpedoed VW's share of the U.S. car market, dropping it from 6% to 2% as VW car dealers stopped distributing the Bug in the retail trade. The company's efforts to salvage its lucrative U.S. operations forced it to produce abroad, particularly in Brazil and Mexico, but the moves failed to overcome the Japanese lead, and in 1979, sales of the old Beetle ended in the United States (Richman 1986, 39).

Beetle Redux

The nineteen-year hibernation of the Beetle in the world's principal car market did not spell the end of the lovable Bug in the minds of nostalgic North and South Americans who continued to hold dear this ugly icon of a halcyon age when cars did not exceed sixty miles per hour. In Brazil, the Bug captured 50% of the emerging market, and in Mexico, it was locked in battle with the Nissan Tsuru, with the lead in passenger car sales seesawing between the two as indicated in Table 6.2. The statistics further show the pronounced falloff in sales of all makers in the peso crisis of 1994–1995 with VW and Nissan undergoing a small recovery. Sales of two U.S. models went to zero in 1996 but were part of Detroit's plans to emphasize the giant U.S. export trade over stagnating Mexican conditions and the related push to highly popular sport utility vehicles and pickup trucks. Indeed, when the latter vehicles are included in 1996 sales, General Motors and Ford are leaders, as listed in Table 6.1. For Volkswagen, the new Beetle plans were influencing its operations in Puebla, where $1 billion was earmarked as early as 1992 for expansion of the only plant that produced the Bug. By 1997 the German car company confirmed that the new Beetle was being built at Puebla for reintroduction in the U.S. market in 1998, with $500 million being invested in facilities that would produce initial runs of 100,000 cars per year, 90% of which would be exported.

The new Beetle received a spectacular reception in the United States, with enough design similarities to evoke memories of its "adorable" and "cartoonish" predecessor together with a new look and price tag of $16,000 to qualify it as "a

Table 6.2
Car Sales by Model and Year

	1991	1992	1993	1994	1995	1996
VW Sedan (Beetle)	86,353	85,989	97,539	77,099	14,830	27,734
Nissan Tsuru	76,267	95,464	74,929	90,329	23,130	21,240
Dodge Sprint (Chrysler)	31,532	40,965	28,222	18,124	228	0
Mercury Topaz (Ford)	25,261	29,862	25,372	7,630	0	0
Chevrolet Cavalier (GM)	18,419	25,780	31,329	24,253	10,410	11,149

Source: Adapted from EIU second quarter 1997, Table 3.16.

truly distinctive fashion statement." Less complimentary comments included "fairly ordinary," "conventional and competent," and "not cheap compared with small cars like the Dodge Neon and Honda Civic" (quotes from Krebs 1998). These comments notwithstanding, the new Beetle greatly boosted VW's sales in the United States and the standing of its Mexican production site. In addition to North America, Puebla exported vehicles and parts to the rest of Latin America, including Mercosur charter members Brazil and Argentina, and was planning to send 350,000 engines in 1998 to factories in Spain and Germany (EIU first quarter 1997, 15).

Supplier Networks

Evolution of Mexico as a global production source can be seen in the headline-grabbing accounts of billion-dollar investments by giant automakers as well as by the less-noticed moves of supplier companies like Siemens AG to erect a $10 million plant in Puebla to supply wire harnesses for the new Beetle. In similar manner, Sommer Alliburti SA of France makes dashboards and door panels for the Bug that it sends in just-in-time synchrony to the 750-acre VW plant. U.S. firms in VW's twenty four-supplier network include TRW, which makes steering columns, and Johnson Controls, which fabricates the seats. As a result of the nearby network formation, 50% of the new Beetle's contents come from Mexican sources. The network has further allowed Volkswagen to meet the strong demand for new and even old Beetles by accelerating production to 450,000 vehicles. The old Beetle, as previously indicated, has always retained a strong following in Mexico with its $7,000 price tag; its durability, furthermore, has made it the vehicle of choice among taxicab owners in Mexico City

(Millman 1998). The extensive supplier network enables VW to make realistic plans for continued growth over the next twenty years; it can even share these plans and large investment costs with its committed suppliers. In 1997–1998 VW anticipated capital costs for expansion and new technology to amount to $500 million, with its integrated network of supplier firms expected to match the outlay as they upgrade in tandem with the main assembly plant. Financial risk is subsequently spread across the network, even though Volkswagen does not exercise management control over the independent suppliers. The lack of control gives these firms the right to strike deals with other auto firms in Mexico like GM and Ford, which could jeopardize VW's trade and technology secrets as well as compromise commercial and design plans. Executive moves can also prompt intense legal battles like the 1993 industrial espionage case between GM and VW, caused by the defection of a vice president from the former to the latter. Such conflicts will continue to plague the industry as it internationalizes and strives to produce cost-competitive global cars in an era of changing alliances and personnel shifts.

In spite of the drawbacks, the principal American, European, and Japanese firms are accelerating the formation of supply networks, with Chrysler de Mexico having 221 production suppliers in 1997. The American parent company is increasingly looking to Mexico as the production site for its China Concept Vehicle, a small car for global, emerging markets. A supporting rationale for this outlook is the nearby location in Monterrey of key suppliers of resins, molds for plastic paneling, and car axles. Ford de Mexico has formed a Mexican Supplier Liaison Bureau to "increase our local suppliers' input in Ford purchasing decisions" (EIU first quarter 1997, 10). The greater interaction occurred while Ford was reducing its key parts firms from 200, to 140. In Aguascalientes Nissan has surrounded its main assembly plant with ten supplier factories owned by its *keiretsu* (industrial group) partners from Japan with four more to open in 1999 (Millman 1998). These *keiretsu* networks tend to be more cohesive than Western ones because of equity and other financial and historical ties that bind the companies together. Moreover, they have always been closely integrated into the operations of the main assembler company, which gave rise to the just-in-time inventory control system for vehicle parts, now universally employed. While spreading the business risk among independent partners, Nissan's *keiretsu* did have negative aspects, which revealed themselves in 1999 when the automaker was seeking an equity alliance with DaimlerChrysler— which turned it down—and Renault SA. Both European firms had difficulty estimating the amount of Nissan's contingent debt, in particular, loan guarantees to affiliate firms that the Japanese company would have to service in the event of default. Nissan would also be responsible for its equity ownership share of the liabilities incurred by those closely related firms that were financially tottering from Japan's decade-long recession. Losses at Nissan alone had propelled its liabilities to $36.5 billion. To rectify these ambiguities on its corporate balance sheet as well as appease its French partner, Nissan moved to merge its parts suppliers as well as encourage them to seek business outside the *keiretsu*. Layoffs and plant closing are expected as Renault weighs in with extensive cost-cutting measures.

GM's Parts Factories. GM's efforts at streamlining its supplier networks by concentrating operations in Mexico go back to the 1970s, when Japanese makers like Nissan began their historic trek to the United States. Before the blitz of cheap, foreign cars began to dampen GM's 60% share of its home market, the giant automaker had steadfastly followed the strategy set out by Alfred Sloan of a vertically integrated production system, including wholly owned parts suppliers that would surround its assembly plants in the American Midwest. The economies of scale inherent in GM's oligopolistic market share meant that the parent could wring all profits from not only assembling motor vehicles but manufacturing their individual parts as well. As Nissan learned, however, an equity share also entails accountability for affiliate liabilities, and such contingencies loom large when consumer demand for the assembled vehicle is dropping.

When GM's market share began to fall following the Arab oil embargo, corporate executives began the highly un-American process of extricating its tightly knit supplier system from the U.S. heartland and moving it to *maquila* plants in Mexico. "Since 1978, General Motors has built more than 50 parts factories in Mexico, which today employ 72,000 workers, making its parts subsidiary, Delphi Automotive Services, Mexico's largest private employer" (Dillon 1998). Cost cutting and better labor relations with the less-truculent Confederation of Mexican Workers prompted GM's move south as the company overtly distances itself from the United Automobile Workers union, which has struck its plants twenty two times since 1990. Just as important, wage rates for Delphi workers in Matamoros, Mexico, come to one dollar to two dollars an hour, while in Flint, Michigan, they are nearly twenty-two dollars.

On June 11, 1998, GM's inexorable outsourcing of its parts operations exploded in Flint, when 6,000 members of the UAW local precipitated a nationwide, eight-week strike against the world's largest manufacturing company, forcing it to close twenty three of twenty eight assembly plants in North America. Nearly 190,000 workers were temporarily laid off, and the company proceeded to lose $3 billion or about 50% of its full year's earnings. Within a week of the strike's settlement, GM moved to fundamentally alter its supplier network. It moved to divest its huge Delphi automotive parts subsidiary with its unionized workforce in an effort to disentangle itself from the suffocating supplier system built by Alfred Sloan (Bradsher 1998, A1).

In these ways, GM's top management is going beyond its domestic borders and implementing a global strategy. A new facility to make 100,000 sport utility vehicles per year was opened in Silao, Mexico, in 1995 for both domestic and export markets. Its Mexican suppliers operate twenty four hours a day to service the Silao plant as well as plants located on five continents across twenty one time zones. Mexican technical support engineers are dispatched throughout the world now that their expertise has reached U.S. standards. Their costs are lower, and they are familiar with GM's new plant designs because so much of the company's recent construction projects have been in emerging markets like Mexico and Brazil. Its parts maker, Delphi Automotive Systems, has matched the parent's move abroad. By October 1997 Delphi had investment plans to open ninety four factories in foreign countries and even supply non-GM assembly plants now that it has become an independent concern (Meredith 1997, 12).

Chrysler's Global Car

Chrysler's merger with the luxury automaker Daimler-Benz will cover its upscale flank in affluent industrialized markets, and for the lowest end, the company is advancing its China Concept Vehicle, or CCV. Under development in Michigan by a special engineering team known as the Liberty group, the CCV is patterned after the old Beetle, and, like the small VW sedan, it is expected to be made in Mexico, where such "popular" cars constitute 40% of total sales. In addition to the country where it is produced, the CCV is expected to be sold in India and China, hence the Chinese designation in its name. Expected to sell for $6,500, the global car is targeting first-time buyers in emerging markets "who are now riding motor scooters" (Krebs 1997). The CCV will challenge Fiat's 178 world car, initially set for production in Mexico, but the option was canceled by its Italian manufacturer after the peso crisis erupted. Fiat, at any rate, appears to be concentrating its Latin American operations in Brazil, where the Palio world car is already being made and exported.

In order to meet its minimum-price target, Chrysler is emphasizing the use of recycled plastic material from soda bottles for the CCV's four-body panels. The lightweight material will help the car hit its fuel-efficiency target of fifty miles per gallon with a two-cylinder engine. The panels will be molded from material equal to 2,132 two-liter bottles, and with dyes already added to the plastic pellets, the paneling will not have to be painted. Savings in energy and fabrication costs will thus be substantial, even though the pellets will have to be heated in the molding process. In contrast, stamping of steel parts is done at room temperature, and in a typical comparison of raw material costs, the metal is usually cheaper than plastic. Nevertheless, steel rusts and therefore must be carefully painted; steel parts also dent easily. Paint shops required by steel body panels cover large areas of an automobile assembly plant and cost hundreds of millions of dollars to build. They are also big polluting operations as opposed to the pollution-reduction recycling of used soda bottles and old, plastic CCV panels, which can be continuously melted down and reused. In its plastic initiatives, Chrysler's Liberty engineering group has filed for more than twenty process patents, and the car is, at times, called the Composite (instead of China) Concept Vehicle (Krebs 1997). Production is expected to begin in 2001 at the company's Saltillo facility pending approval from top management, which is in a state of disarray because of the merger with Daimler-Benz.

HONDA MOVES SOUTH

Always an aggressive competitor since its beginning as a motorcycle builder, Honda Motor Company has also been drawn south from its North American facilities in Ohio and Ontario, Canada. As indicated in Table 6.1, it is in early production of its popular Accord model in Mexico and has earmarked an impressive $900 million for a new site that could produce up to 200,000 units per year. In Japan Honda is pressing the faltering Nissan for the country's second largest market share behind Toyota, while in the United States, its redesigned Accord may upend Toyota's best-selling Camry for the top spot in 2000. To satisfy strong consumer demand, Honda announced in May 1999 that it will build a new $400 million plant in the southern state of Alabama (away from the unionized northern states) that will begin production of minivans or sport utility vehicles in 2001. A 33% expansion of the Ontario plant is also planned, rounding out the company's moves to cover all bases in the three NAFTA nations (Simison 1997, C2).

REFERENCES

Bradsher, Keith. "6,000 G.M. Workers at Michigan Plant Join Auto Strike." *New York Times*, June 12, 1998, p. A1.

Clinton, William J. *Study on the Operations and Effects of the North American Free Trade Agreement*. Washington, DC: White House, July 1997.

Dillon, Sam. "A 20-Year G.M. Parts Migration to Mexico." *New York Times*, June 24, 1998, p. D1.

EIU. "Face to Face with the Leaders of Mexico's Automotive Industry." *Motor Business International*, first quarter 1997, Chapter 1.

———. "Mexico's Motor Industry: The Recovery Continues." *Motor Business International*, second quarter 1997, Chapter 3.

———. "Mexico's Automotive Sector: Rapid Recovery Continues." *Motor Business International*, second quarter 1998, Chapter 3.

Fatemi, Khosrow (ed.). *The Maquiladora Industry*. Westport, CT: Praeger, 1990.

Fucini, Joseph J., and Suzy Fucini. *Working for the Japanese*. New York: Free Press, 1990.

Haigh, Robert W. "Building a Strategic Alliance." *Columbia Journal of World Business*, 27 (Spring 1992): 60–75.

Krebs, Michelle. "A Chrysler for Developing Nations." *New York Times*, October 3, 1997, p. F1.

———. "After Beetlemania Fades, Will the Beat Go On?" *New York Times*, May 3, 1998, section 12, p. 1.

Meredith, Robyn. "The Brave New World of General Motors." *New York Times*, October 26, 1997, section 3, pp. 1, 12, 13.

Millman, Joel. "Mexico Is Becoming Auto-Making Hot Spot." *Wall Street Journal*, June 23, 1998, p. A17.

Nag, Amal, and Steve Frazier. "Despite Ford Venture, Mexico Faces Struggle to Be Competitive." *Wall Street Journal*, January 11, 1984, pp. 1, 25.

Richman, Louis S. "Volkswagen Regains Some Magic." *Fortune*, March 31, 1986, pp. 38–39.

Rubenstein, James M. *The Changing US Auto Industry*. London: Routledge, 1992.

Salpukas, Agis. "General Motors Reports '80 Loss of $763 Million." *New York Times*, February 3, 1981, p. A1.

Shaiken, Harley. "Lean Production in a Mexican Context." In *Lean Work: Empowerment and Exploitation in the Global Auto Industry*, Steve Babson (ed.). Detroit: Wayne State University Press, 1995.

Simison, Robert L. "Honda Expands in America, Eases in Japan." *New York Times*, May 7, 1999, p. C2.

Wilson, Patricia A. *Exports and Local Development: Mexico's New Maquiladoras*. Austin: University of Texas Press, 1992.

Chapter 7

Mercosur and Motor Vehicle Manufacturing

Mercosur (Mercado Común del Sur), or the Southern Cone Common Market, came into existence in 1991 as South America's counterpoise to the North American Free Trade Agreement (NAFTA), which arrived three years later. The high degree of common interests (geography, history, culture) extant among Mercosur nations led to its earlier formation, especially under the leadership roles of its largest members, Brazil and Argentina. Adjacent Paraguay and Uruguay were also natural charter members, with the Southern Cone free-trade bloc expanding in 1996 to include Chile and Bolivia. Chile also seeks membership in NAFTA, with its application stalled in the U.S. Congress, which has not been satisfied by the benefits derived from the NAFTA agreement with Mexico. The dissatisfaction has increased as the U.S. bilateral merchandise trade deficit with Mexico has grown, reaching $18.37 billion in 1996, in large measure due to the devaluation of the peso beginning at the end of 1994 from 3.5, to 8 pesos to the U.S. dollar. The peso's fall accelerated further during the Asian, Russian, and Brazilian financial crises of 1997–1999 as high-growth, emerging markets throughout the world imploded following massive capital outflows and simultaneous crashes in local stock, bond, and currency exchange markets. In August 1997 the Thai baht was the first to fall to foreign speculators, in the process bursting its overly inflated "bubble economy" of speculative lending and investing. Similar implosions ensued in Malaysia, Indonesia, Hong Kong, South Korea, and Russia and hit Brazil at the beginning of 1999. The global crisis knocked the Mexican currency down to 10 pesos to the U.S. dollar in the fall of 1998 as frightened investors sought refuge in the strengthening dollar and U.S. Treasury securities. The collapsing bubble economies induced severe credit crunches in the affected nations as bank lending, even at exorbitant interest rates, dried up, causing massive corporate defaults, subsequent bankruptcies, recession, and high unemployment. Wretched economic conditions, in turn, curbed demand for foreign goods, especially from South

America, which ended up precipitating the Brazilian crisis and the fall of its stock markets and its currency, the real. The panic was short-lived, however, with the robust U.S. economy and its huge demand for foreign goods acting as a locomotive pulling the smaller economies up from severe downturns. In addition, U.S. and West European investments in Brazil's motor vehicle industry—Ford's being a major exception—were not affected by the short-term perturbations since their planning horizons were long-term, and the fundamental attractions remained: the newly formed Mercosur free-trade area, low labor costs, and reduced government regulations in Latin America, as well as the desire of vehicle manufacturers to globalize and diversify their production base.

In addition to reduced protectionist barriers to trade among Mercosur countries, Brazil and Argentina have moved in tandem to open their borders to direct investments and imports from outside Mercosur. Foreign automakers could, therefore, once again compete in the large South American markets and quickly moved to implement plans. The border openings thus had a larger impact on Mercosur countries compared to the effect of NAFTA on Mexico. In the latter, foreign manufacturers could establish *maquiladora* plants (see Chapter 6), prior to NAFTA, that took advantage of low-cost Mexican labor, the absence of duties on imported parts, and the proximity of the U.S. export market, in particular to the megastates of California and Texas. Mexico's borders were therefore opened long before Brazil's or Argentina's, with U.S. auto firms crossing the Rio Grande in the 1970s. In their moves to Mercosur, the foreign car companies are building state-of-the-art, greenfield plants with advanced manufacturing attributes such as country specialization in components and car makes, foreign and local sourcing of parts, and modular manufacturing in which more subassembly is done by independent parts suppliers at their own plants. With just-in-time delivery of parts or modules to the main assembly plant, inventory storage space is reduced, resulting in smaller plant designs and lower construction costs. Such cost-cutting measures are being implemented by the world's major vehicle manufacturers in order to competitively succeed in one of the world's most important emerging markets. Testimony to the importance of the market and Mercosur's impact is given by Renault's president of local operations: "Brazil is a country where we have to be, and Mercosur makes it easy to be here" (Reid 1996, 10). Renault is consequently constructing a $1 billion car plant in Curitiba, Brazil, close to the Argentine border, where the French company has a 33% equity stake in a nearby plant in Cordoba, Argentina. Mercosur will facilitate parts movement and product specialization efficiencies between the two locations, with such cross-border cooperation being rare in the past.

GLOBAL OPERATIONS

In globalizing operations, the major auto companies are reducing capacity in mature markets like the United States, Western Europe, and Japan, where labor costs and union problems are considerable, and constructing factories in Asia, Eastern Europe, and Latin America. To enhance building and operating efficiencies, the new plants are being designed with identical layout to reduce engineering development costs, speed construction schedules, and produce small cars worldwide based on the same vehicle platform. The commonality of plant and car designs, in effect, permits production of the same "global car" at any one of the new facilities, with parts, manufacturing operations, engineering, and maintenance procedures standardized throughout the world. Since many of these facilities will be in Third World, emerging markets, the international transfer of technical expertise from industrialized countries to developing nations is expected to proceed at a rapid pace. "No longer are those countries' lower wage rates the sole driver of global expansion; companies are cultivating engineers, research and marketing experts in nations where they hope to build up their business" (Blumenstein, 1997, A8). As a result, engineering car and plant designs are frequently not coming from R&D centers at corporate headquarters such as Detroit. Moreover, the large vehicles popular in the United States are out of sync with the small, global car most in demand in poorer countries. Similar designs will furthermore enable economies-of-scale production runs because if demand falters in the country of production, output can be shifted to the export market.

The international transfer of technology also means that highly paid engineers need not be detailed from corporate headquarters for start-up, maintenance, and troubleshooting at foreign sites. With comprehensive training, locally employed personnel can acquire the requisite skills for work at a new plant. Manufacturing operations will also be used that take advantage of the lower wage rates, with more manual labor replacing the extensive automation found in industrialized, affluent nations. Reliance on human workers will enable greater work flexibility over dedicated machinery and the enhanced possibility of worker learning from on-the-job experience that reduces production times and costs. Such productivity gains are possible because of the absence of rigid work rules found in American and European factories that were negotiated by powerful labor unions. Affluent countries are also pushing manufacturers abroad with their maturing vehicle markets, which have been reduced to replacement purchases by an aging population. In contrast, a growing population and rising per capita income are spurring a boom in consumer durable goods in emerging markets, with the growing demand prompting a stream of investments by corporate vehicle companies to such newly industrializing countries as Argentina, Brazil, Poland, Thailand, and China. For the Mercosur countries, the commercial shifts represent a major change from the time when they were viewed "largely as dumping ground[s] for obsolete technology and outdated models" (Blumenstein 1997, A1). Significant politicoeconomic reforms by national governments have also created an operating environment conducive to investments by foreign multinational firms. Foremost among these for South America has been the creation of the Mercosur free trade bloc, which was established by the Treaty of Asunción (capital of Paraguay) in 1991.

EVOLUTION OF MERCOSUR

Trade between Argentina and Brazil accelerated with the election of civilian leaders—Raul Alfonsin in 1983 for the former and Jose Sarnay (after the death of Tancredo Neves) in 1985 for the latter—after lengthy periods of military rule. The new presidents, mired in the Third World debt crisis and knowledgeable in global affairs, saw how the booming economies of East Asia had benefited from international trade and investments and used this knowledge to turn away from go-it-alone, distrustful attitudes maintained by prior military junta. The policy shift was further strengthened by the Argentine loss in the Falkland Islands War (1982), which clearly showed how inept its military leaders were as well as how wasteful and inflationary the munificent expenditures to support its armed forces had been. Improving living standards and commercial ties through regional trade subsequently became priority measures with the presidential elections of Carlos Menem in Argentina in 1989 and Fernando Collor in Brazil in 1990, who would proceed to negotiate the 1991 Treaty of Asunción which would reduce or eliminate tariffs on intra-Mercosur trade. Regional exports and imports promptly rose by an average of 27% per year, with member countries planning in 1994 to become a customs union that would have a common external tariff schedule for imports from the rest of the world as well as the free-trade (no tariffs) goal for Mercosur nations.

OPENING OF BRAZIL'S MARKETS

One of Collor's first acts as president was to lift the outright ban on foreign vehicles that had been in place since 1974, causing its industry to languish while innovations and trade initiatives transformed outside motor vehicle markets. The ban encompassed the importing of electronic fuel injection systems and robotic manufacturing systems, resulting in its industry having old product attributes and the lowest productivity and level of automation in the world. In the absence of meaningful competition, domestic carmakers chose to assemble the same designs, year after year, with some models staying in production for more than eleven years. These were derided as "horse carts" by President Collor. To jump-start the industry, the Brazilian government negotiated with the companies and their labor unions "a landmark agreement to cut retail prices by 22% in return for tax breaks and a pledge of labor [union] moderation" (Kamm 1994, A5).

In doing so, the parties to the agreement readily understood that Brazil's archaic auto industry could not continue its torpid practices once the import barriers were lifted. To further prepare for the incoming competition, President Itmar Franco issued a challenge to the domestic industry to build a small, inexpensive "popular car" that could compete against such imports as the Fiat Tipo, which took a sizable 6.4% of total sales in 1994 even after it was hit with stiff tariff rates of 32%. In response to Franco's challenge and Collor's earlier lifting of the import ban, Volkswagen—also taking advantage of government tax breaks offered domestic producers—relaunched the Beetle, ever the world's quintessential small, cheap people's car in 1993, seven years after it had been retired from production by VW's management. The Beetle (which is sold as the Fusca in Brazil) is actually assembled in an Argentine plant; thus, its resurrection in Brazil was enabled by the Mercosur free-trade agreement and was one of the first models to enjoy production synergies between the two large South American markets (Kamm 1994, A5).

The trade liberalization measures also prompted General Motors to introduce its own "popular car," the Corsa, in record time since it could now import parts not made in Brazil. New Omega and Vectra marques were introduced before the Corsa, with the three cars used to replace aging Opala and Chevette product lines, both over twenty years old. Even with the new domestic competition, eye-catching imports like the Fiat Tipo continued to climb in popularity and, in 1995, seized 25.7% of car sales after tariffs were cut from 32%, to 20% at the end of 1994. The startling market share provoked the government into raising duties to 70%, which, together with a slowdown in the economy, caused the sale of imports to nose-dive to 13% of the new car market the following year. Such high tariff rates were also imposed to induce foreign concerns like Renault to invest in Brazil. In addition, the government adopted a program of tax incentives that could be used by producers of affordable, popular cars as well as those vehicles that had at least 50% locally made content (the Fusca easily met this target). Local manufacturers that balanced imports of fully assembled units against an equal number of exports paid tariffs of only 35% on the imports, down from 70%. These rates fell to 31.5% after 1996, to 24.5% after 1997, and to 20% at the beginning of 2000. Importers without domestic production had similar, though not as steep, cuts in their tariff schedules. For example, duties were 63% after 1996, compared to 31.5% for local producers with the imports for nonlocal producers restricted to a quota of 50,000 units per year (EIU 1997, 20). Byzantine in nature, the import obstacles, together with inducements extended by Mercosur and the Brazilian government, had the intended effect of bringing foreign capital, technology, and managerial expertise to the country. Local content regulations as well as the new modular assembly approaches further strengthened domestic parts manufacturers, particularly after the foreign carmakers became satisfied with the quality of locally made parts.

Foreign direct investments in Brazil strongly advanced with the presidential election of Fernando Cardoso on October 5, 1994. Cardoso had impressive qualifications for the job, having served Brazil competently as its foreign and finance minister. Hyperinflation, which in the preceding June alone had reached 45%, had already fallen to 1.5% in September, largely due to the Real Plan implemented by the new president when he headed the finance ministry. In his campaign, Cardoso promised to continue his anti-inflation program, enact greater health care coverage, increase educational opportunities, and pursue the privatization of state-owned enterprises such as TelBrazil, the telephone monopoly. These measures would more closely align Brazil with the advanced economies in the Northern Hemisphere, with the greater social and economic stability encouraging the inward flow of investment capital.

Similar reforms had been proceeding in Argentina since the election of President Carlos Menem in 1989, but because of the importance of Brazil to any regional plans—its population is over four times that of Argentina, with its gross domestic product at $676 billion compared to the latter's $283.7 billion—continued development of Mercosur and trade between the two nations had to await the resignation of the controversial Collor (whose impeachment deadlocked the Brazilian government) and eventual election of Cardoso. Agreement was then reached at the end of 1994 to broaden Mercosur from a free-trade area to a customs union with common external tariff wall. Such integration was prompted by gains in intra-Mercosur trade resulting from earlier tariff cuts. As duties fell, trade between members jumped 47% from 1991 to 1992; 35% from 1992 to 1993; 22% from 1993 to 1994; 14% from 1994 to 1995. Total Mercosur trade stood at $14.5 billion in 1995 compared to $4 billion in 1990. In addition, direct foreign investments increased sharply from $2.5 billion in 1991, to nearly $8 billion in 1996 (Reid 1996, 3–18). Cross-border investments between Brazil and Argentina were slower to develop because of the lack of capital, technology, and managerial expertise in their private sectors compared to what multinational corporations from Europe and the United States could offer. In the motor vehicle industry, therefore, activities by firms like Renault are shaping the industry as they attempt to establish major stakes in newly integrated markets. These stakes, as expected, are along the Atlantic coastline, near the population centers of Rio de Janeiro, São Paulo, and Buenos Aires as opposed to the hard-to-reach hinterland (see Figure 7.1).

The impact of Mercosur is beginning to show in comparisons of country markets in South America: gains of new car sales in 1994 show Argentina and Brazil with hefty increases of 29% and 23%, respectively, while non-Mercosur Colombia rose 15%, and Venezuela's market suffered a devastating drop of 41% (Friedland 1995).

Integration with Argentina

To further capitalize on Mercosur trade, Argentina and Brazil negotiated an agreement at the end of 1998 to streamline the movement of parts and vehicles between the two nations. It had the following stipulations:

1.   Tariff rates that had begun to diverge would be set at 35% on imported vehicles from outside Mercosur.

2.   Tariffs on assembled units and parts would be eliminated in the Mercosur trade.

3.   Local content of 60% would qualify assembled vehicles as Mercosur-made.

4.   Local producers whose output is exhausted by demand would be able to import cars from outside the trade bloc at a favorable 17.5% tariff rate.

5.   Brazilian states would discontinue subsidies to carmakers, although national governments would still be able to award incentives provided approval is obtained from other Mercosur members (Fritsch 1998).

Figure 7.1
Foreign Auto Plants in the Mercosur Region

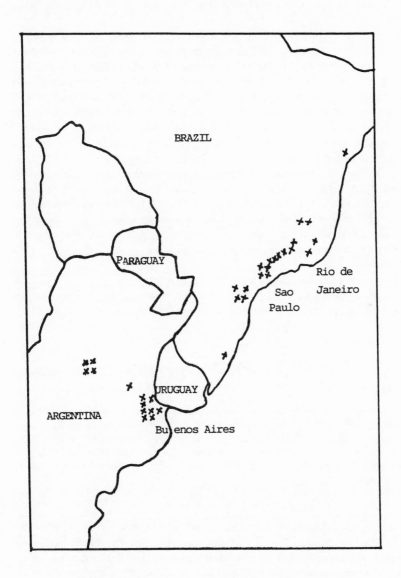

Production Growth in Brazil

From 1986 to 1992 production of vehicles barely grew in Brazil, with units produced in 1986 at 1.056 million and six years later reaching 1.073 million. Production subsequently soared to 1.812 million in 1996, paralleling the advent of Mercosur and other economic reforms. Chief beneficiaries of the growth were the foreign manufacturers, who, as shown in Table 7.1, maintained their lead on Brazil's newly opened playing field and in the absence of formidable local producers.

The lead by European producers VW and Fiat in South America's largest motor vehicle market can be ascribed to the invasion of West European markets by Detroit following World War II. As a countermove, Volkswagen and Fiat attempted inroads in the U.S. car market, were rebuffed, and refocused efforts on less competitive arenas like Brazil. U.S. carmakers subsequently moved to South America as Japanese manufacturers successfully set up operations in the United States and as the home market became mature in terms of slower population and economic growth rates. The Mercosur boom for motor vehicles was also just beginning, and it strained domestic capacity even as output, as shown in Table 7.1, was strongly increasing for the three leading producers. GM was forced to schedule round-the-clock operations at its modern, highly automated São Paulo plant, and the company was still facing more demand than it could meet in April 1997 for its pickup trucks and sport utility vehicles. Additional capital projects have therefore been announced by the company, and these ensure that Brazil will be playing an integral part in the company's global outreach plans.

GM's Priorities. The priorities of General Motors for its global business and for Latin America were set forth by John F. Smith Jr., the company's chief executive officer, president, and chairman, in the 1997 Annual Report (pp. 5–6):

- "Getting common in our processes, parts and vehicle platforms, worldwide, which saves time, confusion, and a massive duplication of effort that translates into savings to the bottom line. . . .

- Competing on a global basis, a priority that is driving the largest international production expansion in the company's history. We have five new manufacturing facilities either under development or up and running in Argentina, China, Poland, and Thailand. These facilities are the cornerstone of our expansion into new markets." (Copyright 1998 GM Corp. Used with permission of GM Media Archives.)

GM's new South American assembly plants are located in Gravatai in the southern Brazilian state of Rio Grande do Sul and in Rosario, Argentina, which has already begun production of the Chevrolet Corsa. The bigger plant in Brazil is expected to be completed in 1999 and will produce the small Opel car at the annual rate of 120,000 units (compared to 84,000 for the Corsa facility). Early estimates of the plant's cost ($600 million) were released by GM do Brasil, with

Table 7.1
Leading Producers

	1992	1996
Volkswagen	347,609	635,255
Fiat	310,272	539,607
General Motors	213,375	443,752
Ford	153,283	147,736

Source: Adapted from EIU 1997, 27.

an additional $500 million alotted for a components plant in Santa Catarina state and $150 million for a parts facility in the state of São Paulo. Minority investors—mainly local suppliers—will hold a 40% equity stake in the assembly plant ("G.M. Is Investing" 1996, D4). Total investments by the world's largest vehicle maker are expected to be $4.18 billion for 1996–2000, more than those by its principal competitors, including Volkswagen at $3.1 billion, Ford at $2.25 billion, newcomer Renault at $1 billion, and Fiat at $0.7 billion (Moffett 1998).

The preceding initiatives are predicated on Brazil's and Argentina's surpassing Germany to "become one of the top three markets in the world behind the United States and Japan," as predicted by Mark Hogan, former head of GM do Brasil (Bradsher, April 25, 1997, D1). GM's investment juggernaut furthermore will be used for the development of a prototype plant centered on the Gravitai project that it has dubbed "Blue Macaw." Hogan, together with G. Richard Wagoner Jr., the company's newly named president and chief executive officer, expects to apply the evolving small-car manufacturing paradigm back in the United States even as it is being contested by the United Automobile Workers union because the development entails the elimination of jobs. Wagoner and Hogan, who has moved up to become general manager of GM's North American small-car group operations, are currently in pivotal executive positions from which to implement the innovation they pioneered as former presidents of GM do Brasil. Still in their forties, both men will undoubtedly be advocating Blue Macaw's modular manufacturing innovations for a long time to come, especially since Wagoner became GM's chief executive in 2000.

MODULAR MANUFACTURING

One of Blue Macaw's distinctive features is the large, 40% minority ownership by Brazilian investors in the GM plant. In earlier North American projects, the firm financed entirely its big-as-several-football-field facilities, thereby retaining full control over production and car design plans. The new partnership with local suppliers implies that the cash-rich American firm is intentionally working with its suppliers on the plant's layout in order to facilitate deliveries when operations begin. The skinny T- or L-shaped facility will entail less operating space (and, therefore, require less investment funds) and provide more walls for loading docks, allowing just-in-time deliveries by the supplying companies. The reduced space at the GM plant further means that more subassembly work will be done at the parts factories, with small components such as speedometers, gas gauges, radios, and glove boxes assembled into dashboard modules and the modular subassembly then shipped, when needed, to the final assembly site (Bradsher, June 17, 1998, D22). The finely tuned deliveries will be based on carefully worked-out procedures between suppliers and GM, with the equity position held by suppliers in the Gravitai venture further cementing relationships with the multinational corporation. Savings from smaller factories (with less space and fewer workers) and strong parts networking have resulted in greater profits for GM, and some of these "lean" practices were learned in the joint venture that the Detroit automaker had with Toyota Motor in Fremont, California. GM's moves abroad furthermore mean that it can easily implement foreign sourcing of parts and adopt innovations without being tied down by labor union contracts or in-house supply systems, both of which are prevalent at U.S. facilities. Local sourcing also translates into higher domestic content in vehicles assembled abroad, satisfying host country objectives while lowering component costs.

Blue Macaw Flies North

GM's concentrated emphasis on cost reduction is tied not only to the low purchasing power of Brazilian car buyers but to the more startling statistic that the company lost about $1,000 on every small car it makes and sells in the bigger U.S. market. Hence, the company had to go beyond Toyota's lean production methods to seek a modus operandi that resolves GM's money-losing dilemma. Modular manufacturing, as fashioned along the lines of the Gravitai project, appears to be an answer. The new plant is expected to produce "the world's cheapest car" by slashing "$3,000 off the retail price of what would otherwise be a $10,000 small car" (Fritsch and White 1999, A8). Modules will be assembled from parts at supplier sites; this will cut installation time and space requirements and reduce the number of workers on the assembly floor by as much as two-thirds.

In the United States, most of GM's workers belong to the powerful United Auto Workers (UAW) union, with their reduced employment having a major impact on factory operating costs. It will also blunt the union's grip on GM's production lines as demonstrated by the nationwide strike against the company in the summer of 1998, which cost General Motors $3 billion in lost profits. Within weeks of the strike's settlement, GM announced plans to build "a new generation of highly efficient assembled plants in North America modeled after the Blue Macaw factory" (Bradsher, August 6, 1998). The company will further distance itself from the UAW by spinning off its principal auto parts supplier

(Delco Automotive Systems) as an independent entity. The new firm will be in competition for GM business with other parts-supplying companies, most of which have nonunion shops in order to be cost-competitive. GM will thus be in a better position to wring cost concessions and greater cooperation from its suppliers just as it has done in Brazil. Indeed, Brazilian operations contributed $1 billion to corporate earnings in 1996.

Based on such bottom-line results, GM developed Project Yellowstone under the direction of Mark Hogan to convert three aging factories in North America to modular manufacturing design. "For the first time, . . . GM will build plants in the U.S. that will depend far more on suppliers delivering built-up chunks of vehicles—whole dashboards, prewired interior panels, and so on—than on UAW laborers bolting and welding thousands of individual pieces at hourly wage and benefit rates of more than $40 an hour" (Blumenstein, Simison, and White 1998, A3). Because of leaner plant requirements, investment costs for the three conversions are expected to be reduced by as much as 50%. Agreement has already been reached with the Canadian Auto Workers union to construct such a plant in Ingersoll, Canada in a joint venture with Suzuki Motor Corporation, the Japanese small carmaker.

The agreement notwithstanding, the American United Auto Workers union angrily vowed to clip the wings of Blue Macaw, as it understood clearly the potential for job losses in its rank and file. In national contract talks during the summer of 1999, its union president announced that modular assembly will be a major sticking point. The Blue Macaw landing in the United States will consequently be bumpy and even delayed, but the strong inroads it has already made in the major Brazilian market ensure that it will spread as small-car assembly and distribution assume global dimensions.

VOLKSWAGEN AND FIAT

GM's moves in Mercosur are being met by the European front-runners, which are adding capacity even faster than the American company. While GM has current planned investments of $2 billion, VW has committed or already spent $2.8 billion, and Fiat, $2.5 billion. Germany's largest private company and car manufacturer intends to use its capital for a modular truck facility in Resende, a new Golf/Audi assembly line in São José dos Pinhais, and an engine factory in São Carlos. The assembly line, when completed in 1998, will have a production rate of 800–1,000 cars per day and significantly boost its capacity by 38%. Prior increases were used by VW to retain its leadership position over archrival Fiat from 1994 to 1995. Its lead position of 508,403 vehicles made in 1994 was slightly ahead of Fiat's at 500,738, but the German company surged ahead in 1995 to produce 600,560 vehicles, while the Italian maker had to reduce its assembly rate to 463,516 because of faltering sales (EIU 1997, 21–27).

VW's lengthy experience in Brazil has produced disappointments in modular manufacturing that GM, still in a construction stage, may yet encounter with its Blue Macaw plant. In 1996 VW, with seven of its local suppliers, established a truck production facility in Resende based on modular supply techniques that VW hoped would set new standards for plant productivity. As much as 75% of the labor force was hired by supply companies, and these workers together with VW employees would cooperate in final truck assembly. When operations began at the new plant, results were highly disappointing, with productivity at only half the level of comparable European facilities and quality problems so pervasive that a third of the output needed additional corrective work ("The Modular T," 1998, 60–61). The setback, however, has not deterred the company or its rivals from continuing with the experiment in new manufacturing techniques in the small-car market.

Fiat, for example, is employing just-in-time inventory systems with its strong network of seventy three nearby suppliers linked to its Betim plant through on-line computer terminals that track 1,400 parts and subassembled modules. Productivity gains were so large that the Italian car company successfully boosted daily output at the site from 800 in 1990, to 2,300 in 1997. The capacity expansion enabled Fiat to begin production of the Palio, its world car, in 1996 with a hefty beginning output of 157,730 units per year, which compares favorably to the production number of 227,244 for its best-selling small car, the Uno. Production rates complement sales figures for 1996, as shown in Table 7.2, which indicate how popular the Palio has proven to be among car buyers.

In the first six months of 1997, Palio sales tripled those of the Uno but still trailed the VW Gol. Its production for the full year totaled 386,901, compared to the slumping Uno at 115,160 and the sales leader Gol at 474,670. While the new Palio cannibalizes sales from the older Uno, its popularity also came at the expense of Ford's two lagging models, the Escort and Fiesta, as listed in Table 7.2. (The lackluster performance led to thoughts in the early 1990s that Ford might quit the Brazilian market.) In addition to being Fiat's entrant in the small, world car competition, the Palio is becoming Fiat's answer to the Brazilian government's push to significantly increase exports since the Italian firm has already begun exporting the Palio station wagon (made at Betim) to Europe (EIU 1997, 25, 28, 51).

VICISSITUDES OF FORD

The world's second largest vehicle maker, Ford has suffered ignominiously in South America as it attempts to secure the major industrial role it is accustomed to playing in such an important emerging market. While sales and profits of other foreign producers advanced, Ford reported a massive $600 million loss in Brazil for 1996, with the red ink continuing (but halved) for 1997 and a modest break-even hoped for in 1998. Instead, the Asian financial crisis spread to Latin America, and Ford's sales in 1998 dropped by a third. The company's travails go back to a money-saving joint venture, named Autolatina, that was formed with Volkswagen in 1987 in response to an environment of low growth, high inflation, and closed markets characteristic of Brazil and

Table 7.2
Brazil's Top Sellers in 1996

Gol (VW)	390,828
Uno (Fiat)	203,239
Corsa (GM)	190,462
Palio (Fiat)	156,930
Escort (Ford)	60,711
Fiesta (Ford)	54,055
Santana (VW)	53,032

Source: Adapted from EIU 1997, Table 2.16.

Argentina, *aprés* Mercosur. Output for the joint venture was centered in Pacheco, Argentina, where an old Ford factory was shared with VW and used to produce the Ford Falcon, designed in 1960 for the U.S. market. Adequate for the 1980s, the Falcon proved no competition for smaller, newer marques that emerged in the 1990s as Mercosur car sales surged upward. In Brazil sales were assisted by the reduction of sales taxes on small cars with one-liter engines. By 1995 Autolatina was headed for dissolution, with Ford left without a subcompact model for the booming market. The giant car firm scrambled to fill the void with imports, only to be thwarted by the Brazilian government's increase in tariff rates to stem foreign exchange losses and force car manufacturers to build local factories. As inventory at dealer showrooms fell, Ford began supplying second-rate vehicles from unsold stock that dealers only could sell at discount. This prompted angry Ford dealers to file an antitrust complaint against the company in July 1996, placing a damper on Ford's introduction of the Fiesta model, which the company had developed in Europe. While the new nameplate was successful in regaining some market share (13% in 1996, up from 10.9% in 1995), profits for Ford nose-dived since parts for the car had to be imported from Europe (Moffett 1997).

To rectify the situation, as well as assist in the assembly of a second small, "popular car," the Ka, Ford initiated a $3 billion program to:

1. Develop a network of Mercosur parts suppliers.

2. Close two foundries and redesign assembly lines to meet small-car production.

3. Reduce salaried and hourly employment rolls.

4. Build its new "Amazon" plant for small cars in southern Brazil to produce a "vehicle line for the coming century, developed on a world platform" (Reitman 1997).

The $1 billion Amazon project was announced on October 2, 1997, and planned for the same southern state of Rio Grande do Sul, close to the Argentine border, where GM is building Blue Macaw. In the announcement, the president of Ford do Brasil indicated: "The intention is to integrate our operating strategies in Mercosur, considering that our installations in São Paulo [farther north] are already operating at full production capacity" (Reuters 1997). The company's integration plans call for 30% of the output of 100,000 subcompact vehicles per year to be exported to other Mercosur nations, with start-up to begin in 2001. Brazil's National Development Bank provided $700 million in financing for the huge project, while Ford contributed about $800 million. The state government of Rio Grande do Sul also promised $240 million in financing and infrastructural development such as roads, gas and electricity service, and wastewater treatment facilities. Twelve to fifteen supplier companies will invest $300 million for a module-supplying network that will include $500 million from Ford.

THE ASIAN CRISIS

When Thailand's currency, the baht, was allowed to float by its government in July 1997, Brazilian automakers barely noticed the pinprick that would burst the bubble economies of Asian "tigers," namely, Thailand, Malaysia, Indonesia, Hong Kong, and South Korea. Thailand, after all, was an irregularly shaped thumbprint on the world map in a corner of the Pacific Ocean mixed up with other tiny Asian nations, while Brazil was a huge Latin landmass fronting the Atlantic Ocean. A collapse in Japan, the world's second largest economy, could have elicited a more startled response but even there, a prolonged downturn since 1989 had failed to dent Brazil's booming auto industry, which was achieving record production and sales in 1996 as a result of the regional free-trade pact and economic reforms. Industrial car output was expected to grow by 100% from 1992 to the end of the decade, a forecast upended by the developing worldwide currency crisis.

Despite its size and distance from Thailand, Brazil, by opening its borders to trade and investments, had inextricably linked its currency and capital markets with those of financial centers throughout the world. Its economy, moreover, had a lot in common with Thailand's since both were classified by international investors as emerging markets characterized by high economic growth rates, volatile stock markets, and weak currencies compared to the U.S. dollar, Japanese yen, or German mark. In Latin America hyperinflation and national budget and trade deficits often sent currencies plummeting, with foreign investors rushing to exit the country before devaluation overwhelmed any capital gains earned. To prevent capital flight, central banks have engaged in a "dirty float" where official reserves of hard currencies like the dollar are sold and where the domestic currency is bought to prop up its value. Other government measures used in supporting a country's currency include raising interest rates or taxes to curb inflation. Higher interest rates also attract short-term portfolio investments and are frequently used by monetary authorities because they can be quickly raised to help ward off a potential run on the currency. Interest rate increases, however, are the instrument of last resort because they frequently choke off economic growth, precipitating unemployment and severe recession. The dirty-float support of the currency also carries huge risks because developing (poorer) countries have limited official reserves, which are quickly drained. Support then ends, and the currency plunges on foreign exchange markets as it did in Thailand, Mexico (in 1994), Russia, and Indonesia.

By October 1997 such turmoil, begun in Thailand in July, had spread to Malaysia, Hong Kong, and South Korea. In order to prevent the crisis from undermining the Brazilian real, its central government doubled interest rates, raised taxes, and reduced budgetary expenditures while concurrently bolstering the real on foreign exchanges through the selling of hard currencies from official reserves. The measures, which had been quickly implemented, precipitated a severe downturn in business activity. Motor vehicle sales were especially impacted, and production slowdowns were scheduled by GM and Volkswagen. Only months after announcing the construction of its new plant in Rio Grande do Sul, Ford Motor Company halted production at its factories for a week because of climbing inventories.

Quick action by the government temporarily quelled the financial turmoil, but as 1998 began, severe instability broke out in Indonesia, and in August Russia crashed. Brazil was forced to devalue its currency in January 1999 as international banks and investors tallied huge losses from loans and investments in these shaky markets and resolved to keep their funds in hard, convertible currencies like the dollar. Money was drawn out of Brazil at the panic-stricken rate of $1 billion a day. Interest rates as represented by the interbank lending rate were raised by the Brazil central bank, Banco Central do Brasil, from below 30%, to 50% after trending downward for most of 1998. In the ensuing recession, domestic sales are expected to fall along with exports as adverse conditions hit all Latin American markets. Competitive pressures are further coming from significant (20%) currency devaluations in Asian and Latin American nations as they attempt to move exports by undercutting foreign prices with cheaper exchange rates.

Because of the recessionary pressures, Volkswagen idled up to 20,000 workers for ten days, with General Motors doing the same with 7,000 workers over eleven days. For VW, the 1998 situation followed voluntary retirements for 4,000 workers in 1997 after the company threatened a mass layoff of 10,000 workers. To reduce the layoffs to 4,000, VW's labor union agreed to give management greater authority to deal with the austere economic times. VW's management was allowed to alter work schedules, for example, sending workers home on slow days with full pay provided the time is made up when the plant is busier. Employees could also be forced to take paid holidays or vacations when work is not available, again with the proviso that missed days are made up (Schemo 1998, C1, C14). At the end of 1998, the union, again attempting to prevent layoffs, accepted a 15% cut in pay.

The downturn in sales hit Ford Brazil particularly hard with its vehicle sales dropping 33.8% compared to the industry's 27.5% for 1998. Ford subsequently instituted layoffs of 6,000 workers for twelve days in Brazil and the idling of 1,400 Argentine employees in tandem with the removal of one plant shift there. As sales continued to fall, Ford Brazil, before Christmas, laid off 2,800 assembly-line workers at its São Bernardo plant, outside São Paulo, which produced its Fiesta and Ka models. The move slowed production by about one-half of its normal rate of 1,000 units per day. Operations were further disrupted in 1999, when the fired workers began occupying the factory in a massive protest against the layoffs. The plant was then closed for all of January.

Forced Devaluation

On January 14 the sword of Damocles, hovering over the Brazilian government since the crisis in Thailand began, fell, cutting the country's currency loose to find its own market value without support from the central bank. Global speculators had won another round in toppling a giant, albeit tottering, economy. Nor would the $41.5 billion bailout package negotiated between São Paulo and the International Monetary Fund appear to offer much salvation. Such aid had been extended to Indonesia under President Suharto, who agreed to such stringent measures that layoffs, starvation, and deadly riots paralyzed the archipelago and forced the president from office. Similar grim conditions now confronted Brazilian officials, and one decision by the newly elected governor of Rio Grande du Sol had a major impact on Ford operations in the state.

Amazon Is Canceled. Sworn in, in January, as financial panic was gripping the nation, Olivio Dutra decided to eliminate millions of dollars' worth of programs from his state budget because they could no longer be afforded. The $280 million subsidies to Ford and GM, given by his predecessor during better times, were targeted in March, with quick responses from the giant firms, especially Ford, which had the greater share ($250 million) to lose. GM delayed the construction of its Blue Macaw plant for six months, but because it was nearly complete, the company had little choice but to proceed with the plant's opening, now scheduled for the middle of 2000. GM's Brazilian operations, moreover, had contributed handsomely to corporate profits in the past, and Blue Macaw was the centerpiece of the firm's globalization drive. The decision to continue was therefore an easy one for top management, just as the decision to cancel the Amazon project at Ford—whose losses in South America had reached $165 million in the first quarter of 1999—was a plausible alternative. In addition, Ford's move did not entail an exit from Mercosur, and the company stated in its April 28 press release that it was seeking another suitable location for its plant. Neighboring states, Parana and Santa Catarina, immediately welcomed Ford to their jurisdictions, as did the northeastern state of Bahia, which further maintained that it would honor any commitments made to the motor company.

Ford's decision to stay while Brazil's sales of motor vehicles were experiencing their slowest year since 1994 can probably be ascribed to the responses of its principal competitors to the devaluation and recession:

1.   GM's decision to complete and start up Blue Macaw was undoubtedly the most important. The company also announced a small increase in the operating rate of its São Caetano factory.

2.   In March 1999 Volkswagen increased output of its Gol model in response to price and temporary tax cuts by dealers and the government to spur car sales.

3.   The following month, Renault, which had opened its minivan factory the preceding year, announced the construction of a $120 million plant in the state of Parana adjacent to the new van factory.

4.   The following day, DaimlerChrysler AG began production of its A-class compact car at its $820 million plant in the Ninas Gerais state, 110 miles northeast of Rio de Janeiro. A company director acknowledged, "A lot of people questioned this enterprise. Competitors have slowed or stopped investments because they see dark clouds on the horizon. At DaimlerChrysler, we see beyond the day-to-day ups and downs, and we see a bright future for Brazil and Mercosur" (Yamaguchi 1999).

The DaimlerChrysler outlook should further strengthen Ford's resolve to compete in Mercosur, especially since its profits from the U.S. market are at record levels, with its market share edging closer to that of perennial leader General Motors. Ford also realizes that business cycles could flip-flop, with North America falling into recession while Mercosur recovers. Then, investing in Brazil will be too late.

Ford's plant cancellation, moreover, occurred while emerging signs began indicating that the panic was ending. The country's real currency, which was worth $.80 before the devaluation, bottomed out at $.45 at the end of February and trended upward to $.60 at the beginning of April. The interbank lending rate had eased from 50%, to 31%, sending the Bovespa index on the São Paulo stock market up 50% over its January low point. Equally significant was the return of foreign investor confidence to the country, enabling Brazil to borrow $2 billion by selling five-year government notes. During the depths of the crisis such investment instruments had been shunned by international lenders, forcing the government to seek bailout financing from the International Monetary Fund (Rohter 1999, C1, C17).

OTHER INVESTORS

Bad times in their part of the world help to explain why Japanese firms like Honda and Toyota have invested so cautiously in Brazil. With a decade-long recession still gripping their large domestic market, both companies are reluctant to undertake billion-dollar commitments abroad. Nevertheless,

The Japanese in particular have concluded that Brazil and Argentina represent the largest and most attractive of the world's emerging markets and are beginning to set up factories here. By comparison, the smaller auto market in Thailand is becoming saturated; China and Indonesia pose political difficulties; India still has too few roads, and demand is only beginning to rise in Eastern Europe, said Koichi Kondo, president of Honda Motor of Brazil Ltd. (Bradsher April 25, 1997, D4)

The preceding comparison of world markets led Honda to the construction and 1997 start-up of a $400 million facility in Sumare to produce as many as 100,000 Civic sedans per year. Toyota has also begun production of the Corolla at the smaller, $150 million factory in Indaiatuba. No Mercosur move is planned by Nissan Motor, Japan's second largest motor vehicle company, undoubtedly because of the string of losses the firm has had in the long Japanese recession. With the advent of the financial crisis, Asia Motors of South Korea reneged on an announced $700 million new van plant in Brazil. All Korean vehicle makers have retreated from global markets as its domestic recession has forced massive downsizing and even the bankruptcy of Kia Motors (EIU 1997, 22).

Chrysler's Outsourcing

The financial inhibitions prevailing in Asia did not deter Chrysler, prior to merging with Daimler-Benz, from opening a $350 million pickup truck plant in Curitiba, Brazil (near São Paulo) in July 1998. The company has avoided the small car market, but it still is adopting modular manufacturing methods at its new facility. The plant's layout is small because the chassis for the Dakota pickup is built at a supplier's factory, one mile away, and arrives at the Chrysler site with wires and hoses installed and tires mounted. Seating modules are also assembled at another supplier's plant, and Chrysler is further contemplating the subassembly of the instrument panel outside its facility ("The Modular T" 60–61). Irrespective of its megamerger with Daimler-Benz, Chrysler is proceeding with its joint venture with rival German maker BMW to invest in a $500 million engine plant, close to the Curitiba factory, for the production of 400,000, four-cylinder, small-car engines per year. Although some of these may be used in a possible mini-Neon car or at the newly operational DaimlerChrysler plant in Minas Gerais, Chrysler intends to export most of the engines (EIU 1997, 24).

ARGENTINA'S MOTOR INDUSTRY

Similar to developments in its bigger neighbor, Argentina's production, sales, imports, and exports of motor vehicles expanded significantly since 1990 and the signing of the Mercosur treaty. In tandem with the landmark trade pact, the Menem government attacked its chronic inflation (averaging an astounding 600% per year for 1983–1991) by adopting the Cavallo Plan in 1991, named for its economics minister Domingo Cavallo, who pegged the Argentine currency to the U.S. dollar. Called the austral at the time, the nation's currency was anchored by congressional legislation in March 1991 at 10,000 australes to the U.S. dollar. In January 1992 the austral was supplanted by the peso at 10,000 australes to one new peso, resulting in one new peso equal to U.S.$1.00. The enactment of the "convertibility law" essentially stripped the central bank of its policy-making role, particularly its ability to print money to finance government deficits. The exacting measure succeeded in bringing inflation down to 4.6% from its torrid rate, and economic growth climbed from 0.4% during the hyperinflationary period to 3.9% (Velde and Veracierto, 1999).

In the fight against inflation, car prices in particular came down, reduced, in large measure, by productivity gains achieved through the use of innovative manufacturing technology. Regulatory reforms and developing Mercosur trade facilitated economies of scale and other production efficiencies as the vehicle trade brought 70% of Brazil's exports to Argentina and as 90% of the latter's exports went to Brazil. A 1991 automotive decree in Argentina also attracted local production and enhanced intrafirm shipment of goods and parts that crossed the country's borders. As an example, Ford increased the production of its Escort and Ranger models, with the additional output earmarked for the Brazilian market. In turn, large numbers of Ford's Fiesta and Ka marques made in Brazil go to Argentina. Such country specialization was made possible by Ford's $2.1 billion investments in the two countries for the refurbishing of old facilities like the Autolatina plant and the construction of new ones. These and other investments—some as early as 1960 in Pacheco, north of Buenos Aires—pushed Ford close to the top among production leaders in 1997 with the assembly of 87,546 passenger cars all having the Escort marque. Italy's Fiat with 97,631 units assembled at its new, $600 million Cordoba plant leads all carmakers, and its output includes 13,501 Palio "world cars." Volkswagen at 89,772 units stands behind Fiat and just ahead of Ford (EIU second quarter 1998, 88–96).

Industrial Resurgence

The heightened economic activity has lifted Argentina's auto industry from its moribund, pre-Mercosur days, as indicated in Table 7.3, where total sales for the country included imported units. The downturn in production and sales in 1995 resulted from the spreading financial crisis of the Mexican bailout and peso devaluation. Transient portfolio investments that had flowed into Mexico City's Bolsa (stock market) took flight as government foreign reserves tumbled and as the current account turned negative. Argentine exports, however, remained exceptionally strong, and U.S. efforts to financially support the Mexican government of newly elected President Ernesto Zedillo successfully dampened the shock waves leading to a recovery in Argentina in 1996.

Comparison of the three nations' motor industry is given in Table 7.4, with Argentina having the smallest. Its production is little more than one-fifth of Brazil's and about one-third of Mexico's. It is heavily dependent on exports,

Table 7.3
Argentine Motor Vehicle Data

Year	Production	Total Sales	Exports
1990	99,639	95,960	1,126
1994	408,777	508,152	38,657
1995	285,424	327,982	52,746
1997	445,869	426,338	208,217

Source: Adapted from EIU second quarter 1998, Table 6.1, p. 86.

with 46.7% of production mainly going to Brazil, but this is nowhere near the large number of exports (74.3%) going from Mexico to the United States. Its size and export dependence make the Argentine industry vulnerable to perturbations elsewhere in Latin America, as the 1995 downturn in Table 7.3 indicates. Brazil's much larger economy was hardly affected by the Mexican peso crisis, enabling exports from Argentina to remain strong, thus promoting its recovery.

Cross-Border Integration

The NAFTA synergy, with Mexican production exported to the U.S. market, is replayed on a smaller scale in Mercosur, with less than half of Argentine production slated for the larger Brazilian market. The actual production-export scenario is, of course, orchestrated by the American (General Motors and Ford) and European (Volkswagen, Fiat, and Renault) companies that have operations in both countries. Table 7.5 lists their Argentine activities. Of the five firms, only Renault did not have significant Brazilian production in 1996, which it rectified with the opening of its Curitiba plant in 1998 and the announcement of a new plant at the same location. GM appears to be the laggard in Argentina, a circumstance it seeks to reverse with a $1 billion investment program. Several of the firms are putting forth new models like the Ford Escort, VW Polo, and Fiat Siena to compete against or replace older nameplates like the Renault 9, Fiat Duna, and Peugeot 504. Mercosur's impact on Argentine production is evident in the huge Escort production run in 1997—the largest annual output of a brand name ever made in the country—made feasible by sizable exports to Brazil. Other model runs will have similarly large export percentages, with the smallest planned still reaching a hefty 20% of Renault 19's production scheduled for export (EIU second quarter 1998, 96).

Table 7.4
Argentina, Brazil, and Mexico's Motor Vehicle Industry, 1997

	Production	Domestic Sales	Import Sales	Exports
Argentina	445,869	228,493	197,845	208,217
Brazil	2,067,452	1,640,683	302,625	411,772
Mexico	1,322,045	496,672	N/A	982,952

Sources: EIU second quarter 1998, Table 6.1 for Argentina; fourth quarter 1998, Table 4.1 for Brazil; second quarter 1998, Chapter 3 for Mexico.

GM Returns

The relatively weak GM ranking in Table 7.5 reflects its withdrawal from Argentina in the late 1970s to concentrate efforts on its home turf in battle with the Japanese. A nearly bankrupt Chrysler also withdrew in 1980, only to return in the 1990s. In the United States Detroit's Big Three automakers shrewdly joined with Japanese counterparts to learn the latter's modus operandi in designing and producing "lean" plants and small cars. These methods accompanied GM's return to Argentina in 1993 in its intention to build its "leanest production facility in the world" in Rosario (EIU second quarter 1998, 90). The assembly plant will cost $350 million, little more than a third of the usual $1 billion new-plant cost. Its design—mainly done by Brazilian engineers—is based on GM's Eisenach plant in Germany, the prototype that incorporated the manufacturing lessons learned in its joint ventures with Toyota and Suzuki. With its start-up, Eisenach has become "Europe's most efficient auto-making operation and the best in GM's empire, with a productivity rate at twice that of most of its assembly facilities in North America" (Blumenstein 1997, A1). At Rosario, other planned features include:

1. Modular manufacturing and close involvement with suppliers.

2. Common design facilities (as in the paint shop) with other emerging market facilities.

3. Reduced automation to take advantage of lower labor rates.

4. A high-speed stamping press.

5. Subassembly of the engine, air conditioning, transmissions and belts, in an ancillary new engine plant, prior to delivery to the assembly line.

6.   Multi-tasking by employees assigned to autonomous work teams with little of the infamous GM hierarchy and union work rules (Blumenstein 1997, A8).

Autolatina Ending

Unlike GM and Chrysler, Ford stayed in Argentina, even though it was preoccupied with the Japanese in its home market and the start-up of its landmark plant in Hermosillo, Mexico. Its attention diverted, the American auto giant elected to keep its Argentine operations at a minimalist level, with the Autolatina plant in Pacheco to be shared with Volkswagen AG. At the time, Ford could see little reason for a bigger investment, as it assumed that the ennui that had characterized South America for much of the twentieth century would continue into the new millennium. Its outlook was perfectly reflected in Ford's decision to assemble the Falcon model at the Pacheco plant, a car that was too old and too big for the local market, which would include Brazil with the advent of Mercosur. For its part in the 1987 Autolatina joint venture, Volkswagen

Table 7.5
Company Production and Investments

COMPANY	Model	1997		1995-1998
		Company Production	Model Production	Investments
FIAT		97,631		$ 600 million
	Sienna		35,438	
	Uno		32,938	
FORD		96,381		1,000
	Escort		87,546	
VW		89,772		500
	Gol		49,538	
	Polo		40,234	
RENAULT		79,226		200
	19		36,150	
	Clio		24,500	
GM		20,258		1,000
	Silverado			

Source: EIU second quarter 1998, Tables 6.2, 6.4, 6.5, 6.6.

redesigned its subcompact Gol model, which would become the best-selling car in Brazil (see Table 7.2), and its huge lead there would put it at the top for car sales throughout South America.

To reverse its lagging predicament in Mercosur, Ford in 1995 moved to end the joint venture and go after the small, popular car segment that had contributed so much to VW's success in boosting its Argentine market share from 10% in 1987, to 18.6% in 1996. Ford's share dropped from 20%, to 10%. The subsequent dissolution called for the physical division of the Pacheco plant, with each side going its own way. In a billion-dollar retooling effort, indicative of how seriously it is taking its Argentine operations, Ford proceeded to refurbish its half of the plant and is assembling the Escort subcompact at record levels for the domestic and Latin American export markets (Bradsher, May 16, 1997, D1, D3).

Devaluation Slowdown

Even with its peso pegged to the U.S. dollar, the turmoil in Brazil leading to devaluation of the real had a significant impact on the smaller Argentine economy, particularly on slowing exports to Brazil. This was then a negative aspect of Mercosur integration, where recession in Brazil would spread quickly to its principal trading partner. Statistics for 1998–1999 track the spreading malaise. In the third quarter of 1998, Argentina's gross domestic product (GDP) was still growing, with a 2.9% increase over the same period in 1997. Brazil's GDP had already declined with a -0.1% drop. In the next quarter, Brazil's GDP further dropped by -1.9%, dragging Argentina's down by -0.5%. With its greater dependence on exports, Argentina's industrial production in November 1998 was -6.9% as markets dried up in Brazil. The latter's drop in industrial production was only -2.6%. By March 1999 Argentina's loss in industrial production swelled to -11.7% ("Emerging Market Indicators" 1999).

For the motor vehicle industry, exports fell 13% in October 1998 over October 1997 levels, causing vehicle production to decrease by 27%. By November all principal vehicle manufacturers had reduced work hours and suspended production. By the end of the year, Ford Argentina was planning on firing 1,500 employees from its 4,000-person workforce. In negotiations with the labor union and government, the company instead agreed to the suspension of 1,400 workers for fifteen months and no permanent layoffs during the period. The agreement came after Brazil had sunk further into chaos with its surprise devaluation in January. Suspended workers got a $600–700 a month subsidy from the Labor Ministry to tide them over the jobless period. Similar suspensions have occurred at other plants as the foreign companies wait anxiously for recovery to take hold in Brazil. By March 1999 Asian, Russian, and Brazilian financial crises had abated, and small increases in motor vehicle production were scheduled by GM and VW (Reuters news release, 1999).

REFERENCES

Blumenstein, Rebecca. "GM Is Building Plants in Developing Nations to Woo New Markets." *Wall Street Journal*, August 4, 1997, pp. A1, A8.

Blumenstein, Rebecca, Robert L. Simison, and Joseph B. White. "GM Chairman Lays Out Plans for Change." *Wall Street Journal*, August 6, 1998, pp. A3, A6.

Bradsher, Keith. "In South America, Auto Makers See One Big Showroom." *New York Times*, April 25, 1997, pp. D1, D4.

————. "One Thrives, the Other Doesn't." *New York Times*, May 16, 1997, pp. D1, D3.

————. "G.M.'s Plant in Brazil Raises Fears Closer to Home." *New York Times*, June 17, 1998, pp. A1, D22.

————. "General Motors Plans to Build New, Efficient Assembly Plants." *New York Times*, August 6, p. A1.

Brooke, James. "Brazil's Big Winner." *New York Times*, October 5, 1994, p. A1.

EIU. "Brazil's Motor Industry: Output Poised for 40% Growth to 2000." *Motor Business International*, fourth quarter 1997, Chapter 2.

————. "Argentina's Motor Industry: In the Aftermath of the Crisis." *Motor Business International*, second quarter 1998, Chapter 6.

————. "Brazil's Motor Industry: A Temporary Blip or an Ominous Warning?" *Motor Business International*, fourth quarter 1998, Chapter 4.

"Emerging Market Indicators." *The Economist*, February 6, 1999, p. 110; May 22, 1999, p. 116.

Friedland, Jonathan. "Car Wars: Latin Consumers Gain as Makers Upgrade." *Wall Street Journal*, June 23, 1995, p. A10.

Fritsch, Peter. "Latin Nations Take Big Step on Car Tariffs." *Wall Street Journal*, December 11, 1998, p. A10.

Fritsch, Peter, and Gregory L. White. "Even Rivals Concede GM Has Deftly Steered Road to Success in Brazil." *Wall Street Journal*, February 28, 1999, pp. A1, A8.

"G.M. Is Investing in 3 New Brazil Plants." *New York Times*, December 3, 1996, p. D4.

Kamm, Thomas. "Brazil Swiftly Becomes Major Auto Producer as Trade Policy Shifts." *Wall Street Journal*, April 20, 1994, pp. A1, A5.

"The Modular T." *The Economist*, September 5, 1998, pp. 60–61.

Moffett, Matt. "Bruised in Brazil: Ford Slips as Market Booms." *Wall Street Journal*, December 13, 1997, p. A10.

Moffett, Mathew. "Brazil's Auto Industry Maneuvers a Comeback; GM, Ford, Others Benefit." *Wall Street Journal*, May 14, 1998, p. A18.

Reid, Michael. "Mercosur Survey." *The Economist*, October 12, 1996.

Reitman, Valerie. "Ford to Invest up to $1 Billion in Brazil, Revving an Already-Competitive Market." *Wall Street Journal*, October 3, 1997, p. A4.

Reuters Internet news release via Yahoo.com/October 2, 1997, "Ford, Brazil State Sign Accord to Build Car Plant."

Reuters news release via Yahoo.com/January 18, 1999, "Ford Argentine Unit, Union Agree [on] Suspension."

Rohter, Larry. "There's a Lot of Grit in Brazil." *New York Times*, April 23, 1991, pp. C1, C14.

Schemo, Diana Jean. "Economic Detour in Brazil." *New York Times*, September 26, 1998, pp. C1, C14.

Velde, Francois R., and Marcelo Veracierto. "Dollarization in Argentina." *Chicago Fed Letter*, Federal Reserve Bank of Chicago, June 1999.

Yamaguchi, Noriko. "DaimlerChrysler Rolls out First Brazil-Made Car." Reuters news release via Yahoo.com/April 23, 1999.

Chapter 8

Foreign Development of China's Motor Vehicle Industry

While China's economic development in the last decades has been remarkable, it is still a poor country highly dependent on foreign capital, technology, and managerial expertise for implementing its ambitious industrialization plans. Foremost among these efforts are Beijing's plans for a modern motor vehicle industry with minimal loss of central government control to foreign multinational enterprises and to "reform-minded" domestic politicoeconomic forces that such industrialization tends to provoke. China's political hierarchy is especially haunted by the Tiananmen Square massacre, even though the violent government reaction failed to deter foreign manufacturers from investing in the world's most populated country or inhibited its workers from embracing the new opportunities for improving their livelihood. The resulting rise in living standards is increasing the demand for transportation in general and motor vehicles in particular, a development that comfortably fits in with the industrial plans of government officials, who have anointed the automobile industry as a major engine of economic development and mass production.

MODERN DEVELOPMENT

The beginning of China's contemporary moves toward a motor vehicle industry can be traced to 1976, the year that witnessed the passing of Mao Zedong and Zhou Enlai and the returning to power of Deng Xiaoping (Zhou's protégé), who became the modern architect of China's economic development. Among his radical moves, the communist leader:

1. Established private (as opposed to state) ownership of farms and the market setting of prices for farm output.

2.   Opened China's closed economy to investment funds and technology from abroad, allowing foreign ownership in joint ventures with local partners.

3.   Rehabilitated the status and work of scientists and engineers in Chinese society, who under Mao's Cultural Revolution had been "reeducated" in menial tasks under peasant, rural conditions.

4.   Encouraged young Chinese to study abroad.

5.   Negotiated the return of Hong Kong to Chinese sovereignty while allowing the former crown colony to retain its free enterprise mode of business.

Deng's imprimatur on these revolutionary moves was publicly emblazoned on his historic trip in 1979 to the United States, in the process restoring normal diplomatic and economic relations with the United States.

The reforms accelerated economic output in China's agricultural sector, and foreign capital and technology fostered industrialization and trade, which, in turn, gave rise to a business class with needs for efficient means of communication and transportation for the distribution of goods and services as well as for domestic/international business travel. These needs ran up against China's antiquated infrastructure (roads, ports, telecommunications systems), a result of neglect under the communist regime. To rectify the situation, Beijing turned to the West, Japan, and overseas Chinese for aid, direct foreign investments, and technical and managerial expertise in exchange for business opportunities in its large consumer market.

FOREIGN AID

On a net disbursement basis, official development assistance (ODA) from the government of Japan to the Chinese government was pronounced over the five-year period 1989–1993. In 1989 such aid came to $832.18 million, constituting 55.7% of total aid extended to China on a bilateral, government-to-government basis. The numbers for subsequent years were 1990: $723 million (51%); 1991: $585.29 million (46.3%); 1992: $1,050 million (50.6%); and 1993: $1,250 million (60.2%). These sums were mainly used for the construction of water plants and sewage facilities, bridges, railways, chemical fertilizer plants, ports, and some highway and subway (in Beijing) projects. Second to Japan's ODA to China in 1993 was Germany with $247.8 million, followed by Spain ($140.1 million), Italy ($135.5 million), and France ($102.6 million). In 1994 Japan's ODA to China grew to $1,479.41 million, which can be broken down into grant aid of $99.42 million, technical cooperation ($246.91 million), and loans ($1,133.07 million). Among international organizations, the International Development Agency (the soft loan section of the World Bank) came in first in 1993 ODA disbursements to China of $865.1 million, followed by the United Nations Development Program at $44.8 million (*Japan's Official Development Assistance Annual Report 1995*, 305–309).

Highway Construction

Part of the developmental assistance is used for highway construction as the Chinese government inexorably moves to put its masses behind the wheel of a compact "people's car" costing close to $5,000. While the growth of paved highways is impressive—from 1952 to 1992, paved roads increased from 34,300 miles to 575,300 miles—"the few dozen short stretches of modern freeways built in the last decade are almost lost in a rural landscape where dirt paths and narrow farm-to-market lanes still predominate" (Tyler 1994, D8). Such road building is needed to support the state's plan of producing 3 million motor vehicles in the year 2000, half of them automobiles as opposed to trucks and minivans, with production up from 1.5 million units in 1994. With rising incomes and growing consumer appetite for autos, state planners view auto production as the driving force for sustained economic growth. From 1996 to 1997, for example, the production/assembly of passenger cars was expected to expand by 25.7 %, while the increase in other commercial vehicles was only 4.8%. This is a sharp break from prior statistics, which favored the production of trucks and buses for both military and economic development purposes and not for use by a poor populace that could hardly afford to buy cars in the first place.

TRUCK MANUFACTURING

With close ties to the military and especially during the hypersensitive period of the Cold War between East and West, China's motor vehicle manufacturing shunned reliance on firms from the West or Japan, with the mainly state-owned companies using old, available designs and technology from the 1940s. The principal manufacturers included the state-affiliated First Automotive Works (FAW), Dong Feng Motor Corporation (Second Automotive Works or SAW), and Nanjing Motor (FAW and SAW are more recently known as First Auto Group and either Dongfeng Motor or Aeolus Automotive Corporation, respectively). An exception was Beijing Jeep (a joint venture with the Chrysler Corporation, the American owner of Jeep, and Beijing Automotive Works), which in 1995 had an estimated annual production of 90,000 vehicles, placing it in a tie for third with Nanjing Motor and behind SAW at 175,000 units and FAW with 150,000 (EIU second quarter 1996, 76–78).

Established in 1950 in Changchun, FAW began production of medium-weight (three- to five-ton) trucks using antiquated Soviet Union technology as well as its vertically divided labor system. In such a system, parts manufacturing (beginning with rudimentary operations like forging and casting, to final assembly of the motor vehicle) was done within the confines of a single enterprise like FAW or SAW. This permitted supervisors and unskilled workers to visualize how their work fitted in with the end product, and the making of their own parts from raw materials obviated any dependence on external suppliers as well as the need to interact with slovenly government bureaucracies in order to obtain parts from another manufacturer. Moreover, in the 1950s, there were few parts suppliers around. The elementary work system was on the order of a large job shop (going back to the time before Henry Ford's mass-production methods), leaving little in the nature of cost cutting through economies of scale. In addition, the crude industrial times and geographic expanse of China encouraged the proliferation of these vertically integrated, low-production factories as each region adopted similar self-reliant systems for the start-up of its manufacturing needs. Productivity numbers illustrate how backward such systems were compared to those in the modern world: in 1981 the Chinese motor vehicle industry employed 904,000 workers to make 176,000 four-wheel units, while Japan in 1980 used 683,000 workers to make over 11 million vehicles (Marukawa 1995, 330–355).

Enterprise Amalgamation

With such comparisons, even the central government came to understand the need for rationalization in the industry, and in 1980 FAW began the process of taking over smaller companies, with the number coming to ten by the end of 1982. It included a merger with Automotive Research Institute, China's only motor vehicle research center at the time. The amalgamation process continued in 1986 as FAW wrested control of auto-making firms from municipal governments like those in Jilin and Changchun, whose managerial and technical expertise as well as financial resources were, at best, quite limited. By 1992 FAW had grown to 149 firms and six institutions, but the transition did not go smoothly, as the company's top administrators had to share control over segments of the massive enterprise with powerful city governments that may have relinquished their authority over local plants but still retained regulatory rights and even received profits from these units. Considerable regulations and challenges were also forthcoming from the central government in the guise of the First Ministry of Machine Building, which was, in turn, supplanted by the more specific China Auto Industry General Corporation as the industry grew and subsequently by the China National Auto Industry Corporation (Yang 1995, Chapter 4). The latter may have exercised some power over foreign exchange spending, but it had its own budgetary problems, which often placed it at a disadvantage vis-à-vis other state and local authorities.

Up until the late 1950s, the mandate for the fledgling industry was the meeting of government production targets by simple reproduction of available technology. The design and development of new products and processes were strictly relegated to the military on behalf of its efforts to keep up in the East–West arms race. The resulting moribund approach to civilian needs may have been fitting in a peasant economy, but as industrialization continued to spread in China, the inherent inefficiencies began consuming inordinate amounts of scarce capital. Thoughts of earning foreign exchange through exports were also dashed by the low-quality production even as surrounding Asian "tigers," led by Japan, were charging into the transpacific trade. FAW's lack of innovation was apparent to the First Ministry of Machine Building even as it was turning the state enterprise into a truck-making monopoly. Nevertheless, during the technologically static times and political turmoil under Chairman Mao, little innovation was dared or expected by the manufacturing enterprise and its governing agency.

Formation of SAW. By the early 1960s, technical assistance from the Soviet Union was breaking off as the two erstwhile comrades began fortifying their long border against possible attack. This led Mao in 1967 to plan a second truck-making facility in the remote village of Shiyan of Hubei province in an effort to disperse his industrial base and camouflage it from the Soviet Union whose engineers had been intimately associated with the construction of FAW's Changchun plant (see Figure 8.1 for plant sites). Progress of the new enterprise proceeded slowly because of the site's remoteness, the lack of Soviet technical input, and the marauding of the Red Guard, who were running amok in Mao's Cultural Revolution. SAW's start-up therefore had to wait until 1978, when Deng, following Mao's death, restored order. SAW also became a manifestation of the new leader's economic reforms, introducing limited competition but not privatization in the critical activity of truck production. Reform accelerated in 1979 as legislation was introduced paving the way for purchase and licensing of foreign technology. In the new work environment, SAW quickly established its own research center at Shiyan and manned it with graduates of Qinghua University and Jillin University of Technology, which had the best auto engineering programs in the country. Such profit-enhancing R&D was heavily pushed in the early 1980s by state and military enterprises to make up for the deep cuts that Deng was inflicting on their budgets. (In this push for profits, the army came to control 10,000 business entities, both foreign and domestic.) SAW also began its own amalgamation process, with member firms rising to "109 in 1984, 202 in 1987, and 301 in 1989" (Marukawa 1995, 337–338).

The corporate members of Dongfeng Motor Group (as SAW is now called) are spread over twenty eight provinces and collectively have close to 350,000 employees. The group's operating entity is Dongfeng Motor Corporation, and it has three main manufacturing divisions located in Shiyan for trucks, Xiangfen for engines and gearboxes, and Wuhan for passenger cars (EIU 1997, 69–78). Other truck manufacturers have also appeared on the scene, but these have had minimal impact: by 1992 Dongfeng and FAW held 98% of the medium-size truck market. To further assist their product and process development, both enterprises turned to foreign technology to get in on the government's embrace of passenger cars. Nevertheless, First and Second Auto Works principally remained truck manufacturers, as the data in Table 8.1 indicate, with Dongfeng overtaking FAW in truck production but lagging badly in the more important passenger car business.

Privatization Plans. In the mid-1990s Dongfeng Motor Corporation undertook the streamlining of its managerial decision making in an effort to diversify its product line following a dramatic fall in market share—from 34% in 1990 to 14.5% in 1996—endured by medium-weight trucks, which the company mainly produces. The revamping was also instituted to undergird management plans to tap foreign capital markets by selling stock on, for example, the New York Stock Exchange. The effort failed, however, when

Figure 8.1
Motor Vehicle Production Sites

Source: Leslie S. Hiraoka. "Foreign Development of China's Motor Vehicle Industry," *International Journal of Technology Management* (in press), Figure 1. Inderscience Enterprises Ltd. (IJTM@inderscience.com)

Table 8.1
Production and Sales of Principal Manufacturers, 1992

		Production, units	Sales (in 10,000 yuan)
FAW	trucks	82,460	1,019,551
	chassis	18,320	
	passenger cars	15,127	
SAW	trucks	97,913	730,623
	chassis	30,106	
	passenger cars	801	
Beijing Jeep Corp.	BJ 2020 Jeeps	36,244	348,989
	Cherokee Jeeps	20,001	
Jinbei Auto Co.	light trucks	24,855	341,501
	light buses	8,111	
	vans	4,715	
Nanjing Auto Works	light trucks	43,970	283,203
	chassis	13,930	
Tianjin Light Passenger Car Works	light vans	3,069	207,663
	passenger cars	30,150	

Source: Tomoo Marukawa, "Industrial Groups and Division of Labor in China's Automobile Industry," *The Developing Economies*, 33(3) (September 1995): 336.

corporate revenues sagged from 13.4 billion renminbi (rmb) in 1994 to 10.9 billion rmb the following year. This caused profits before taxes to drop precipitously from 1.74 billion rmb, to 360 million rmb, clearly showing that bloated operating costs were still the norm. The dismal income statement resulted in the company's failure to meet listing requirements of a prominent stock market.

Other state enterprises, however, have met with success, and their shares now trade on New York's Big Board, reflecting the government's relaxed attitude toward foreign, private equity participation in state companies. The privatization move was further boosted in September 1997, when a Communist Party Congress endorsed the sale of the bulk of China's 13,000 largest state entities to private share owners. Ideologically, the party is explaining its turn to capitalism as a move to a diversified public ownership of the government's assets. The radical departure, moreover, is illustrated by the absence of a legal, judicial canon governing free enterprise and private ownership in China. No doubt, its leaders will be looking to the West and Japan for the basis of a new business law system with the emphatic proviso that changes in industrial structure will not adversely impact the existing political setup (Faison, September 17, 1997). Such reconciliation may prove difficult given China's tremendous need for foreign inputs to meet the rising demands of a burgeoning consumer economy.

JOINT VENTURES WITH FOREIGN MAKERS

The manufacture of light trucks, Jeeps, and passenger cars, almost all with foreign technical assistance, is presented in Table 8.1, with Jeeps a transition vehicle between trucks and cars (or automobiles). Currently, the Jeep is considered a light truck, or more commonly, sport utility vehicle in the United States, whereas in China it is more akin to the passenger car. Its hybrid characteristics enable the transportation of goods and people, making Jeep an ideal car—as government authorities thought—for China's massive population and rugged land area. At the time of China's initial interest in Jeep, its parent, American Motors Corporation, was a floundering enterprise that had failed to seize market opportunities during the gasoline shortages of the 1970s. In 1979 a controlling 46% of AMC was purchased by Renault of France, where it became a major drain financially on its new French owner. AMC's precarious state may have paradoxically endeared it to a xenophobic Chinese government, which was cautiously looking abroad for foreign technology and partners and extremely fearful of being railroaded by giant multinational corporations like GM and Ford.

Negotiations began in 1979 between American Motors and Beijing Automotive Works and culminated in the signing of a joint-venture agreement— the first of its kind between a Chinese government enterprise and foreign company—on May 3, 1983. Beijing Automotive Works would own 68.15% of the daughter Beijing Jeep Corporation, with the remaining interest held by AMC. The American firm committed $16 million to the joint venture as well as operating and design technology for a light, durable, and inexpensive vehicle for China's huge consumer market. Until the new design and production plant was in operation, Beijing Jeep worked off the old design, designated BJ 212, which had been produced earlier by Beijing Automotive. It also assembled AMC's Cherokee XJ Jeep from completely knockdown kits imported from the United States (Harwit 1995, 67–70).

Along with the formation of the Beijing Jeep joint venture, a second set of successful negotiations occurred between Volkswagen and the Shanghai Tractor and Auto Corporation. The landmark deals confirmed China's turn to the West and the use of foreign, advanced technology, especially for the development of its passenger car industry. The joint ventures were also geared to stem the outward flow of foreign exchange to Japan for imported automobiles, which were seen more frequently on China's roads. The turn to indigenous production and import substitution also produced twenty six other technology transfer projects with foreign makers, these centering on auto parts manufacturing. The new projects, however, failed to stem the shortage of quality parts during the 1980s that constantly plagued the production schedules of final product assemblers.

Money Crisis

The lack of foreign exchange also became a severe problem for the government even as it was attempting to curb imports with domestic production. The licensing of foreign technology, payments to foreign engineers and technicians needed to transfer the technology, purchase and translation of design manuals, and import payments for completely knockdown kits assembled by both Beijing Jeep and Shanghai VW, the second joint venture, precipitated a financial crisis in the mid-1980s, when American Motors stopped shipments of the kits until Beijing Jeep caught up with back payments. The problem for Jeep Cherokee financing was inevitable since the imported kits were paid for in hard currency, while vehicle sales in China were denominated in the country's soft currency. The crisis was resolved when Zhu Rongji, the vice minister of the State Economic Commission and future prime minister, brokered a deal that essentially limited imports of the Cherokee kits, with assembly concentrated on the homegrown 212 model and local sourcing of parts for use in the Cherokee. Production resumed under this arrangement, with 24,000 units made in 1986; 26,000 in 1987; 31,000 in 1988; and nearly 40,000 in 1989, which included 6,600 Cherokee Jeeps (Harwit 1995, 77–78). The latter number grew to 20,000 units in 1992 (see Table 8.1) as industrialization, growing Chinese exports of light manufactures like apparel and toys, and direct foreign investments from abroad allayed the shortage of hard currencies and increased consumer purchasing power. By the 1990s China was building a growing surplus in its merchandise trade account with the United States, which reached $22.8 billion in 1993. Government officials now actively promoted the automobile as an export earner and sought entry into the World Trade Organization. The economic activity produced sizable gains in real growth of China's gross domestic product, with annual gains averaging 8.6% from 1989 to 1993 and climbing to 13.4% in 1993. The positive statistics, however, did not enhance the relative positions of either American Motors or the Beijing Jeep joint venture. AMC became a wholly owned subsidiary of Chrysler in 1987, and Beijing Jeep was forced to share the still-small Chinese car market with Volkswagen and Toyota. Chrysler subsequently failed in its attempt to expand when its bid in 1995 to build a $1 billion van and engine plant lost out to Mercedes-Benz of Germany. Two years later, the company closed its office in Beijing, citing slow growth in vehicle production and lack of opportunity in China compared to other areas such as Latin America.

AUTOMOBILE PRODUCTION

Failing to penetrate the military monopsony in trucks, except for Jeep, foreign manufacturers (other than Chrysler and Peugeot) are participating in the faster-growing car market in partnership with China's central and local governments, among them the country's largest city, Shanghai. Production leaders in passenger cars include Shanghai Volkswagen, Beijing Jeep, Tianjin Auto (with Daihatsu technology), FAW (with VW), Changan (Suzuki technology), FAW Audi, Guangzhou Peugeot (terminated), and Dongfeng with Citroen. Table 8.2 lists the manufacturers with production numbers and sales figures for 1995. The lengthening list of international arrangements confirms China's acknowledgment that foreign companies are needed to supply vital expertise in product and process design, cost and quality control, and start-up and production scheduling to meet the more sophisticated demands of a car-buying public that is becoming aware of what is available in the West and Japan.

German Entry

Volkswagen clearly remains the largest producer in China, with Shanghai VW, FAW-VW, and FAW (Audi) ventures. Audi is a subsidiary of VW, accounting for over 58% of 1994 production. VW's early success can be attributed to Beijing's geopolitical concerns about becoming too involved with Japanese and American firms. The Chinese government probably felt that there was enough commercial interaction with Japan Inc. and, as discussed, seized upon an import substitution program in the mid-1980s designed to limit Japanese imports. Beijing also remains irritated with Washington's public pronouncements about the Tiananmen Square massacre, China's human rights violations, and rampant piracy of U.S. intellectual property rights (books, films, computer software). In comparison, distant Germany was much less threatening and also possessed the requisite technology.

Consequently, even before Deng Xiaoping's return to power, a machine-building vice minister was sounding out Volkswagen's interest in a joint venture that would transfer German technology to China and upgrade manufacturing facilities and capabilities to eventually result in an export industry. Four years of discussions had elapsed when, in 1982, VW proposed a trial assembly of completely knockdown kits of the Santana nameplate exported from Germany for fabrication in the Shanghai auto plant. The experiment demonstrated the feasibility of assembling the VW kits, and in product comparisons the Santana easily bested the sedans that the Shanghai plant was producing based on an old Mercedes model. Chinese officials also pursued VW's assistance in designing the blueprints and accompanying assembly lines for a new model car to be made in the renovated Shanghai facilities, with its production obviating the need for imported kits. VW engineers deemed this request highly impractical given the substandard plant conditions and immediately vetoed it (Harwit 1995, 94–97).

Even without agreeing to this key issue, Volkswagen, following its successful demonstration, was asked to join a 50–50 joint venture in October

Table 8.2
1995 Chinese Production and Sales (units) of Automobiles

	Production (est.)	Sales
FAW-VW	20,200	20,000
FAW (Audi)	17,000	20,000
Dongfeng (Citroen)	4,400	30,000
Shanghai VW	149,000	160,000
Changan (Suzuki)	18,000	20,000
Tianjin Auto (Daihatsu)	66,000	65,000
Beijing Jeep	25,900	30,000

Sources: EIU, *Motor Business Asia-Pacific*, first quarter 1998, p. 48; EIU, *Motor Business International*, second quarter 1996, pp. 76–78; "The Long Drive into the Middle Kingdom," *The Economist*, June 8, 1996, pp. 63–64.

1984 with three state and municipal authorities led by the Shanghai Tractor and Auto Corporation (name changed to Shanghai Automotive Industry Corporation), having a 25% equity share, a trust and consultancy arm of the Bank of China (15%), and the China National Auto Industry Corporation (10%). The Shanghai VW joint venture was capitalized at close to $40 million and was signed by no less than Chancellor Helmut Kohl of West Germany and China's Premier Zhao Ziyang (Harwit 1995, 96–97).

The exuberant fanfare at the signing failed to mask the backward state of manufacturing that VW engineers had uncovered in their demonstration. Extensive renovation of the Shanghai car plant, infrastructural development for movement of parts and product to and from the plant, retraining of Chinese plant personnel (many in Germany), and establishing financing and banking services all became immediate concerns, with frequent slow progress accompanying halting production of the completely knockdown kits. In its first year, Shanghai VW turned out 3,356 Santanas which rose to 10,470 in 1987; 34,000 in 1991; 66,000 in 1992, and 115,300 in 1994 (EIU, first quarter 1996, 8–12). The lack of quality parts suppliers became VW's greatest obstacle, and the problem was compounded by both the government's insistence on 80% local content of assembled units and the lethargic productivity gains of the communist-indoctrinated workforce. Chinese parts suppliers made some quality improvements through licensing of foreign technology, but this was offset by the frequent use of substandard parts produced locally. With such defective parts usage, the 80% local content target was reached in 1992–1993. VW had encountered similar makeshift production in prior operations in East Germany and had come to expect frustratingly slow progress in dealing with China's unmotivated workers and slothful bureaucracy.

The 1990s ushered in a surging Chinese economy and concurrent amelioration of foreign exchange shortfalls. These developments rebounded to Shanghai VW's benefit by allowing the joint venture greater freedom in importing and the use of foreign parts. The access to quality parts accelerated production at the plant, with profits rising to $154 million in 1991 and falling in 1992 to $87 million, reflecting the usual vicissitudes of doing business in China. The earnings further financed continued capital investment and retooling, which reached about $300 million at the end of 1992, allowing Shanghai VW to overtake Beijing Jeep as China's showcase venture for motor vehicle production (Harwit 1995, 103–104).

The country's considerable success in international trade also brought government demands for a high-quality product that could compete against foreign imports once protectionist barriers were phased out. These included a 260% tariff on completely built-up units, with all imports accompanied by mandatory licenses issued by a slovenly and byzantine bureaucracy. Such barriers would have to be removed if China's sought-after membership in the World Trade Organization was to be approved. Production costs would also have to come down if the Santana, with ex-factory price of $20,000 in 1992, was to compete in its own and world markets. The seeming paradox of high operating costs in a poor country with labor rates of $125 a month is understandable from the perspective of communist state dogma, which forbade the layoff of workers, leading to vastly inflated payrolls. Political graft and employee theft also added to costs. The dated design of the Santana model— which may have been suitable for China's needs— further made competition in global markets highly problematic; in the blunt words of Shanghai VW's managing director, Fang Hong, "It will not be easy to export. The Santana is an old car and no one wants an old car" (Meyer 1992, 50–51). Volkswagen's engineers, however, are not enthusiastic about redesigning the model and its assembly lines. Their simpler and more tenable plan calls for increased output to decrease per unit production costs, which may make the Santana price competitive in less-developed markets in and around China.

Expansion Agreements

As the preceding shows, the auto industry made a measurably successful beginning using foreign technology, and rising output prompted government officials to approve two more production sites in addition to the Shanghai VW and Beijing Jeep factories. One of them was in Changchun, where in 1988 VW entered into a licensing agreement with FAW to assemble the Audi 100 model. The first Audi came off the assembly line in 1988, with production rising to 20,000 units in 1994. The licensing agreement was terminated in 1997, although production continued based on the German technology. A letter of intent was also signed in 1988 between FAW and Volkswagen to form a joint venture to assemble the Jetta car at the Changchun Audi location beginning with construction of a greenfield, 150,000-car-per-year assembly plant as well as engine and transmission factories. These negotiations took only eighteen months to complete, indicating the close cooperation between China and VW that had ensued from the Shanghai VW project. FAW would own a majority 60% of the joint venture, which began meaningful production of 8,000 Jettas in 1992 (EIU, first quarter 1996, 8–12).

Volkswagen's earlier experience in Shanghai and with FAW operations through the Audi licensing deal permitted the simultaneous production of parts and finished vehicles even as the new plant was being built. To assist in this effort, FAW had shrewdly purchased a body shop in North America that was disassembled and shipped to the new production site, where, with welding equipment from VW, the reassembled shop began rudimentary body production in 1992. Painting and final assembly were subsequently done at the nearby FAW (Audi) plant, where production was temporarily stopped to accommodate the Jetta work. Such makeshift production was possible even before the Jetta assembly line was completed because all three companies had vested (equity) interests in the Jetta joint venture: FAW, 60%; VW, 30%; Audi, 10% (EIU, first quarter 1996, 8–12). By early 1998 VW had invested $1 billion in the new facilities, with operating losses reaching close to $100 million because of poor sales. In contrast, the Shanghai VW plant is running at 80% of capacity and is making money through the captive sales of Santana cars to the city of Shanghai for use by municipal employees and taxi fleets (Smith and Blumenstein 1998, A8). VW is further benefiting from the export sales of Santana completely knockdown kits to the Shanghai joint venture for which it is paid in Chinese renminbi exchangeable for deutshemarks at a preset, profit-making currency rate. In the south of China, VW is earning licensing fees from FAW for the production technology of its CitiGolf car now being made at a plant in Shunde (EIU, first quarter 1996, 8–12).

Volkswagen's front-running status in the world's largest country should be juxtaposed against its retreat in the United States, the largest and richest market for motor vehicles. With its 7.2% U.S. market share in 1970 and strong brand loyalty among American Beetle drivers, VW appeared poised to capture the small-car market once the Arab oil embargo began in 1973. The Japanese imports, however, proved formidable with sleeker, new designs, easy handling, swifter acceleration, and low emission of pollutants, and these attributes overwhelmed the slow, noisy VW Bug, whose market share sank to 2.6% in 1983. The company attempted to stem the downturn in the mid-1970s with introduction of new Golf and Rabbit models and movement of production to the United States with the purchase of a mothballed Chrysler plant in Pennsylvania. In this, VW would be ahead of Japanese direct investments in the United States just as it would be a decade later in China. U.S. sales, however, did not revive, and in 1988, the Pennsylvania plant was closed after experiencing considerable labor turmoil.

Other Losses

Following a diplomatic dispute over the president of Taiwan's visit to the United States in July 1995, Beijing, once again playing its geopolitical cards, awarded a $1 billion van project to Mercedes of Germany for the production of 60,000 vans and 100,000 engines a year in Nanfeng. Among the losing bidders were both Chrysler and Ford from the United States. Mercedes has a 45% minority interest in the joint venture, with South China Automotive Corporation holding 55% (Nash 1995). Even with production yet to begin, interest by Mercedes in the project is flagging, and it may consider withdrawing from it (Smith and Blumenstein 1998, A8). Furthermore, the megamerger between Daimler-Benz (parent company of Mercedes) and the Chrysler Corporation will undoubtedly refocus additional attention away from the China market.

Mercedes' early disappointment follows losses suffered by PSA Peugeot Citroen of France in its two joint ventures: Guangzhou Peugeot and Dongfeng Citroen, the latter in Wuhan. In early 1997 PSA abandoned its factory in Guangzhou due to problems with its local partner, low output, lack of quality parts, and mounting losses. The low output at both plants is mirrored in production for 1993 and 1994, when it crashed at the Guangzhou plant from 16,700 to 5,200 units and at the Wuhan site from 17,100 to 8,000 units (EIU, second quarter 1996, 76–78). The end of the Peugeot project follows Renault's earlier retreat in 1987, when it sold its interest in American Motors and Beijing Jeep to Chrysler.

ENTRY BY GENERAL MOTORS

GM's bid to take over the abandoned Peugeot plant also met failure, but it has not slowed the company's effort to invest $2 billion in China over the next two years beginning in 1998. The principal focus for the world's largest carmaker is a $1.5 billion plant that GM is constructing with Shanghai Automotive Industry Corporation (SAIC) to make 150,000 Buick Century sedans a year with production begun before the end of the century. SAIC is the same agency involved with Shanghai VW and is "one of the nation's most profitable state-owned companies with an expert distribution and servicing network" (Faison 1995). It enjoys strong political support from Zhu Rongji, China's new prime minister and mayor of Shanghai from 1988 to 1991, who helped broker the Shanghai VW deal and resolve the Beijing Jeep payments crisis.

China has been intensely interested in GM's technical and financial prowess and, in exchange for awarding it the Shanghai project, received from the American corporation two R&D centers located in Beijing and Shanghai, which were established and run by GM's Delphi Automotive Systems as well as "a huge pan-Asian technical-training center to groom as many as 1,000 engineers a year" (Smith and Blumenstein 1998, A8). GM, furthermore, has twenty one parts-making operations in China and hopes to mass-produce two light trucks and a small car in the future. The corporate giant's surging investments signal China's growing confidence in dealing with the world's largest industrial corporation and in turning the country toward a market-oriented economy. Both changes survived the death in 1997 of principal advocate and reformer Deng Xiaoping and were advanced in the same year when the new president, Ziang Zemin, like Deng, made a historic visit to Washington, D.C., to promote better relations between the transpacific nations. Concurrently, the Fifteenth Communist Party Congress voted to sell off most of the state-owned enterprises, giving a further boost to Western style capitalism.

GM's current ambitious program in China, while, in part, responding to Beijing's new capitalistic pursuits, can be equally ascribed to the global plans of its chairman and chief executive officer, John F. Smith Jr., who became CEO in 1992. At the time, GM was still reeling from the twin competitive blows of the Japanese export blitz of the 1970s and its transplanted factories in the United States of the 1980s. Comparatively high production and labor costs resulted in GM's losing money on the majority of vehicles it sold. By continuing the aggressive downsizing started in the 1980s, which, under Smith, resulted in the closing of twenty nine factories and more massive layoffs, the company's North American Automotive Operations underwent a startling financial recovery. Even with domestic operations revived and showing strong profits, GM's CEO realized that future growth would have to come from abroad because the home market where the company had most of its sales had become a mature, replacement, enormously competitive arena. Consequently, to maintain corporate growth and profits, GM was forced to pursue global economies of scale in new growth markets like Asia/Pacific, which was expected to grow by 40% over the next ten years to constitute 30% of the world's market. Direct foreign investments to add production capacity are subsequently occurring at the highest rates in GM's history.

In this global game plan, the huge, dynamic Asian continent mainly revolving around China has naturally become a focal point for the world's largest manufacturer, with its CEO explicitly citing these national attributes motivating GM's thinking:

1.   China's strong growth rate would make it the second largest economy in the new millennium.

2.   While still poor, its per capita income could double every eight years, with growth at a high 9% per year.

3.   High level of personal savings—nearly 50% of income—would generate internal funds for needed capital investment.

4.   A very young workforce with 45% of China's 1.2 billion population under the age of twenty six, which results in a youthful subpopulation greater than the total population of the United States, Japan, Germany, Great Britain, and Canada (Smith 1997).

Prompted by the preceding incentives, GM is gearing up for a sustained effort in the Chinese market even as Asian economies in South Korea, Thailand, and Indonesia stumble into recession. The outcome of GM's momentous effort will have a profound impact on the world's motor vehicle industry and will determine if the company continues to play its preeminent role in the new millennium.

JAPANESE ROLE

Japan's Honda, Toyota, and Suzuki are also moving to the Asian mainland, but in slower, smaller steps than GM. Honda was recently approved by the government to produce 30,000 cars per year at the Guangzhou Peugeot plant abandoned by the French. The Japanese carmaker plans to invest $200 million in partnership with Guangzhou Auto Group and Dongfeng Motor, with the latter already producing engine and suspension components in China, using Honda's technology, for export to Honda plants outside China. Honda, like GM, intends to begin commercial production before the year 2000 provided approval is given by the government for a feasibility study currently being drafted by the company (Faison, November 14,1997).

Also planning to invest is Suzuki Motor in the Changan Automobile company, which already makes a minicar under license from Suzuki. Altogether, Suzuki has five plants in the country, making 260,000 motor vehicles per year, which are known for their durability and fuel-efficiency (Reitman 1998). Suzuki cars are, furthermore, showing the fastest growth in market share among car manufacturers, especially in China's huge countryside, where they are suitable for travel over very rugged terrain (Smith and Blumenstein 1998, A8). The Japanese maker is also well known in India, another giant developing country, where its Maruti model sells for $5,200 and has an 80% market share.

The popularity of Toyota vehicles both in and outside China is also evident. In 1995 sales, the Toyota Charade, made under license to Tianjin Automotive by its Japanese affiliate Daihatsu, moved to a clear second ranking, surpassing all other car companies except Shanghai VW (see Table 8.2). Outside China, Toyota's nameplates ended first in sales in the following countries: the Corona in Taiwan, the Corolla in the Philippines, the Hilux in Thailand, and the Kijang in Indonesia ("Lands of Opportunity"). To strengthen its China ties with Tianjin Automotive, Toyota will be entering into a joint venture with the local producer to manufacture 150,000 engines a year ("The Long Drive" 1996, 63-64).

SHIFTING OUTLOOK

Under the guidance of its central and local governments, China has moved into the production and marketing of a people's car for its huge consumer population. Technically backward and fearing much innovation, Beijing turned to Germany, and in particular, Volkswagen for the creation of Shanghai VW, which is becoming a business model for joint ventures between state agencies and foreign multinational enterprises. The objectives of the former—local development and technology transfer from advanced nations—clash constantly with the profit-oriented goals of the foreign makers, and such fundamental antagonism may yet doom China's industrialization plans. Already, the chairman of VW has indicated that being first in China was not enough; his global plans have shifted to being a major player in the United States, and VW is planning considerable investments there if the relaunched Beetle is successful. The patience for sales and profits in China is thus wearing thin, and it would behoove its government officials to understand this basic tenet of modern capitalism.

Table 8.3 numerically lists production projections for the growing passenger car market obtained from the Economist Intelligence Unit (EIU). Total production is expected to climb to 480,000 units in 1999 and 555,000 in the year 2000—far below the government's target of 1.5 million cars. Among manufacturers, Beijing Jeep and Dongfeng Citroen will probably become minor players, although the former is still expected to be a major producer of commercial trucks and vans. As the new millennium arrived, GM and Honda were still starting up operations, and, therefore, the increase in production will come from the two VW joint ventures and from the Chinese firms using Audi, Daihatsu, and Suzuki technologies. From 1994 to 1999, the percentages of technically based German cars grew from 40.2%, to over 55% of total

Table 8.3
1991 and 1994 Actual and 1999 Projected Production of Automobiles

Producer	1991	1994	1999
Tianjin Auto (Daihatsu)	11,300	58,500	110,000
Changan (Suzuki)	0	17,200	50,000
Shanghai VW	33,900	115,300	205,000
FAW (Audi)	7,000	20,000	25,000
FAW-VW	0	10,100	35,000
Beijing Jeep	11,000	13,900	32,000
Dongfeng Citroen	3,000	8,000	20,000

Sources: EIU, *Motor Business Asia-Pacific*, first quarter 1998, p. 48; EIU, *Motor Business International*, second quarter 1996, pp. 76–78.

production, a commanding lead for Volkswagen. Changan and Tianjin Auto will also see surging production, but the lack of an equity position in each may hamper the role played by the Japanese car companies whose technologies will be used.

Revival of Imports

The Japanese companies, however, do have strong market positions in the rest of Asia, and if foreign pressure such as from the World Trade Organization, which China wishes to join, forces Beijing to reduce its import barriers—erected to protect domestic production and save foreign exchange reserves—popular Japanese nameplates may once again pour into the Chinese market. The probability of such trade shifts is particularly high because the Asian currency crisis has sent demand crashing in those countries where the Japanese makers have significant production. Sales slumped 51% in both Thailand and Malaysia in the current recession beginning in July 1997, while in Indonesia, the Philippines, and South Korea, the downturn has been 49%, 21%, and 16%, respectively ("Car Trouble"1998).

The import picture should a priori share an inverse relationship with domestic production, particularly with the government's emphasis on local content and technology transfer. This was borne out in the 1980s, when Japanese imports took the lion's share of China's briefly opened market. Of 148,700 motor vehicles (trucks, Jeeps, and cars) imported in 1984, Toyota's share can be approximated by its sales in the same year of 40,000 units. As domestic production increased during the latter half of the 1980s, total imports fell from 354,000 in 1985, to 65,000 in 1990 (Yang 1995, 144–145). In the 1990s, however, both imports and production increased in concert, reflecting a booming economy and the popularity/competitiveness of Japanese imports. Despite the protectionist barriers, total imports climbed to 225,000 in 1992, paralleling strong increases in domestic output. The Japanese share of the import market was about 150,000, and Nissan sales tripled to 60,000 units in the same year (Harwit 1995, 39-40). The government's efforts at managing its trade consequently appear to be weakening with the rise of business activity and the continuing penchant for foreign goods.

CONCLUSIONS

While China's economic reforms were begun with a bang under Deng Xiaoping, its move into heavy industries like motor vehicle manufacturing has been stymied by the political straitjacket imposed by the Communist Party. This has meant delay and losses for both foreign and domestic firms, and while the outlook appears encouraging, a few major firms like Chrysler are looking elsewhere for opportunities. The bottom line is that profits have proved highly elusive even after sizable investments.

Overriding the business concerns are the global economic shifts such as the current currency crises gripping most of East Asia. Growth areas in Europe as well as North and South America are proving highly attractive to many auto executives in terms of their technology sharing and capital investments. A shift away from China could leave its fledgling motor vehicle industry with an obsolete base with few modernization possibilities, which will leave it a minor player in evolving global markets.

REFERENCES

"Car Trouble." *Business Week*, March 9, 1998, p. 48.
EIU. "Face to Face: With FAW-Volkswagen of China." *Motor Business Asia-Pacific*, first quarter 1996, Chapter 2, pp. 8–12.
———. "The Vehicle Markets of China, India and South Korea: Prospects Beyond 2000." *Motor Business International*, second quarter 1996, Chapter 6, pp. 76–78.
———. "A Strategic Profile of Dongfeng: Ambitious Agenda." *Motor Business Asia-Pacific*, fourth quarter 1997, Chapter 5.
———. "A Strategic Profile of Tianjin: China's Number Two Producer." *Motor Business Asia-Pacific*, first quarter 1998, Chapter 4, pp. 42–50.
Faison, Seth. "China Beckons and Car Makers Pant." *New York Times*, June 29, 1995, p. D7.
———. "A Great Tiptoe Forward: Free Enterprise in China." *New York Times*, September 17, 1997, p. A3.
———. "Honda Beating Out G.M., Plans to Build Cars in China." *New York Times*, November 14, 1997, p. D2.
Harwit, Eric. *China's Automobile Industry*. Armonk: NY: M.E. Sharpe, 1995.
Japan's Official Development Assistance Annual Report 1995. Tokyo: Ministry of Foreign Affairs.
"Lands of Opportunity." *New York Times*, June 6, 1996, p. D1.
Marukawa, Tomoo. "Industrial Groups and Division of Labor in China's Automobile Industry." *The Developing Economies*, 33(3) (September 1995): 330–355.
Meyer, Richard. "Beijing or Bust." *Financial World*, December 8, 1992, pp. 50–51.
Nash, Nathaniel. "China Gives Big Van Deal to Mercedes." *New York Times*, July 13, 1995, p. D1.
Reitman, Valerie. "Frugal Head of Suzuki Drives Markets in Asia." *Wall Street Journal*, February 26, 1998, p. A2.
Smith, Craig S., and Rebecca Blumenstein. "In China, GM Bets Billions on a Market Strewn with Casualties." *Wall Street Journal*, February 11, 1998, pp. A1, A8.
Smith, John F., Jr. Remarks at the General Motors Corporation annual stockholder's meeting, May 24, 1996.
———. "GM's Thinking on China." CEO Series Issue No. 12, Center for the Study of American Business, Washington University in St. Louis, January 1997.
Tyler, Patrick E. "China Planning People's Car to Put Masses behind Wheel." *New York Times*, September 22, 1994, pp. A1, D8.
Yang, Xiaohua. *Globalization of the Automobile Industry: The United States, Japan, and the Peoples's Republic of China*. Westport, CT: Praeger, 1995, Chapter 4.

Chapter 9

India: Out from the Nehru-Gandhi Shadow

The Himalayan contrasts between Asia's land giants derive from the democratic-socialistic institutions of India and the authoritarian, opaque nature of its northern neighbor's politicoeconomic system. A splintered leadership, entrenched bureaucracy, and eternally powerful vested interests in the status quo have produced painfully slow progress and considerable controversy in India, whose loud, but free, media continually broadcast the nation's shortcomings to the world. Westerners hear the din and routinely dismiss it as the ranting of the world's biggest beggar nation even as they are mesmerized by China's economic growth—conveniently forgetting the People's Republic of China's aggression against United Nations forces in the Korean War, the strife and bloodshed of the Cultural Revolution and the Tiananmen Square massacre, and the sale of nuclear weaponry to Pakistan and perhaps others. China's devaluation of its currency in the early 1990s to preempt Asian competitors in Western markets also helped instigate the economic crises racking Indonesia, Malaysia, Thailand, and Hong Kong. In contrast, India's highly regulated economy escaped the ravages of capital flight from domestic sources and the sudden exodus of "hot" foreign money, which East Asian countries initially welcomed at the behest of the International Monetary Fund and other advisers from the West and then found impossible to control.

The two giants will switch positions in the new millennium as India becomes the world's most populated country, but size alone will not be its greatest attribute. New Delhi's relatively peaceful transitions in freely elected governments contrast markedly with the political vicissitudes in Beijing, which may yet encounter the severe conditions that upended the Soviet Union. The uncertainty—at times, erupting into chaos—will continue to plague business in China, while the more transparent political system in India with its predictable government changes facilitates long-term business planning, especially in large, capital-intensive industries like motor vehicles because the major problems are visible before investments are made. In India's case, foreign multinational corporations escaped massive losses because they were simply kept out. The country extended no welcome mat after its people suffered through the imperialist exploitation of the British raj, and India would go it alone until circumstances proved that the outside world had something concrete to offer. China, on the other hand, was seeking foreign contacts and investments in the late 1970s, when Deng Xiaoping attempted to spur economic growth as a subterfuge for the lack of political freedoms that were being demanded by domestic and foreign voices.

NEHRUVIAN SOCIALISM

At the time of its independence in 1947, India was a poor, agrarian nation with considerable religious and caste strife requiring a strong central government to hold the subcontinent together. There was no industrial blueprint from Japan that would encourage it to seek foreign technology, investments, and markets. India's priorities centered on feeding itself and strengthening its forces against internal turmoil and foreign adversaries. Toward these ends, the nation came under the leadership and socialist, self-reliant policy of its founding father, Jawaharlal Nehru, who was India's first prime minister after independence until his death in 1964. Steering clear of Western capitalistic practices, Nehru embraced the Soviet style of planning and control of the fledgling industrial sector and received technical assistance and foreign aid from the Eurasian communist giant, with such assistance increasing as Sino–Soviet relations began to fray in the early 1960s. At the same time, serious land disputes separated China from India. These led to a massive Chinese invasion in 1962 of Aksai Chin, an area adjacent to the Indo-Pakistani hotly contested state of Kashmir. While a cease-fire was called the same year, Sino–Indo relations have been tense ever since with a de facto India/Soviet Union alliance facing a Chinese–Pakistani partnership. The warfare with communist China did little to alter Nehru's socialist views, primarily because it occurred toward the end of his life. At any rate, the prime minister had always articulated a middle-of-the-road foreign policy between East and West, choosing to be a Third World spokesman for nonaligned nations. While many of these nations succumbed to dictatorial regimes, Nehru persevered in keeping India's democratic institutions strong and did not dismantle the private enterprise system set up by the British.

Industrial Policy

The entire business sector came under stringent government regulations with the Industrial Policy Resolution of 1948, earmarking state monopolies in such key areas as munitions, atomic energy, railway transportation, aircraft manufacturing, and coal, iron, and steel industries. Initiatives left to the private sector included the assembly and manufacture of motor vehicles, although these operations came under the purview of the Industries Development and

Regulation Act of 1951. Motor vehicles—so important in modern transportation—largely escaped from government ownership because powerful British interests such as Morris Motors had formed ties, before independence, with local producers, and they withstood the challenges from a young, floundering central government. The cream-colored Hindustan Ambassador car—practically the only passenger vehicle on India's roads in the three decades following independence—is a classic example of vested interest's maintaining their hold in the absence of competition and innovation. The Ambassador, based on the 1950s technology and design of Britain's Morris Motors, was built by Hindustan Motors Ltd. of Calcutta, and it was easy to make and operate and, just as important, was affordable by a poor customer base. Foreign imports were not allowed, giving the Ambassador a huge, captive market. Furthermore, the automobile industry remained static during modern India's developmental stage, because trucks, not passenger vehicles, had the government's priority. Few new business permits were consequently given for carmaking ventures.

FORMATION OF TELCO

India's origins in commercial motor vehicles, as a result, came in the heavy vehicle manufacturing of trucks, buses, and locomotives. This is exemplified by the Tata Engineering and Locomotive Company (TELCO), which was formed in 1945 by the takeover of Singhbum Shops of the East India Railways by Tata Sons. From its first locomotive produced in 1952, TELCO has become one of the largest motor vehicle manufacturers in the country. The company's evolution to making trucks and buses was assisted by technology imported from Daimler-Benz, with the German firm making a 10% equity investment in the Tata enterprise. Other foreign tie-ups approved by the government because of the need for motor vehicles included Ashok Motors of Madras with the U.K.'s Leyland Motors and Premier Automobiles of Bombay with Fiat of Italy to make cars and Dodge, U.K. for trucks. Most of the Indian companies had incorporated before independence, giving them considerable leverage with the new government for approvals to take on foreign partners. Hindustan Motors, for example, was formed in 1942, followed by Premier Automobiles in 1944, Mahindra & Mahindra (as well as TELCO) in 1945. The early incorporations later facilitated the formation of joint ventures as Ashok Motors did with Leyland in 1948 soon after independence.

As Nehru's leadership became firmly established, government regulations increased, and in 1956 guidelines defining a motor vehicle manufacturer were published by the Tariff Commission. These stipulated that vehicle makers were required to be vertically integrated, with the capability of producing integral components (namely, engines, transmissions, rear axles, suspensions, and the chassis) from raw materials. Assembling completely knockdown kits, by itself, was not sufficient to be deemed a manufacturer, and the Tariff Commission specified only four firms—Hindustan Motors, Premier Automobiles, Standard Motor Products of India, and Ashok Motors—as qualified to make motor vehicles (Bowander 1998a, 647–648). In order to compete against the preceding four, TELCO teamed with Daimler-Benz and, with the foreign technology together with its own developmental efforts, became the least-cost manufacturer of diesel trucks in 1964. TELCO and other vehicle firms also invested in machining and press tools used in the making of dies, forges, and castings, which were then used to make vehicle component parts. Such requisite action by TELCO and others helped them assume leadership positions in the industry from start-up in the mid-1970s to current times, as shown in Table 9.1.

In the twenty one years separating the production listings, TELCO's leading position was relinquished to Maruti Udyog as the latter became the principal supplier of cars to a growing middle class. Maruti had actually been a government-sponsored enterprise before 1983, when, due to financial difficulties, it entered into a joint venture with Suzuki Motors of Japan. With the foreign technology, Maruti Udyog has captured upward of 77% of the small-car market. Also listed is Bajaj Tempo, formed in 1959, whose specialty in two-wheel vehicles is not reflected in the preceding statistics. TELCO's dominance survives in light commercial vehicles, where it held 61.5% of the domestic market in 1995 and an even larger 73.7% of medium and heavy vehicles which include the various weight classes of trucks, buses, dump trucks, and military vehicles, but no longer locomotives. TELCO has a puny 2.5% of the passenger car market, which it is trying greatly to improve. The effort is being hobbled by the firm's early success in truck manufacturing, which the government attempted to curb because of a supposed monopolistic threat.

ENTER MOTHER INDIRA

The restrictions began in the 1960s, when New Delhi itself came under tremendous pressure internally by the death of Nehru and failure of his socioeconomic policies and externally by the Chinese invasion of 1962 and a second war with Pakistan in September 1965 over Kashmir. In 1966 Indira Gandhi, daughter of Nehru, became India's third prime minister and used the tumultuous times as an excuse to increase the government's manipulation of the private sector and economy to enhance her political self-interests.

In fact, it could be persuasively argued that the Indian economy would have fared much better had Mrs. Gandhi been more attentive to economics than to politics. A good economic policy requires much more than political rhetoric to fuel it; it needs sound management, and sustained supervision. Mrs. Gandhi did not have it in her temperament to supply either. And so vague socialist shibboleths [like getting rid of poverty or producing a people's car] became the magic mantras of Indira's time [which ended violently in her assassination in 1984]; and her promises of an egalitarian society created instead an elite bureaucracy that prospered and perpetuated itself. (Gupte 1992, 18-19)

In the early 1970s, India invaded East Pakistan.

Table 9.1
Major Vehicle Producers

Company	Production of Vehicles	
	1974–75	1995–96
TELCO	22,595	181,401
Maruti Udyog	---	277,776
Mahindra & Mahindra	10,417	112,910
Hindustan Motors	17,202	30,822
Premier Automobiles	19,017	20,322
Ashok Leyland	7,251	37,901
Bajaj Tempo	3,713	28,027

Source: Adapted from B. Bowander, "Competitive and Technology Management Strategy: A Case Study of TELCO," *International Journal of Technology Management*, 15(6/7) (1998): 651, Table 2.

The People's Car

Among the favored elite was the playboy son of the prime minister, Sanjay Gandhi, who had come up with a technically unsound prototype for an inexpensive "people's car" dubbed the Maruti. Using his mother's influence, Sanjay easily raised millions of dollars in start-up capital for his new venture, persuaded the chief minister of Haryana state to evict residents from the site outside New Delhi where his car plant was to be built, and secured a license to make 50,000 cars annually (Gupte 1992, 441). Other manufacturers fell on harder times. TELCO's technology licensing agreement with Daimler-Benz was terminated by the government, which had co-opted heavy industry into supplying its military needs at the expense of civilian and export markets. Commercial motor vehicles, except for Maruti, had become secondary to other priority sectors such as coal, power, steel, munitions, and armaments, and foreign purchases of technology and capital equipment were approved only for the latter industries.

In 1971 the war machine under Indira Gandhi was reactivated when India invaded East Pakistan, defeated the Pakistani army, and established the independent state of Bangladesh. These were followed by the explosion of an atomic device in 1974. The weapon's buildup and armed conflicts further drained the central treasury and the situation was exacerbated when the oil crises struck in the 1970s and when the government had to bail out Sanjay's floundering Maruti car company. In June 1980 Sanjay Gandhi was killed in a plane crash, with his people's car yet to debut on the streets of India.

Government Restrictions

In contrast, progress—though slowed—was still under way at other vehicle firms. TELCO's leading manufacturing position, for example, had already been developed to such an extent that even with the loss of technical assistance from abroad, it could proceed using its own substantial resources. This continuance can be illustrated by the construction of a new production facility in Pune that began with considerable input from Daimler-Benz and was completed in 1977, even though the foreign collaboration had ended. An engineering research center was established in 1967 that provided in-house R&D as the company expanded in truck manufacturing with little foreign assistance. The expertise in trucks, however, had little relevance for carmaking, and, at any rate, the government was in no mood to approve investments that would increase the supply of passenger cars. To further its micromanagement of the private sector, New Delhi passed the Foreign Exchange Regulations Act and the Monopolies and Restrictive Trade Practices Act, which it hoped would help it redress the deficits building in the nation's balance of payments and the accumulation of market power by large private enterprises like TELCO. Both measures proved highly counterproductive. Advanced foreign technology was kept out of the country, slowing India's industrialization while other nations like Japan were making tremendous strides in catching up with the West. The antimonopoly act raised barriers to potential competitors entering an industry by requiring extensive government approvals. The barriers to entry, in effect, froze the leadership positions of companies already operating in an industry by keeping out new competitors. India's economy consequently stagnated in the 1960s and 1970s because of these and the following measures:

1.   High defense expenditures.

2.   Licensing restrictions on imports of technology and capital goods.

3.   High tariff and other protectionist trade barriers.

4.   Severe restrictions on foreign investment and ownership of domestic companies.

5.   Government policy of keeping the currency inconvertible and overvalued, thus hindering exports.

6.   Capacity regulations requiring private firms to obtain government approvals to increase production and engage in new product development.

7.   Implementation of barriers to exit an industry were forcing nonviable firms to continue operating in an effort to maintain employment rolls and the state's tax base.

Large domestic firms also came under the scrutiny of the Monopolies Inquiry Commission, which had already deemed that concentration in the motor vehicle and parts industry was excessive. TELCO, then the industry leader, was investigated when the firm sought approvals for its new Pune facility and capacity additions and investments at various locations. The bureaucratic wrangling and delay, inherent in the commission's modus operandi, were the principal weapons used to curb industry concentration, but time was on the side of the established private firms because the same tactics were employed to keep out foreign and domestic entrants (Bowander 1998a, 646–680, 1998b, 622–645).

THE JAPANESE ARRIVE

Only when the government-backed Maruti company encountered severe setbacks in the early 1980s was a foreign firm, Suzuki, allowed entrance. Now owned by the government following Sanjay's death, Maruti had become such a scandalous mess, entailing huge financial losses, that the state was forced to seek competent management from abroad. The selection of Suzuki was prompted by the oil crises resulting from the Arab oil embargo, 1973–1974, and the Iranian revolution in 1979, which quadrupled petroleum prices and greatly altered the world's motor vehicle industry. The inflationary spiral suddenly increased the need for compact, fuel-efficient cars and the process technology—principally owned by Japanese manufacturers like Suzuki—for making these vehicles. The oil shocks also unleashed recessionary forces, moving the government to reverse many of its industrial policies that had stunted economic growth in the prior three decades. In concert with the Suzuki entrance in 1982, four other local concerns were permitted to team up with foreign manufacturers, namely, DCM with Toyota, local investors with Mitsubishi Motors and Eicher Goodearth of Germany to form Eicher Motors, Punjab Tractors with Mazda Motors to form Swaraj Mazda, and Mahindra & Mahindra with Nissan of Japan. For the most part, these partnerships have had limited impact on India's motor vehicle industry, with the major exception, of course, being Maruti Udyog, the joint venture between the Indian government and Suzuki Motors of Japan, which quickly became the largest maker of commercial vehicles in India due largely to its government backing and Suzuki's business expertise. The Suzuki juggernaut was also assisted by regulations that kept other firms out during the rest of the 1980s and prevented heavy vehicle manufacturers like TELCO from acquiring advanced technology to move into passenger-car making. Some established car companies like Hindustan and Premier became complacent in the closed economy and failed to modernize even as technology advanced in the outside world.

In turning to Suzuki, the Indian government was attempting to incorporate the foreign advances into its moribund people's car company while minimizing the exploitation it knew that multinational corporations were capable of. Suzuki was consequently offered a minority 26% interest in Maruti Udyog in 1982, which was raised to 40% in 1988, then 50% in 1992. The greater degree of ownership was secured by Suzuki as it financially underwrote the upgrading and expansion of the Maruti plant, which included the losses suffered by the joint venture until 1992, when it turned profitable (EIU 1997, 4).

END OF NEHRUVIAN SOCIALISM

The death of Mrs. Gandhi in 1984 did not end her family's dynastic rule because by the end of the year, her other son, Rajiv Gandhi, succeeded her as prime minister. Times had changed, however. The bankrupt state of the country's economy, progress by Asian neighbors, and shifting geopolitical forces collectively moved the new leader to adopt much-needed economic reforms. The desperate straits also prompted Rajiv to journey to Moscow in May 1985 to seek $1.15 billion in trade and investment funds from the Soviet Union, which itself would implode at the end of the decade. India's poor performance is illustrated in Table 9.2 as its growth fell behind even that of its archenemy Pakistan.

The information revolution, moreover, which was propelling much of this growth during the 1980s, was also communicating the dismal state of India's poverty, poor health care, and high illiteracy rate not only to its domestic population but to the rest of the world as well. As more and more Third World countries began the transition from "public-sector-based socialism to private-sector-led economic growth," India's new administration was obliged to follow (Gupte 1992, 37). The reorientation was outlined in the Five Year Plan for 1986–1990 that stipulated the following:

1.   De-licensing of some industries such as auto parts manufacturing.

2.   Reducing regulation under the Monopolies and Restrictive Trade Practices Act.

3.   Permitting the use of foreign technology.

4.   Exempting from licensing requirements capacity increases up to 49% of already approved limits.

5.   Broad-banding of production licenses, which gave motor vehicle and other manufacturers the opportunity to implement innovations in product and process designs (Bowander 1998a, 650, 1998b, 628–629).

The preceding reforms, however, were too little, too late for a populace that had waited too long for promises of "greatness" and prosperity to materialize. In 1989 Rajiv Gandhi was voted out of office and was murdered two years later when attempting to make a political comeback.

INDIGENOUS R&D

While progress may have been too limited to satisfy impatient voters, there were definite signs that economic reforms were having an impact. Productivity growth, for example, climbed steeply from the decade of the 1970s, when it averaged an anemic 0.9, to 4.4 in the 1980s, exceeding the numbers of such Asian "tigers" as Hong Kong at 3.7 and Thailand at 3.1 (Bowander 1998b, 638).

Table 9.2
Growth of Asian Countries, 1960–1990

Country	G D P	Industrial Output
India	4%	6%
Pakistan	5%	8%
Indonesia	6%	9%
Thailand	7%	9%
Taiwan	8%	12%
South Korea	9%	10%

Source: Clive Crook, "Time to Let Go: A Survey of India," *The Economist*, February 22, 1997, 3.

Suzuki Motors also began introducing Japanese cutting-edge technology and quality improvement programs, with the new techniques revamping the industry.

In addition, quite a bit of productivity enhancement could be ascribed to in-house R&D, which was begun by large firms before the monopolies commission began curbing enterprises that it deemed too powerful. As an example in motor vehicles, TELCO had mean annual R&D expenditures of 27.99 million Rs. (rupees) in the 1974–1978 period over five times the 5.42 million Rs. of its closest competitor, Hindustan Motors. The emphasis on R&D was carried into the 1980s, with TELCO increasing mean expenditures to 126.26 million Rs. in 1986–1990 while Ashok Leyland, its rival in truck production, came in second with 32.1 million Rs. The consequences of such efforts increased both productivity and production numbers for TELCO, with its productivity ratio rising from 1.38 in 1977, to 2.12 ten years later. In the same period, Ashok Leyland's ratio increased from 1.24, to 1.46. Rising productivity furthermore spurred increased production and economies of scale at TELCO, with the total number of commercial vehicles rising from 25,269 made in 1975, to 81,829 in 1990, while production expansion at Ashok Leyland was from 7,711, to 24,297 (Bowander 1998a, 658–659). The comparison shows that foreign technology was by itself insufficient in developing a leadership position in India's vastly heterogeneous and politically harassed motor vehicle industry. After all, both TELCO and Ashok Leyland had infusions of foreign technology, but the former's output in 1995–1996 exceeded the latter by over 4.5 times.

Product Design

TELCO, furthermore, did not have a product entrant in the important light commercial vehicle category in the mid-1970s, as Ashok Leyland did, and was frozen out of the product category when strict government licensing regulations were imposed. As these regulations were lifted, TELCO began a crash design program to develop the TATA 407 light commercial vehicle, using in-house engineering capabilities and computerized numerical control machining systems imported from Japan. The machining systems included in-line, dedicated equipment that greatly streamlined production of TELCO's high-output requirements and enhanced productivity by cutting per unit costs. The TATA 407, furthermore, was the industry's first indigenously developed light commercial vehicle, and its introduction in 1986 was quickly followed by LCV-TATA 609 the following year and the LCV Tatamobile in 1989 (Bowander 1998a, 663–664).

TELCO's new models were developed based on strengths in the firm's engineering and output supply capabilities, but in competitive markets, of course, the demand side guarantees sales and profits. Marketing and service outlets are thus critical in the huge expanse of the heavily populated Indian subcontinent, and this is especially important at a time when foreign firms like Ford and Honda are entering the market. TELCO's network of ninety four dealers gives it one of the strongest sales and distribution systems in the country, and they complement the engineering and design prowess of the company. The marketing network includes specialized service centers located in high-growth areas to meet after-purchase customer needs and instill brand loyalty. TELCO has furthermore gone into the export market as a means of understanding the foreign competition that is invading its previously closed home territory. It is also proposing to raise $200 million on international capital markets to underwrite the expansion of its product range.

Shift to Passenger Cars. TELCO's Achilles' heel can be seen in Table 9.3, which lists the vehicle types made by the firm in 1995. The company's vulnerabilities lie in passenger cars and sport utility vehicles, which are incurring heightened demand due to personal and business travel needs. Abetting this shift are rising personal incomes resulting from 5–6% economic growth rates since 1994. In order to meet the new demand, TELCO has entered into a second joint venture with Mercedes-Benz of Germany, which began producing the Mercedes 220E car model in 1995. The $150 million joint venture, known as Tata-Daimler-Benz, is 51% owned by the foreign partner and 49% by the Indian firm. Production occurs at a Pune facility with annual capacity of 30,000 units. In addition, the first partnership formed in 1954 and still 10% owned by the parent, Daimler-Benz, geared up production in 1998 of a small car to directly compete against the Maruti 800. For this effort, a massive investment of 40 billion Rs. was planned by TELCO whose corporate sales in 1994/1995 were 57 billion Rs. The company intends to use its in-house R&D for the design of the car and the vehicle's manufacturing process. A 100,000-car-per-year facility is planned that TELCO feels will provide minimum scale economies to enable it to challenge the front-running Maruti 800 (EIU 1996a, 22, 35–36).

The growth in the passenger car market has also tempted Mercedes-Benz into going it alone and introducing its own people's car independently of TELCO. The effort will be under the direction of its wholly owned subsidiary,

Table 9.3
TELCO's 1995 Production

	Units
Passenger cars	10,548
Sport utility vehicles	0
Light commercial vehicles	69,347
Medium & heavy commercial vehicles	89,993

Source: EIU, *Motor Business Asia-Pacific*, third quarter 1996, "A Strategic Profile of Telco: Facing Up to the Challenges Ahead," pp. 37–45.

Mercedes-Benz India, which was incorporated in 1994. The move paralleled strong car sales nationwide that increased by 28% from 1993 to 1994 and moved up another strong 26% the following year.

While the government's liberalization measures have also prompted foreign investments—along with the strong demand—in India not all regulatory and tariff barriers have been removed. The government has kept a 110% duty on built-up vehicle imports as well as on imports of completely knockdown and semiknockdown kits. Duties on auto parts fall in the range of 10% to 50% ad valorem, with the differential in tariffs used to encourage foreign investment in domestic production facilities (EIU 1996a, 30–31). These are usually made with a local partner, and such plans must still be approved by the Foreign Investment Promotion Bureau. The tariff schedule and necessary approvals have failed to deter foreign competitors from entering India's huge, growing vehicle market, where many of them will be attempting to duplicate Suzuki's success in passenger cars.

Maruti Udyog

As detailed earlier, the Gandhian vision of a "people's car" may have paved the way for Suzuki's initial 26% equity stake in bankrupt Maruti Limited, but the foreign maker's rugged vehicle designs and lean manufacturing processes greatly altered India's automobile industry. Based on these strengths, Suzuki introduced a small van in 1984, only two years after signing on with the Indian government. This was followed in 1985 by the best-selling Maruti 800 subcompact (powered by an 800 cc engine) and the Gypsy sport utility vehicle, patterned after the Jimny model. Greater-powered cars were introduced in the 1990s, including the Maruti 1000, Zen, and Esteem models, to tap the market for better-performance vehicles now sought by more affluent customers. Suzuki's stake in the joint-venture firm climbed to 50% as the sales of Maruti Udyog reached $600 million in 1992–1993. For the same fiscal year, the Indian affiliate leaped into the black with an operating profit of $29 million. In 1995–1996 sales climbed to $1.8 billion, and operating profit was $232 million, with the escalation noticed in several corporate boardrooms around the world. The $1.8 billion result comes from domestic and export sales of 260,000, units which can be broken down as follows: sales of the Maruti 800 led at 103,000, followed by the Zen at 46,000, the Omni van at 35,000, the Maruti 1000 at 26,000, the Esteem at 19,000, Gypsy SUV at 6,000, and the total export market for all models at 25,000 (EIU 1996a, 36–38). The breakdown highlights Maruti's strength in the small-car segment, and this is where other foreign and domestic firms are planning on challenging.

With government barriers to foreign entry lowered in 1993 and the turn to profitability of Maruti Udyog, foreign car manufacturers, many of which had not been in the country as recently as 1991, came pouring in. After all, giant multinational firms like General Motors, Ford, Toyota, and Volkswagen could hardly be participants in global markets if they were not in India, which was on the verge of becoming the world's most populated country. In this industry of giants, with huge financial and technical resources, deals and plans began to be implemented in rapid order (Dunne 1997, 14):

1.   Ford Motor Company sought approval for an $800 million joint venture with Mahindra & Mahindra to produce the Ford Escort and Fiesta beginning in mid-1996.

2.   Toyota reduced its stake in DCM-Toyota to go it alone in the Indian market.

3.   Daewoo Motors of South Korea acquired 51% of DCM-Toyota, in the process changing the affiliate's name to DCM-Daewoo Ltd. It planned to invest $1 billion and boost capacity of the joint venture to 160,000 vehicles per year by the end of the 1990s.

4.   India's Hindustan Motors entered into a joint venture with GM-Opel in 1994, with output planned for 106,000 units per year of the 1600 cc Opel Astra, which will eventually have a 70% local content.

5.   Honda invested $280 million in a joint venture with SIEL of India to begin production of its Civic car in 1997.

6.   Premier Automobiles of India teamed up with Fiat Auto of Italy to manufacture the Fiat 178 in 1997.

7.   Volvo planned to manufacture trucks in partnership with the Indian government in Bangalore by 1998 and contributed 500 million kroner to the venture.

8.   Hyundai planned a huge $1.1 billion investment by itself to produce the Accent in Tamil Nadu, with start-up expected in 1998. This and the preceding Daewoo project were cancelled or put on hold when the currency crisis crippled South Korea.

9.   Volkswagen teamed up with Eicher to make Skoda and Audi cars in 1997, with an initial investment of $200 million.

Of the numerous foreign investments, Ford's 50–50 joint venture with Mahindra & Mahindra, the Bombay-based leading maker of sport utility vehicles, appears to have the greatest chances of success. The $800 million partnership is planning to erect a 100,000 annual capacity Fiesta car plant outside Madras, close to India's major auto parts makers. This will enhance the possibility of assembling vehicles containing substantial local content, in the process taking advantage of the country's low wage and manufacturing costs. The Ford joint venture is thus intent on emulating the Suzuki strategy of producing a competitively priced car like the Maruti 800, whose $5,800 price tag has made it extremely popular in the poor country. Ford is also famous for having a full product range of vehicles in the event that demand develops for bigger, more expensive cars. As the world's second largest and most profitable commercial vehicle manufacturer, Ford is further planning to make its Indian operations an export base, especially to developing countries in South Asia and Africa. Production is therefore planned in a number of models, with the Escort already being built at an existing Mahindra plant in Maharashtra state. The activities all fit in the giant company's tentative ambitions for developing a cheap, utilitarian "Asia car" for the region's masses (Jordan 1996).

Response by Suzuki. The new challenges for the front-runner have prompted Maruti Udyog to increase its output of 250,000 vehicles per year in 1996, to 320,000 in 1998 at a cost of $430 million. Suzuki, the Japanese parent company of Maruti, further envisioned capacity expanding to 500,000 by the end of the twentieth century, with capital costs rising by $500 million. This would cover expected demand increases from both domestic and export markets, add to economies of scale, and preempt other firms from taking market share from Maruti. Suzuki's strategic response to the competition, however, has not met with approval from the Indian government (its 50–50 partner in the Maruti joint venture) especially if the expansion is funded by the sale of stock that reduces the government's ownership. Suzuki, moreover, feels that debt financing is out of the question with interest rates at a lofty 17%.

In the fight to set corporate policy, the Japanese firm's president, Osamu Suzuki, strongly feels that the government should leave the management of the joint venture to Suzuki simply because it does not know anything about carmaking. The state should furthermore reduce its holdings in the joint venture and realize an attractive gain on its original investment, mainly attributable to Suzuki's efforts. The car company also feels that the selection process of top management—which it shares with the Industry Ministry in New Delhi—is too bureaucratic for current competitive conditions. Set up in 1992, when Suzuki was given 50% joint parity with the government, the selection process calls for alternating appointments every five years for Maruti's chairman and managing director. Each side takes turns appointing one of the two top executives, and a new round was scheduled for August 1997. Already upset by the disagreement over funding for the $1 billion expansion and the ending of its monopoly in small cars. Suzuki objected to the ministry's choice of a senior Maruti manager for the managing directorship and took the issue to court. It was settled the following year when the government's director agreed to step down after an abbreviated three-year term, paving the way for Suzuki's nominee to take over (Karp 1997).

In an August 1997 interview, Osamu Suzuki elaborated on the firm's dispute with the Indian Ministry:

It has been a longstanding belief of mine that when governments attempt to engage in business, they are doomed to fail. I see no alternative for the Indian government but to leave management of Maruti to us. If it refuses, it should assume responsibility for the company's (eventual) failure. In almost every country in the world the government sector is in decline. Maruti simply will not succeed unless the government reduces its role. (EIU 1997, 3).

REFERENCES

Bowander, B. "Competitive and Technology Management Strategy: A Case Study of TELCO." *International Journal of Technology Management*, 15(6/7) (1998a): pp. 646–680.

———. "Industrialization and Economic Growth of India: Interactions of Indigenous and Foreign Technology." *International Journal of Technology Management*, 15 (6/7) (1998b): 622–645.

Crook, Clive. "Time to Let Go: A Survey of India." *The Economist*, February 22, 1997, p. 3.

Dunne, Michael. "Asia's Epic Poker Game." *The JAMA Forum*, 15(3) (1997): 9–17.

EIU. "A Review of the Automotive Sector in India: The Expansion Continues." *Motor Business Asia-Pacific*, first quarter 1996a, Chapter 3, pp. 21–45.

———. "A Strategic Profile of Telco: Facing Up to the Challenges Ahead." *Motor Business Asia-Pacific*, third quarter 1996b, Chapter 4, pp. 37–45.

———. "Face to Face: With the Chairman of Suzuki." *Motor Business Japan*, third quarter 1997, Chapter 1.

———. "A Strategic Profile of Maruti Udyog: In Search of a Strategy for Growth." *Motor Business Asia-Pacific*, fourth quarter 1998, Chapter 3, pp. 36–38.

Gupte, Pranay. *Mother India*. New York: Charles Scribner's Sons, 1992.

Jordan, Miriam. "Ford to Build Fiesta Model in India, Investing $400 Million in Joint Venture." *Wall Street Journal*, January 4, 1996, p. A7.

Karp, Jonathan. "India Alarms Multinationals by Battling Two Investors." *Wall Street Journal*, September 22, 1997, p. A19.

Chapter 10

The New Millennium Arrives

As the industry globalizes, severe competition for consumers plays the pivotal and defining role in foreign markets as it does in mature, domestic ones. The automakers are subsequently using new designs, hybrid vehicles, low-cost global cars, environmental initiatives, and electronic commerce over the Internet to gain strategic advantage. As their moves increasingly cross national borders, analysis and planning must be undertaken to account for different cultural backgrounds, regional economic shifts, governmental regulations, and major disruptions in world financial and currency markets, that can send nations into deep recessions. Moreover, as over-capacity grips the industry, consumer marketing moves to the fore at corporate headquarters, displacing capital investments and production in the intense struggle for market share and profits.

Even if supply and demand numbers come into balance, however, it will not mitigate all business problems because, with incomes rising worldwide, individual transportation uses are in flux, giving rise, for example, to growing sales of Buicks—a luxury nameplate made by General Motors—in China, still a very poor country, with annual per capita income of less than $800. The decision to assemble and market the $40,000 car was, furthermore, made during China's transition period from a centrally planned to a more capitalistically oriented economy. In the turmoil, the gamble was undertaken, based on the already rising number of affluent buyers, that there would be sufficient demand for the prestigious brand name. The decision, moreover, was based on the closed domestic market to imports that the Chinese government had imposed on its huge, but undeveloped, economy, and now, to Buick's chagrin, it is planning to dismantle the trade barriers to advance its entrance into the World Trade Organization. This will allow other luxury nameplates, manufactured outside China, to enter the market, and Buick will enter a new round of competition against such potent nemeses as Mercedes-Benz, BMW, Lexus, and Acura. The competition from the Japanese carmakers will be especially fierce because of their nearby production facilities and their dominance of Asian trade. In its own strategic moves, General Motors has continued to shore up its Asian resources by making alliances with Japan's Suzuki, Isuzu, and Fuji (Subaru). These were undertaken as the Asian currency crisis waned and economic growth resumed in virtually all nations of the huge continent, prompting rivals to match GM's moves, with Ford taking over Mazda and Renault of France buying a significant share of Nissan. The two U.S. giant firms are furthermore battling for control of South Korean automakers, like Kia and Daewoo, that were financially crippled in the downturn. Back in China, Volkswagen, another global contender, holds on to its paramount position while DaimlerChrysler, following the downsizing of its Beijing Jeep operations, remains one of the few major companies lacking a strong base in or near the world's biggest emerging market. How it addresses this shortcoming will determine its role as a global enterprise even as it recovers from the throes of its landmark merger between Daimler-Benz and Chrysler.

The specifics of the small Chinese auto market show how entangling the competition grew for projected 1999 sales of only a half million units. Volkswagen's Sentra and Jetta models were expected to take 40% and 15%, respectively, of the market, with the Daihatsu Charade, Suzuki Alto, and Citroen ZX following with 20.1%, 9.2%, and 7.7% per car. A stumbling Jeep Cherokee, the DaimlerChrysler entry, retained a 1.7% toehold, while VW's Audi luxury car division, the GM Buick, and the Honda Accord were expected to elevate their minute portions of 2.9%, 1.6%, and 1.5%, respectively. Indeed, the growing business class of buyers along with the usual high-level bureaucrats— "who get a chauffeur-driven car as a perk"—are no longer content in being transported in a boxy, economical vehicle, singularly lacking in prestige, and are clamoring for expensive foreign brands with all passenger comforts (Landler 1999). Trading up and keeping abreast of the neighbors thus remain effective marketing ploys by the automakers, whose high-priced models, developed for the West, are increasingly clogging the limited road network in the Chinese countryside. The main problem for the industry, however, remains the production overcapacity resulting from sustained investments, most of which have never been profitable (Simison 1999).

GM SHANGHAI

Indicative of the huge flow of direct foreign investments is the $1.5 billion factory constructed by a 50–50 joint venture between GM and Shanghai Automotive Industries, which "is selling Buicks as fast as it can make them. It has speeded up production twice in the seven months of operation. There is even a waiting list" (Simison 1999). Moreover, "Its spit-and-polish assembly plant in an industrial zone here has become a sort of shrine for Chinese and foreign business people, who come to gawk at the cars and the camaraderie" (Landler 1999, C10). GM is also using the plant to broaden its product line to include a minivan for transplanting the new soccer mom in China as she strives to meet a demanding family schedule. The steep price tag on the second vehicle of about $40,000 further promotes the upscale appeal that GM is cultivating, and this pricing strategy may even allow a small profit margin, which has been elusive among carmakers. The profits, however, may prove fleeting when China relaxes its 100% tariff level imposed on imported vehicles. The protected market enjoyed by foreign producers like GM will subsequently erode, but the Detroit automaker will still retain the invaluable experience of operating in this quixotic environment.

GM's problems in China, moreover, have been exacerbated by its own government which signed a historic agreement with Beijing opening the country's economy to foreign imports—that GM wanted to be kept out—in exchange for U.S. assistance in getting China membership in the World Trade Organization. Parts of the bilateral accord centering on motor vehicles include:

1.   Large tariff cuts on imports from the current 80%–100% level to 25% by 2006.

2.   An average of 10% tariff cuts on auto parts by 2006.

3.   Elimination of import quotas by 2005.

4.   "Foreign auto companies and banks would for the first time be able to offer consumer loans for cars, a critical concession in a country where few can lay out the money for such a large purchase" (Eckholm and Sanger 1999, A17).

5.   U.S. auto firms, in addition to the retail loans would be allowed trade distribution rights, such as maintenance and repair service of their brands, that had been severely restricted by the government in the past (USTR 1999).

Also important for foreign businesses in China is the general opening of the huge undeveloped economy to trade and investments within the rules negotiated by members of the World Trade Organization and its predecessor rubric, the General Agreement of Tariffs and Trade (GATT). Since its inception in 1947, GATT has been highly successful in increasing international trade and prosperity through the elimination of barriers that protect inefficient elements of a domestic economy. In particular, the U.S.–China accord will remove trade barriers in agriculture and such important services as telecommunications, banking, and insurance that underwrite commerce between nations as carried out by private firms. The new economic order will probably spell the end of many, if not all, of China's regulatory agencies and state-owned industrial enterprises that have been responsible for its economic backwardness, compared to other East Asian nations both large and small. This will undoubtedly spur economic growth in the world's largest emerging market and increase its importance to foreign carmakers.

As such, even with the signing of the accord reducing trade barriers, efficient producers like Toyota and Honda will continue to invest in China and not depend on the export trade. Both companies were highly successful in their moves to the United States and realize that huge, complex markets like those in North America and Asia are best targeted by well-planned and strategically located facilities that complement their exports from factories in Japan. They will further maintain their competitiveness by erecting small operating plants and expanding them to meet demand for their well-designed models, which are frequently well received by consumers. Similar to their migration to the New World, transplants from Japan to China will be led by the maverick firm Honda, which has formed a 50–50 joint venture with the Guangzhou Auto Group to produce 30,000 Accords per year in a new $140 million facility in the booming southern Chinese region. Engines for the Accord will be supplied by a second 50–50 joint venture between Honda and Dongfeng Motor, which will cost $60 million. The tied projects parallel the carmaker's earlier investments in Marysville and Anna, Ohio ("Honda Details China Auto Ventures"). In November 1999 Toyota Motor signed with Tianjin Automotive Industrial Company to produce a small car that would be affordable to the average Chinese family. With the successful start-up of its Shanghai Buick plant, General Motors is also considering plans for the same market segment in small family cars, and its candidate will be the Opel Corsa, which will be made at the Shanghai plant. Not to be outdone, Volkswagen will be joining the small-car fray with its "people's car" costing less than $10,000 (Smith 1999).

ASIAN REVIVAL

The stepped-up activity in China is part of a larger global phenomenon whereby multinational corporations like General Motors, Ford, Honda, and VW are taking huge profits from the booming American market—which had record sales of 16.89 million vehicles in 1999—and aggressively investing them in potentially large markets in Asia. The competition in the former middle kingdom with its 1.3 billion population remains ground zero in the scenario, but its puny 1.5 million vehicle sales per year have conditioned the automakers to include smaller countries like South Korea and Thailand in their Far East plans, especially since these "tiger economies" are expected to resume their torrid growth trajectories. Both stumbled badly during the currency crises of 1997–1999, with Thailand igniting the implosion by its sudden devaluation of its currency, the baht. Government officials subsequently had to ignominiously negotiate bailout loans from a supercilious International Monetary Fund (IMF), with Seoul especially humiliated because it is being forced to auction off prime industrial assets like Daewoo and Samsung Motors to foreign interests. The situation was less exacerbating in Thailand because, unlike South Korea, the smaller Southeast Asian kingdom did not have independent, indigenous automakers that could be sold to such giants as GM and Ford. Factories owned by the foreigners were merely shuttered during the depths of the Thai recession and are now being revived because of rising demand.

Twilight of the *Chaebol*

"Transported by the whispers of workers and housewives, a wave of impending doom is descending on this auto factory town [Pupyong, South

Korea], whose fortunes have always marched in lockstep with those of the Daewoo group" (French 1999, C1). Daewoo Motor Company, the jewel in the industrial crown of the Daewoo conglomerate, or *chaebol*, was going insolvent under the crushing $16 billion of debt that it had incurred as the weakening won (South Korea's currency) savaged the country's economic accounts. A financial transfusion from the parent was out of the question because the second largest *chaebol* was itself being pulled under by the weight of $78 billion worth of loans that it was no longer servicing. Too big to fail—or so the group's founder had thought—it was now being dismantled as subsidiaries like the motor company were being sold to assuage the creditors, many of them Japanese and American banks that had also believed in the self-indulgent words of the *chaebol*'s founder. Equally important to these lending institutions was the long-standing backing by the South Korean government, whose industrial policy had anointed the *chaebol* as the principal private enterprises that would lead the nation's industrialization in the manner of Japan's *keiretsu*. They indeed filled this role as Korean industrial exports began competing in world markets like the United States. In automobiles, Hyundai, Daewoo, and Kia became familiar brand names, but their later appearance did not give them the distinctiveness and market power garnered by the Japanese. Strenuous efforts were made to leapfrog, or at least gain more of the stature of their Japanese competitors, and this required inordinate sums to fund their international aspirations. When capital markets and institutions even in Japan failed to save a sinking Nissan, the tottering and fall of Korea's industrial dominoes were assured. At the end, Daewoo's debt exceeded the $58 billion in hard-currency loans extended by the IMF to the South Korean government. As a condition for the funds, the government was ordered to restructure the conglomerates and curb many of their ill-conceived and debt-ridden expansion plans.

In comparison, why did Japan, in the midst of its own severe economic recession, not require IMF assistance? Its economic and finance ministries had certainly succeeded and become highly confident, even arrogant, over the past three to four decades due to the nation's export and investment success, which had created an economic superpower. This was furthermore achieved in the crucible of U.S. competitive markets where American business, political, and government leaders continuously recommended reforms that actually led to the strengthening of Japan's economy and industries. They included the lowering of protectionist barriers, liberalization of investment rules, less government interference in capital and foreign exchange markets, and reduced subsidies for inefficient industries. The measures were grudgingly implemented because Tokyo had little desire to antagonize its principal trading partner. Seoul, on the other hand, stubbornly clung to its archaic, largely inefficient ways of doing business, with the private sector adding to its massive debt load. In Japan corporate executives were forced to streamline their operations to compete internationally, especially when the yen began surging on foreign exchange markets. The balance sheets of Japan's major companies, unlike their Korean counterparts, were consequently strong enough to weather weakness in the domestic economy. Those that buckled, such as Mazda and Nissan, were readily taken over by foreign competitors with considerable expertise in turning these companies around. In addition, both export earnings and the yen remained strong throughout the recession, which added to official government reserves used to prop up the shaky banking sector. The central banks of Korea and Thailand, in contrast, sold billions of dollars of reserves from their treasuries in futile attempts to strengthen their plunging currencies. As reserves emptied, devaluation of the currency became inevitable. This action guaranteed default on hard-currency (yen and U.S. dollar) loans that private firms like Daewoo had taken out from foreign commercial banks.

In the end, Daewoo, one of South Korea's spectacular success stories, also proved to be perhaps the most spectacularly egregious case of failure. In the midst of the Asian financial crisis of 1997, even as managing its own huge debt was becoming nearly impossible, the conglomerate pressed ahead with expansion plans, opening an expensive new automobile factory in Vietnam and buying a troubled Korean car maker, the Ssangyong Motor Company. (French 1999, C4).

In the aftermath of the group's collapse, the reorganization plan forced on the *chaebol* by its creditor banks with oversight by the government, which was also mired in its own debt problems, called for the outright sale of Daewoo Motor. Because most of its sister conglomerates were also being dissolved, the government could turn only to foreign interests in the fire sale of not only Daewoo but Samsung Motors as well. In the prior sale of Kia Motors, which had entered court receivership in April 1998, the government had managed to keep Kia in Korean hands by arranging for Hyundai to take over the bankrupt firm, even though Ford held a 9.4% stake in Kia and was actively seeking to bid for it. Weighed down by the $5 billion in liabilities that accompanied the Kia acquisition, Hyundai, by itself, became too shaky to consider buying another insolvent carmaker. Ford and General Motors were thus the major bidders on Daewoo Motor, while Renault SA announced that it was negotiating for Samsung Motors. The three foreign concerns had concluded that the Asian auto industry would be growing again and were adding to operating assets as opportunity arose. Renault had, in 1999, formed a formidable alliance with the ailing Nissan Motor Company and was looking to buy Samsung for as little as $2 billion. The price tag was low because the French company was refusing to assume the $5 billion debt of the Korean firm that had sent it into court receivership. The American auto companies were similarly intent on repudiating Daewoo Motor's $16 billion of mainly overdue, short-term loans, simply because, as in the case of Samsung, the massive debt of Daewoo exceeded its intrinsic value. This naturally did not sit well with government officials, who were seeking capital infusions from foreign interests to retire the debt and bolster the nation's financial reserves. If the foreigners were not interested in paying even parts of the overhanging debt, political and ministerial personnel began to rethink the Daewoo situation and search for ways to keep the automaker in Korean hands. This would dangerously inject a chauvinistic ploy into a floundering case, with government bureaucrats with limited, if any, industrial experience attempting to solve a corporate insolvency problem that they had helped to create. Moreover, the action could easily backfire by invoking retaliatory measures from foreign governments that would limit the sale of Korean vehicles in their markets.

GM Invests in Asia

GM's Daewoo bid complements its Asian moves into China and Japan, where the Shanghai Buick plans, discussed previously, are being followed by a joint venture in Jinbei that will begin production at the start of the new millennium. In Japan GM has taken a 49% stake in Isuzu, 20% share of Fuji Heavy Industries, and a 9.9% equity interest in Suzuki, which, in turn, has a major share of the Indian car market as well as 9.2% of Chinese car sales. The American firm has also forged an agreement with Toyota to cooperate on the research and development of environmentally clean vehicles and energy sources and is in talks with Honda, where it plans to buy the latter's LEV6 low-emission engines. Environmental concerns for the automakers have increased in the aftermath of tough pollution control standards on emissions adopted by the state of California as well as the European Union. These and safety issues are being readily addressed by top management especially since industry sales have reached record levels, making funds available for investment in breakthrough technologies that could give a firm a huge competitive advantage among increasingly environmentally sensitive consumers. Corporate headquarters have also witnessed the never-ending legal battles that have crippled the U.S. cigarette industry, giving it a pariah image that other executives are not interested in sharing.

Thai Recovery

In Southeast Asia, Thailand is now being dubbed the "Detroit of the East" because both GM and Ford are racing to produce vehicles at new $500 billion truck and auto plants as demand returns. The former will be making the Opel small car at its facility, which was postponed during the Asian crisis, while the Ford Ranger pickup truck is already being assembled at the Ford factory. Both manufacturers are hoping that Asian sales will grow to 10% of their worldwide sales, which they plan to achieve by offering attractive models to customers. Hence, Ford is producing pickup trucks, a product area in which it has excelled, while GM is making the Opel, probably its strongest small car. GM will furthermore be producing 40,600 minivans annually "and is preparing a Thai marketing blitz that includes everything from billboards to Buddhist flower ceremonies" (Frank 1999). Ford's product development program centers on a new passenger car, part of investments totaling $1 billion that it is allocating for markets in Thailand, India, Vietnam, Malaysia, and the Philippines. Such moves by the Americans are meant to capitalize on the area's financial crises, which paved the way for increased equity ownership as well as hamstrung the Japanese automakers because of the slowdown in their own domestic economy. They are consequently reversing the earlier challenge (when the Japanese exported and built transplants in the United States) by moving westward across the Pacific and competing aggressively for markets that they had heretofore left alone. The ebb and flow of these global efforts are furthermore coinciding with major changes in Detroit's executive suites and the altered plans of new leaders to keep their firms at the forefront of a rapidly changing industry.

NASSER OF FORD

Jacques A. Nasser became Ford's chief executive officer (CEO) at the beginning of 1999, when the large firm was successful in acquiring Volvo Cars over rival bidders Fiat and Volkswagen. Most of the work for the acquisition can probably be attributable to Nasser's predecessor, Alex Trotman, and the company's predisposition of buying into well-regarded brand names like Jaguar and Mazda when they encountered financially turbulent times. While Volvo was different because of its profitable situation, Ford's interest in Daewoo Motor continues the modus operandi. This type of business continuity is also evident in Nasser's declaration of "war on the industrial giant's stodgy, overly analytic culture," which appeared remarkably similar to Trotman's global 2000 restructuring of the firm when he became CEO on November 1, 1993 (Kerwin and Naughton 1999, 131). In the latter's shuffling of his executive staff, Nasser was elevated to group vice president of product development with a mandate to cut costs and spearhead the development of "'world' cars at five 'vehicle development centers' in Europe and Dearborn, Mich." that would lead the fleet into the new millennium (Templin 1994). Trotman's objectives centered on consolidation of the huge North American and European operations, which Nasser, in 1999, promptly reversed because the move left headquarters increasingly isolated from foreign markets such as Europe and Latin America, resulting in missed opportunities. Nasser is subsequently planning to give regional managers primary responsibility for marketing and design redevelopment of numerous car models in hopes of rejuvenating sales. In the scramble, not much is being said about the world car that was to be the nexus of Ford's hope in 2000 and beyond. Such strategic flip-flops, often by the same person, have unfortunately been endemic to large multinational corporations that are pursuing globalization by simultaneously investing in various parts of the world on a scale never before seen. Many of these initiatives will fail, but such are the risks of diversifying the assets of a $100 billion enterprise. Moreover, if the acquiring company can pay a reasonable price for a floundering firm and brand name and possesses superior managerial capabilities, the outcome could turn out positive and worth the risks. In Ford's case, its hefty investment in Mazda Motor Corporation finally turned profitable in 1999, Nasser's first year as chief executive. The takeover had been engineered by Alex Trotman in June 1996 during the midst of Mazda's money-losing decade, which began in 1991. Throughout the fiscal drought, Ford and Trotman doggedly pursued the turnaround, sending three American executives to Hiroshima, Japan, to take their turn at reducing the company's bloated costs. These actions included:

1. Reducing employment from 46,000 to 36,000.

2. Closing or merging 20% of Mazda's parts suppliers.

3. Removing 100 mostly unprofitable sales outlets from Mazda's Japanese dealership network.

The strenuous cost cutting led to $375 million in net income for Mazda for its fiscal year 1999, and the amount is forecast to increase slightly in 2000. In the interval, sales are expected to climb by about 20% as Asian recovery occurs. With revenues at not a-trivial-level of $20 billion for fiscal 1999, Mazda, Japan's fifth largest automaker, will undoubtedly play a pivotal role in Ford's Asian trajectory (Shirouzu 1999).

Domestic Concerns

While 1999 produced a brightening picture for Ford in Japan, yearly statistics covering the company's sales performance in its large U.S. domestic market may raise some problems for Nasser and his new top management team in Dearborn, Michigan. A record sales year for trucks and cars in the United States was indeed heartening for Ford, except that the industry's overall increase of 8.7% from the prior year outran the company's gain of 6.1%, and hence, its share of the important U.S. market fell from 25.5% in 1998, to 24.4% the following year. The company's 6.1% sales gain, moreover, was held down by the smaller 4% rise in its sale of light trucks, a market area that the company has led and from which it derives the bulk of its profits. The importance of light trucks to Ford can be seen in the sales figures for its top-selling vehicles: in 1999 Ford's F-series pickup (considered a light truck) was the top-selling vehicle in the country with 869,001 units sold. Its best-selling sport utility vehicle (SUV), the Ford Explorer, also a light truck, led SUV sales in the United States at 428,772 units. In contrast, Ford's top seller in passenger cars was the Taurus with 368,327 units sold, and this figure represented a 0.7% decline from year-ago sales (Meredith 2000, C1, C17).

Despite the bright spots in light-truck sales, Ford's shrinking market share for the vehicle category can be particularly problematic for CEO Nasser because 64% of the firm's operating income comes from the product in contrast to 12% from cars. Translated into per vehicle profits, the trucks contribute $1,785 per unit while margins on cars are only $489 (Kerwin and Naughton 1999, 135). Increased competition is the reason for this downturn, with the Chevrolet Silverado, GM's large pickup, rising in annual sales by 18.2%, while Ford's F-series was up by only 3.9%. The Explorer SUV was actually down by 0.6%, paralleling the drop in Taurus sales. DaimlerChrysler's Dodge Ram, another major competitor for the F-series, rose 4.6%, also outdoing the Ford pickups, and, just as significantly, the Jeep Grand Cherokee—DaimlerChrysler's leading SUV—saw sales rise by a strong 30.9%. The Cherokee was redesigned for the 1999 model year, which definitely aided the popularity of this descendant of the venerable Jeep military vehicle that first saw service in World War II. As unsold light trucks pile up in dealer inventory lots, Ford has resorted to giving cash discounts and rebates on them, which it did not have to do in the past. This will erode profit margins and bring back the old style of operating, namely, "cranking out huge runs of products, then discounting to move the metal" (Ball 1999, A3).

In addition, aging sport utility vehicles are facing competition from new hybrid ones like the Lexus RX 300 of Toyota, which combines the rugged external image of an SUV with the comfortable internal amenities of a passenger sedan. American drivers are generally receptive to such changes, resulting in major shifts in consumer demand as automakers strive to keep up and even lead significant turning points on demand curves. Europeans are also reacting positively to the new SUVs, which they had initially shunned as too clumsy to drive and park on narrow, old-city roads. Smaller designs prompted sale increases of 26% in 1998 and 21% in 1999 as Europeans tired of boxy little cars with limited appeal and comfort. On both sides of the Atlantic, the smaller SUVs are also being promoted by important considerations of pollution control and fuel efficiency, which becomes a bigger factor as gasoline prices climb. The older, bigger vehicles have notorious reputations as gas-guzzling, polluting behemoths, and their size, after crash studies and high insurance claims, is now deleteriously affecting their image as safe, secure vehicles. Injury and death rates involving large sport utility vehicles and minivans have been rising because of their tendency to roll over upon impact. In addition, the false sense of security that these large vehicles give their drivers often make them reckless because of incorrect expectations that they would survive an accident with minimum injury. The resulting higher claims will prompt increased insurance premiums, and this as well as its more dangerous image could curb SUV sales, although they remained brisk in 1999. The supply side of the market, on the other hand, could be crimped by government standards on company-wide fleet emissions. The trucks are heavy polluters, and because of their robust sales, this has pushed the emission average for new vehicles sold close to the ceiling of federal government guidelines. To lower its new fleet averages, Ford is actively introducing smaller cars to its product lineup like the Ka and Focus, which it hopes will become best-sellers like the earlier Escort and thereby reduce its fleet's emission numbers.

In the U.S. minivan segment, Ford, because of increases by its Winstar, was the sole gainer in market share. From 1998 to 1999 it increased its share of the minivan market by 0.6%, while the front-running DaimlerChrysler, because of slippage in sales of the Dodge Caravan, saw its share fall significantly from 42.7%, to 37.6%. Again, intense new competition caused the drop, especially from the Odessey, which drove Honda's minivan share from only 1.7% in 1998, to 5.8% the following year (Ball 2000). What the Odessey has done to shake up the American market, the Renault Scenic minivan has done for its European competitors. Introduced in 1997, the Megane Scenic saw its sales climb quickly to 275,000 in 1998, placing it second to the Volkswagen Golf car in overall vehicle popularity. To capitalize on this successful introduction, Renault is out with the Avantine hybrid nameplate, which combines the acceleration of a sports coupe with the roominess of the Scenic family minivan. In such novel ways, the newcomers keep ratcheting up the competition in hopes of eroding sales and profits of front-runners like Ford in its light-truck division, which has brought in so much money to the American firm.

Faltering Cars. For Ford, the threat of diminishing sales for its light trucks is compounded by the relinquishing of so much market share in passenger cars to the Japanese and Europeans. Its Ford Taurus, once the best-selling car in the United States, now runs third behind the Toyota Camry and Honda Accord. Moreover, annual sales of the Taurus dropped from 1998 to 1999, even though it was redesigned for the 1999 model year, while sales increased for the other two. The reception given the new makeover is partly to blame because it was critiqued as "how undistinguishable it is from all other midsize sedans" (Bradsher, March 31, 1999). Why would Ford be so blasé about its main entrant in the important family sedan market, especially at a time when Nasser had already taken the company's helm and was railing about its bureaucratically encrusted, stodgy image? The new CEO, moreover, had been an integral member of his predecessor's management team and therefore must have had some input on Ford's best-selling car. A plausible answer concludes that the millennium redesign of the Taurus had come under the control of the accounting department—the functional staff manned by the so-called bean counters—which had stood by as cost overruns in the preceding 1996 Taurus design priced the car out of the market. Its earlier debut in 1986 was also afflicted by huge development costs that, although popular from the time of its launching, did little for the company's bottom line. Toward the end of the 1990s, at any rate, Ford's profit center had gravitated to the light-truck business end, bringing along with it most of the firm's engineering and design talent as well as top management's attention. The lack of direction thus left the family sedan as well as other car lines in the hands of the cost cutters, resulting in minimal changes, because they would cost more, and ho-hum designs. The luxury, high end of the business was particularly impacted.

In the United States, the GM Cadillac was the perennial winner among expensive, luxury sedans, and it was followed by the Ford Lincoln. In 1998 the American nameplates switched places, with Lincoln ousting Cadillac from the top spot, and in 1999 both cars were outsold for the first time by Mercedes-Benz of Germany and Lexus of Japan. Cadillac fell to No. 3, followed by Lincoln and BMW, another foreign model. Analysis of each car's sales pattern show that the three foreign brands had been gaining ground for most of the decade at Detroit's expense. During this period, the Lexus had a 192.6% gain in sales, and Mercedes-Benz, 141.7%, while Cadillac and Lincoln suffered losses of 30.9% and 23.8%, respectively. In their upward moves, the foreigners offered the American consumer a greater selection of new, eye-catching designs, especially at the entry-level end (beginning at $30,000) of luxury cars. For example, buyers have been attracted to the C-class Mercedes-Benz sedans, priced at $30,000 to $35,000, because the prestigious nameplate is affordable to many buyers at that money range. Hybrid luxury models that combine the rugged attributes of a sport utility vehicle with a full-size car have also spurred sales of the Lexus RX 300 "sport wagon" and the BMW X5 "sport activity wagon" (Bradsher 2000, C1, C4). New models introduced by Mercedes-Benz and Lexus, moreover, have reached eight apiece, while Lincoln had only five, and this helps explain the Ford fall in the highly prominent, luxury-car class. Nasser is attempting to retake the lost ground and has hired Wolfgang Reitzle, formerly of BMW, with authority over Ford's luxury cars and a mandate to return them to top-selling positions.

At the lower end of the price range, the new CEO is actively changing the way models are redesigned. He has "banished Ford's longtime practice of updating aging models to match those of top competitors" (Kerwin and Naughton 1999, 136). Instead, greater personal interaction with consumers is being emphasized where engineers elicit ideas that produce better designs and, of course, sales. This objective led to Nasser's decentralizing of authority, giving more say to local managers, who, he feels, are closer to the customer. Thwarting this grassroots approach will be the corporate hierarchy and funding authorities that rarely approve new ideas because of their inherent risks and greater costs. Creative competitors are thus given an opportunity to nibble away at parts of Ford's vast market. Status-quo managers are willing to see this occur so long as the enterprise keeps prospering, as it is currently doing. They may also have an ally in William Clay Ford Jr., who now represents the Ford family's 40% equity ownership as chairman of the board of directors. Elected by the shareholders, the directors, besides overseeing top management, act on behalf of the owners, particularly in terms of the company's profits and stock price. For most of them, the price of the stock is their principal concern, along with receiving dividend payouts, and the powerful shareholders will vigorously protest any corporate action that could threaten their financial well-being. The situation is made more difficult for Nasser and his management team because among the stockholders are large mutual and pension funds whose investment personnel would quickly sell Ford shares if financial returns are not being met. The falling stock price can easily deflate any reforms suggested by Nasser in his attempts to make Ford into a more competitive company. This would also pertain to initiatives in the global arena since most of its profits are derived from domestic operations, and the board and its constituent body, the shareholders, are not interested in seeing profits undermined by risky projects abroad or way-out designs at home.

CHANGE AT GM

The situation is similar at General Motors, whose chief executive officer and chairman, John F. Smith Jr., is expected to retire in May 2000. While he has been successful at leading the giant automaker into a number of foreign markets with an array of investments and equity alliances, Smith has been unable to arrest GM's continuous slide in the U.S. market share that began in the 1970s. From 1982 to 1999, the company went from 44%, to 29.5%, and while its vehicles perennially used to lead their counterparts at Ford, the reverse is now true in pickup trucks, sport utility vehicles, and midsize cars. As an example, 1999 sales of the Taurus were ahead of those of GM's Chevrolet Cavalier sedan by 368,327 to 272,122. Boring vehicle designs at GM, especially in its cars, as well as exciting new competitor models are causing the reversals in the company's fortunes and its prolonged slump in domestic markets. To his credit, however, Smith executed an important turnaround at the giant company from the time of his appointment to CEO and chairman in the early 1990s, when GM might have expired because of its myriad operating losses. Extensive streamlining and cost cutting by Smith stemmed the flow of red ink, and the ensuing strong U.S. economy led to record revenues and profits for 1999 of $176.6 billion and $6.002 billion, respectively. He thus leaves the company in an excellent financial position to attack the problems of falling market share and becoming a global competitor. Smith's spin-off of Delphi Automotive Systems, GM's in-house parts supplier, will also give the automaker increased flexibility in its worldwide purchasing program even as Ford attempts to accomplish the same feat with its own parts maker, Visteon. In another streamlining move, GM is about to sell its Hughes Space and Communications unit, which manufactures satellites to the Boeing Company for a hefty $3.75 billion. The funds will complement the reserves that the company has raised from profitable North American operations to acquire stakes in foreign automakers like Fiat and launch a major program in design innovations and new features to redo the unexciting image of its vehicles. The latter effort now centers on:

a team of idea-generators working out of a converted garage at GM's technical center north of Detroit. The staff members—mostly in their 20s and 30s—are charged with tracking trends in society that will determine what consumers want from cars and trucks in the future. They scour design exhibitions and toy stores for ideas, bypassing the auto industry's usual circuit of car shows. Teamed with an anthropologist, they spend days shadowing Generation Xers to see how cars and trucks will fit into their lives. (White 1999)

Based on marketing research that predates the recently formed idea-generation team, General Motors is implementing a massive new model-launching program centering on twenty cars and forty light trucks that will be offered throughout the world from 1999 to 2003. This will be used to counter DaimlerChrysler's $47 billion effort for the development of sixty four new vehicles as well as the smaller BMW's planned introduction of twelve models in the United States from 1999 to 2000. GM is, in this manner, gamely addressing one of its most fundamental problems with a new respect for competitors that grabbed so much of its home territory that it once took for granted (Meredith 1999).

Global Network

Struggling in the United States, General Motors, under John Smith, has steadily built the foundations of a global corporate empire that may be the company's saving grace in the twenty-first century. Ford, Toyota, and Volkswagen have all followed suit but are nowhere near GM's global reach. As the Buick Shanghai successful start-up has shown, the Detroit automaker is widening its lead in important emerging markets. Recent events indicate how this is being done. GM is in competition with Ford and Hyundai Motor, South Korea's largest automaker, to take over the bankrupt Daewoo, the nation's second largest vehicle firm. While the U.S. giants report record profits for 1999, Hyundai's distributorship in South Africa has been placed in liquidation by a South African court, resulting in the closing of its dealers and service centers after creditor banks refused to roll over the company's $120 million in loans or ease repayment terms. Another Hyundai asset caught up in the financial mess is a new assembly plant in Botswana that was to be a part of the company's supply network for the region. The liquidation raises immense questions regarding its bid for Daewoo and its viability of servicing the latter's debt, especially when Hyundai Motor and its parent conglomerate are already weighed down by their own extensive debt loads. With time and huge financial reserves on their side, GM and Ford can purposefully promote their bids for Daewoo with Korean authorities as the debt crisis strangles their smaller, Korean competitor.

Elsewhere, GM continues to add to its global network. Countering Ford's takeover of Volvo Cars, the company will buy the 50% share of Swedish luxury carmaker, Saab, that it does not already control. GM is also experimenting with its new network in less-affluent areas in ways that no other competitor can do. During the past decade, the firm added considerable capacity to its Brazilian operations only to have the region engulfed by the liquidity crisis now smothering Korean manufacturers. Slowing China's growth, the debt mess failed to penetrate the highly regulated economy of Asia's other giant, India, whose demand for moderately priced vehicles has increased as economic reforms, industrialization, and trade have pushed its economy forward. In a $100 million deal connecting foreign affiliates in the huge countries, GM's subsidiary in Brazil will export unassembled compact cars and bigger sedans made in its factories to India, where manufacturing facilities of GM and its partner, Suzuki, do not make the bigger, more expensive units now being demanded by the growing business class. These more affluent buyers on the Indian subcontinent are dismissive of the boxy, plain econocars in their showrooms and, in contrast, hold GM's reputation and product designs in high regard. The fact that it still is the biggest maker and distributor of vehicles in the United States and world is impressive in nations where offerings by its competitors are often unattractive, older models that display a cheap price tag and even cheaper appearance.

In this manner, GM, using its inroads in China, India, Brazil, and Japan, bets its future on a globalization strategy. Currently, there is a glut of production capacity, and General Motors is losing market share because of its lack of distinctive vehicles in advanced markets. In the competitive environment, the global giant is bringing more of the auto business under its control by buying failing enterprises and shifting its excess supply to areas where there is more demand. Better economic conditions in the developing world, moreover, appear to be an inexorable trend that will eat away at the oversupply, permitting global players like GM to eventually price their products to include higher profit margins. It will then be in a situation akin to its golden years in the United States, where it was the market leader because of widespread control of operating assets and because the capital-intensive nature of the industry precluded smaller companies from challenging its position. For GM and the handful of global companies that will remain, the risks to this scenario lie in government restrictions on access to their markets. Temperamental leaders of poorer, developing countries have always used the threat of expropriation and expulsion to keep foreign multinationals in line. To counter such action, the global automotive industry has evolved to accommodate the concerns of political leaders by joining with government agencies and local suppliers to share ownership, management accountability, and profits with host countries. Moreover, the large, multinational companies provide technology, capital, and jobs in viable enterprises whose output is well received in consumer markets and gives the host government an added measure of economic prestige.

The cooperative partnerships are being formed even in industrialized nations where concerns like environmental pollution are being addressed. In September 1993, for example, Detroit's Big Three car companies signed an agreement with the U.S. government to share resources in developing a vehicle that would be more fuel-efficient and, consequently, would produce less exhaust emissions and be cheaper to operate. The pact was a major turnaround for the industry because it had always been hostile to emission standards mandated by the U.S. Environmental Protection Agency. Environmentalists, moreover, have gained a powerful new ally in William Clay Ford Jr., Ford's young chairman, who is actively and vocally seeking to reduce pollutants emitted from the company's products and factories. Ford is advancing the strategy that a better environmental image will help promote the sale of more vehicles at home and abroad as better-informed consumers become more convinced that the health of the planet directly influences their well-being. Moreover, the technology developed to meet emission standards in the advanced nations will have a longer shelf life as markets develop overseas and as pollution control devices are installed in vehicles and factories in foreign countries. Development cost will thus be spread over more units, yielding economies of scale that will be another distinct advantage for a globally operating company.

From the preceding analysis, it appears that Ford and General Motors are moving to the front ranks of world markets, having recovered from the Japanese invasion of their home markets and ratcheted their leadership roles in the United States to overseas markets. Volkswagen and Toyota also appear well positioned, with the Japanese firm somewhat lagging in Europe. DaimlerChrysler, in contrast, has major shortcomings in Asia now that the huge continent is growing again, contributing to the strengths of the first four companies that are developing strong positions there. GM is so sure of its global strategy—which, of course, must include Asia—that beginning in 2000, its board of directors "will add world wide market share to the criteria that determine executive compensation" (Meredith 1999, p. 10). Such incentives will probably be adopted at other major automakers except for possibly DaimlerChrysler, which is still working on melding the disparate cultures of its "merger between equals." Such egalitarian expressions notwithstanding, it was clear from the beginning that authority at the top would be held by Juergen Schrempp from Daimler-Benz, with the head of Chrysler, Robert Eaton, exiting the new company after three years. Upon Eaton's departure, the Chrysler or American-derived part of the merger could then look to Thomas Stallkamp, who had become president of DaimlerChrysler AG. Differences between Schrempp and Stallkamp became so acute, however, that within a year, the latter was forced to retire from the firm. In the upheaval, it was revealed that Stallkamp's position was so tenuous that he had "no control even over Mercedes operations in the United States" (Bradsher, September 25, 1999). As such, the German side—capitalizing on Schrempp's high executive office—is moving to absorb the bigger Detroit enterprise. This is occurring not only with the departure of top managers but with the phasing out of Chrysler's Plymouth brand name, which was expected to begin in November 1999. Such decision making has preoccupied management to such an extent that it had to forgo the possibility of an alliance with Nissan. This gave Renault an opportunity in the Asian market, which the French carmaker seized. The gaping hole in DaimlerChrysler's "global" operations, however, remains, and executives of the firm keep searching for partnerships or acquisitions that will catapult it into the small-car business of emerging and most Asian markets.

ARRIVAL OF E-COMMERCE

In major ways, the automotive industry is augmenting its global business by conducting business over the Internet, the already established, worldwide information superhighway. E-commerce is expected to reach a trillion dollars, and impetus toward this awesome amount was given by the megamerger of America Online (AOL), the largest provider of Internet services, with Time Warner, the giant media and entertainment conglomerate. The merger announcement came on January 10 of the new millennium, but even before the startling news, the global power of the fledgling network was connecting 200 million people and transacting $20 billion of retail sales and a much more $109 billion of business-to-business (B2B) activity. Estimates for the latter's growth, mainly in the United States, come to $1.3 trillion by 2003. For the larger automakers, already pursuing a global strategy, the huge merger would constitute an affirmation of their own pursuits abroad and accelerate corporate plans for conducting business in cyberspace, especially in the American market. These plans had progressed to such an extent that, prior to the AOL–Time Warner announcement, General Motors had formed a partnership with AOL to market its vehicles to the latter's subscribers, and Ford had forged its own arrangement with Yahoo! Inc. The GM deal followed a $1.5 billion investment by AOL in the Hughes Electronics subsidiary of the auto company for use of its satellite communication systems. GM, by itself, has also been upgrading its e-commerce capabilities by committing $4 billion per year in the following areas:

1. Integration of auto dealer computer systems with its plants as a means of facilitating orders for custom-made vehicles and reducing delivery times.

2. Launching GM TradeXchange, a B2B on-line network bringing together buyers and suppliers of more than 200,000 parts and services.

3. Extending the use of its TradeXchange to its Japanese affiliates (Isuzu, Suzuki, and Fuji) as well as Toyota and Honda in order to give the automakers greater-volume buying power for attendant price discounts.

4. Installing voice-activated Internet access through AOL in some vehicles beginning in 2000, allowing GM to charge monthly service fees as an Internet provider.

Internet access will probably be in 400,000 GM vehicles by the end of 2000, but not all services will be available. For example, drivers will not be able to send E-mail from their automobiles. In the new partnership with AOL, the advertising of GM cars through the server's on-line auto section will probably be the principal commercial result of the deal.

In the Yahoo arrangement, Ford car buyers will have similar connections to the Internet as the GM–AOL agreement but will also lack the ability to purchase a new vehicle on-line or send E-mail from the car. On-line retailing—a hallmark of the information revolution—is being restrained in the auto industry by the opposing power of existing dealers who do not want to be bypassed in direct sales from factory to individual buyers. Franchise laws in many states, furthermore, do not permit the automakers to sell directly to the customer. General Motors was also taken to court when it attempted to set up its own dealer network to which it would refer its on-line buyers. Another brake on point-and-click buying is the reluctance of customers to make such a large purchase without a hands-on test-drive of the vehicle. The neighborhood dealer thus keeps control over this aspect of retailing. Where it does lose considerable leverage is in negotiations over the vehicle's price because on-line comparisons will easily give potential buyers critical information. Consumers will subsequently make it mandatory to check the Internet before going to the dealer, and ultimately, most of the decisions to buy will be made on-line. The haggling with the dealer, which most buyers detest, will thus be reduced, if not eliminated.

The biggest impact on Detroit's on-line business, however, will continue to be the on-line supply chain, which will cut purchasing costs that exceed $80 billion a year for both Ford and GM. Compared to the retailing end in the independent dealer's showroom, where automakers have little experience, B2B transactions have soared as both companies moved abroad and forged international linkages with local suppliers in Brazil, Mexico, and other emerging countries. Impetus for this globalization of supply networks was also given by

GM's decision to spin off its in-house parts division, and Ford is planning to follow with its Visteon supply unit. The moves allow the automakers greater flexibility in obtaining supplies, especially for overseas plants, and give them the upper hand in negotiating price concessions for their volume purchases. They are further aided by the significant amount of on-line B2B expertise extant in the United States, where such networks originated. Ford, for example, is teaming up with the Oracle Corporation, one of Silicon Valley's most notable software firms, to form Auto.Xchange, its Web site that will facilitate its on-line buying of parts, raw materials, and services. Oracle has the recent experience of launching a similar system, uniting 250 companies, and is committing hundreds of programmers to come up with the software in an accelerated implementation of the Ford on-line joint venture. It will also maintain, manage, and host the electronic Auto.Xchange, which eventually may be handling $300 billion worth of transactions per year. That level of business will undoubtedly include a vast amount of goods and services that cross national boundaries and hence significantly contribute to the industry's globalization.

REFERENCES

Ball, Jeffrey. "Ford, DaimlerChrysler Boost Rebates on Some Very Profitable Light Trucks." *Wall Street Journal*, November 11, 1999, pp. A3, A8.

———. "DaimlerChrysler Fights to Retain Minivan Dominance." *Wall Street Journal*, January 11, 2000, p. B4.

Bradsher, Keith. "Requiem for the Middleweights." *New York Times*, March 31, 1999, p. C1.

———. "A Struggle over Cultures and Turf at Auto Giant." *New York Times*, September 25, 1999, p. C14.

———. "Luxury Wheels Turn to Europe." *New York Times*, January 13, 2000, pp. C1, C4.

Eckholm, Erik, and David E. Sanger. "U.S. Readies an Accord to Open China Economy as Worldwide Market." *New York Times*, November 16, 1999, pp. A1, A17.

Frank, Robert. "How Thailand Became the 'Detroit of the East.'" *Wall Street Journal*, December 8, 1999, p. B1.

French, Howard W. "With Daewoo, a Twilight of Korean Conglomerates." *New York Times*, September 3, 1999, pp. C1, C3.

"Honda Details China Auto Venture." *Wall Street Journal*, May 8, 1998, p. A12.

Kerwin, Kathleen, and Keith Naughton. "Remaking Ford." *Business Week*, October 11, 1999, pp. 131-142.

Klayman, Ben. Reuters press release via Yahoo.com/ "Ford, Oracle to Create Online Supply Network," November 3, 1999.

Landler, Mark. "General Motors Is Using Buicks to Make Inroads in China." *New York Times*, December 18, 1999, pp. C1, C10.

Meredith, Robyn. "Can G.M. Return to the Passing Lane?" *New York Times*, November 7, 1999, section 3, pp. 1, 10, 11.

———. "Car and Truck Sales in 1999 Set U.S. Record." *New York Times*, January 6, 2000, pp. C1, C17.

Shirouzu, Norihiko. "Mazda's New President Vows More Cost Cuts." *Wall Street Journal*, December 16, 1999, p. A17.

Simison, Robert L. "Buick Succeeds in China by Laying Stress on Quality." *Wall Street Journal*, October 26, 1999, p. A18.

Smith, Craig S. "Toyota Plans to Build Car Plant in China as Part of Joint Venture." *Wall Street Journal*, November 2, 1999, p. A20.

Templin, Neal. "Ford's Trotman Gambles on Global Restructuring." *Wall Street Journal*, April 22, 1994, p. A3.

U.S. Trade Representative (USTR) Fax Retrieval System. "Summary of U.S.-China Bilateral WTO Agreement." Washington, DC, November 15, 1999.

Warner, Fara, Kara Swisher, and Nick Wingfield. "Ford and GM Sign Pacts with Web Sites." *Wall Street Journal*, January 10, 2000, p. A3.

White, Gregory L. "GM, Long Too Cautious, Tries to Be Creative and Cool." *Wall Street Journal*, October 11, 1999, p. B4.

Selected Bibliography

Andrews, Edmund L., and Laura M. Holson. "Daimler-Benz Will Acquire Chrysler in $36 Billion Deal That Will Reshape Industry." *New York Times*, May 7, 1998, pp. A1, D4.

Bowander, B. "Competitive and Technology Management Strategy: A Case Study of TELCO." *International Journal of Technology Management*, 15(6/7) (1998a): 646–680.

———. "Industrialization and Economic Growth of India: Interactions of Indigenous and Foreign Technology." *International Journal of Technology Management*, 15(6/7)(1998b): 622–645.

Bradsher, Keith. "In South America, Auto Makers See One Big Showroom." *New York Times*, April 25, 1997, pp. D1, D4.

———. "G.M.'s Plant in Brazil Raises Fears Closer to Home." *New York Times*, June 17, 1998, pp. A1, D22.

———. "Ford Buys Volvo Car Unit in Bid to Lift Profile of Luxury Models." *New York Times*, January 29, 1999, pp. A1, C4.

Cusumano, Michael A. *The Japanese Automobile Industry*, Cambridge: Council on East Asian Studies, Harvard University, 1985.

Dower, J.W. *Empire and Aftermath*. Cambridge: Council on East Asian Studies, Harvard University, 1979.

EIU. "Face to Face: With FAW-Volkswagen of China." *Motor Business Asia-Pacific*, first quarter 1996, Chapter 2.

———. "Face to Face with the Leaders of Mexico's Automotive Industry." *Motor Business International*, first quarter 1997, Chapter 1.

———. "Brazil's Motor Industry: Output Poised for 40% Growth to 2000." *Motor Business International*, fourth quarter 1997, Chapter 2.

Fatemi, Khosrow (ed.). *The Maquiladora Industry*. Westport, CT: Praeger, 1990.

Haigh, Robert W. "Building a Strategic Alliance." *Columbia Journal of World Business*, 27 (Spring 1992): 60–75.

Halberstam, David. *The Reckoning*. New York: William Morrow, 1986.

Harwit, Eric. *China's Automobile Industry*. Armonk, NY: M.E. Sharpe, 1995.

Hiraoka, Leslie S. "U.S. Gasoline Conservation and Japanese Auto Imports." *Energy*, 8(12) (1983): 993–998.

————. "U.S.–Japanese Competition in High-Technology Fields." *Technological Forecasting and Social Change*, 26(1) (August 1984): 1–10.

————. "Japan's Increasing Investments Abroad." *Futures*. 17(5) (October 1985): 495–508.

————. "Japanese Automobile Manufacturing in an American Setting." *Technological Forecasting and Social Change*, 35(1) (March 1989): 29–49.

————. "Paradigmatic Shifts in Automobile Manufacturing." *Engineering Management Journal*, 1(2) (June 1989): 7–15.

————. "Globalization of the Automobile Industry." *Engineering Management Journal*, 3(4) (December 1991): 17–26.

————. "The Industrial Policies of the USA and Japan." *International Journal of Technology Management*, 15(6/7) (1998): 526–541.

————. "Foreign Development of China's Motor Vehicle Industry." *International Journal of Technology Management*, in press.

Ingrassia, Paul, and Joseph B. White. *Comeback: The Fall and Rise of the American Automobile Industry*. New York: Touchstone, 1994.

Kerwin, Kathleen, and Keith Naughton. "Remaking Ford." *Business Week*, October 11, 1999, pp. 131–142.

Levin, Doron P. "Toyota Plant in Kentucky Is Font of Ideas for U.S." *New York Times*, May 5, 1992, p. A1.

Lohr, Steve. "The Company That Stopped Detroit." *New York Times*, March 21, 1982, p. F1.

Mair, Andrew. *Honda's Global Local Corporation*. New York: St. Martin's Press, 1994.

Marukawa, Tomoo. "Industrial Groups and Division of Labor in China's Automobile Industry." *The Developing Economies* 33(3) (September 1995): 330–335.

Meredith, Robyn. "The Brave New World of General Motors." *New York Times*, October 26, 1997, section 12, p. 1.

————. "Can G.M. Return to the Passing Lane?" *New York Times*, November 7, 1999, section 3, pp. 1, 10, 11.

Niskanen, William A. *Reaganomics*. New York: Oxford University Press, 1988.

Reitman, Valerie. "Frugal Head of Suzuki Drives Markets in Asia." *Wall Street Journal*, February 26, 1998, p. A2.

Sakiya, Tetsuo. *Honda Motor*. Tokyo: Kodansha International, 1982.

Salpukas, Agis. "General Motors Reports '80 Loss of $763 Million." *New York Times*, February 3, 1981, p. A1.

Shiomi, Haruhito, and Kazuo Wada. *Fordism Transformed.* New York: Oxford University Press, 1995.

Smith, Craig S., and Rebecca Blumenstein. "In China, GM Bets Billions on a Market Strewn with Casualties." *Wall Street Journal,* February 11, 1998, pp. A1, A8.

Strauss, William A. "Auto Industry Cruises On." *Chicago Fed Letter* Number 121, Federal Reserve Bank of Chicago, September 1997.

Tyler, Patrick E. "China Planning People's Car to Put Masses behind Wheel." *New York Times,* September 22, 1994, pp. A1, D8.

U.S. Department of State. *Foreign Relations of the United States* 1951. Vol. 6: *Asia and the Pacific.* Washington, DC: U.S. Department of State, 1977, part 1.

————. *Foreign Relations of the United States* 1952–1954. Vol. 14: *Japan.* Washington, DC: U.S. Department of State, 1985, part 2.

U.S. Trade Representative press release. "Impact of America's Car Companies on the U.S. Economy." Fax Document number 40102. Washington, DC: Office of Public Affairs (May 10, 1995).

Vickery, Graham. "Globalisation in the Automobile Industry." In *Globalisation of Industry: Overview and Sector Reports.* Paris: Organisation for Economic Co-operation and Development, 1996, 153–205.

Yang, Xiaohua. *Globalization of the Automobile Industry: The United States, Japan, and the People's Republic of China.* Westport, CT: Praeger, 1995.

Index